THE BIBLICAL DOCTRINE OF ELECTION

THE BIBLICAL DOCTRINE OF ELECTION

by

H. H. ROWLEY

*The Louisa Curtis Lectures
delivered in
Spurgeon's College, September 1948*

Πάντα δὲ δοκιμάζετε, τὸ καλὸν κατέχετε
1 Thess 5 : 21

WIPF & STOCK · Eugene, Oregon

Wipf and Stock Publishers
199 W 8th Ave, Suite 3
Eugene, OR 97401

The Biblical Doctrine of Election
By Rowley, H. H.
Copyright©1950 James Clarke & Co
ISBN 13: 978-1-60608-763-3
Publication date 6/5/2009
Previously published by Lutterworth Press, 1950

Copyright©Lutterworth Press1950
First English edition 1950 by Lutterworth Press
This edition published by arrangement with James Clarke & Co

TO THE
UNIVERSITY OF WALES
IN GRATITUDE FOR
THE HONORARY DEGREE OF
DOCTOR OF DIVINITY
AND IN MEMORY OF
FIFTEEN HAPPY YEARS
SPENT IN ITS SERVICE
THIS VOLUME IS DEDICATED

Preface

MUCH of the material of these lectures was given in a course of four lectures which I was invited to deliver at Bangor in December 1946 under the auspices of the Bangor School of Theology, and again in October 1948 at Cardiff under the auspices of the Cardiff School of Theology. My gratitude to former colleagues and enduring friends for the honour of these invitations was only matched by the pleasure I found in being again in their midst and in renewing the fellowship of the years now past.

In their present expanded form the lectures were delivered at Spurgeon's College in September 1948, under the Louisa Curtis Foundation. To Principal P. W. Evans, and to the Tutors and Students of the College, I express my gratitude for the honour of this invitation and for the warmth of their reception, and my pleasure that I have been able thus to repay a little of my debt to Charles Haddon Spurgeon. That giant among men, to whom the Baptist denomination in particular owes an immeasurable debt, died when I was in my infancy, and I never heard the music of his voice or the challenge of his preaching. My debt to him is therefore mediate; yet it is none the less real. For eighteen years, and those including the most impressionable years of my life, I knew the influence of the ministry of W. Y. Fullerton at Melbourne Hall Church, Leicester. For the privilege of sitting at the feet of one in whom so much of the spirit of Spurgeon lived I can never cease to be grateful to both of these great men, and yet more to God.

In the lectures themselves I have little that is new to offer, since the Biblical doctrine of election is not of my creation, but has been to be found in the Bible ever since it was written. In its broad outlines it has been recognized by a number of writers, including not a few contemporary writers. Yet I do not know of any study of the subject on this scale, modest as it still is, and I can only hope that it may serve some useful

PREFACE

purpose to gather together this collection of Biblical material, and that it may inspire some preaching on this neglected theme. For my subject is academic, yet much more than academic. It carries throughout a message of warning on the sacred obligations of spiritual inheritance and the perils of their neglect or repudiation.

That I have not been able to append a bibliography is due to the simple fact that it could not be a bibliography of the general subject of the lectures, since so few recent books and articles have been devoted directly to it. The interested reader will find in the footnotes references to a number of books and articles on which I have drawn for observations on aspects of the subject, but their collection could only yield a list of works cited, and not a bibliography of the subject of the lectures.

The passages of Scripture cited are given in my own translations, which endeavour to indicate the rhythmical arrangement of the original where it is poetical. Such deviation from the Massoretic Hebrew text as I have permitted myself is explained in the footnotes. That that Massoretic text differs not seldom from the original text needs no demonstration and causes no surprise; yet the restoration can rarely be achieved with confidence, and I deprecate the wholesale conjectural emendations which were but recently the main interest of the commentators.

Some of my readers would doubtless have preferred to find quotations from foreign works cited in the original. Others, however, may find it more convenient to have them in translated form. Since the subject of my lectures is likely to be of interest to more than scholars, I have given them all in English, both in the text and in the footnotes. Where an official translation was available, I have employed it, but otherwise I am responsible for the renderings. Where they are not literal I trust I have not unfairly represented the sense.

To many libraries and friends I am indebted for the loan of books to which I should not otherwise have had access, and in particular I am indebted to a number of foreign scholars for copies of their recent books and articles. To record here all their names would be to weary the reader, while to select amongst them a few to record would be both invidious and unjust. Few men can be more fortunate in their friends, or receive more generously from them. That there are points on which I disagree with some of them is but to be expected; yet in my disagreement I would acknowledge that from all I have learned.

To Professor A. R. Johnson I am indebted for help in reading the proofs, and to my daughter, Margaret, I am indebted for the preparation of the Author and Scripture Indexes. To them I express my gratitude, and also to the Lutterworth Press and its Printers for their patience and understanding.

Manchester
November 1948

H. H. ROWLEY

Contents

Preface page 7

Abbreviations 13

CHAPTER
1. THE ELECTION OF ISRAEL 15
2. THE COROLLARIES OF ISRAEL'S ELECTION 45
3. THE LIMITATION AND EXTENSION OF ISRAEL'S ELECTION 69
4. THE ELECTION OF INDIVIDUALS 95
5. ELECTION WITHOUT COVENANT 121
6. THE HEIRS OF ELECTION 139

Indexes 175

Abbreviations

BWANT = Beiträge zur Wissenschaft vom Alten und Neuen Testament.
CambB = The Cambridge Bible.
CentB = The Century Bible.
EB = *Études Bibliques.*
HAT = *Handbuch zum Alten Testament.*
HK = *Handkommentar zum Alten Testament.*
HSAT = *Die Heilige Schrift des Alten Testaments* (ed. Kautzsch-Bertholet).
HSATes = *Die Heilige Schrift des Alten Testaments* (ed. Feldmann and Herkenne).
ICC = The International Critical Commentary.
KAT = *Kommentar zum Alten Testament.*
KHC = *Kurzer Hand-Commentar zum Alten Testament.*
MC = The Moffatt Commentary.
WC = The Westminster Commentary.

Chapter One

THE ELECTION OF ISRAEL

IN modern Biblical studies the doctrine of election has received little attention. Yet it would seem to be fundamental to the thought of the Bible in both Old and New Testaments.[1] To the writers of the Old Testament Israel is the chosen people of God;[2] to the writers of the New Testament the Church is the heir of the divine election. In both Testaments individuals are presented as chosen of God for their particular work. Whether we like it or not, the doctrine of election is a Biblical doctrine, and whatever our view of its validity, it demands some attention from the student of the Bible.

In a recent article Professor G. E. Wright has observed[3] that "modern scholars have done little with this doctrine, perhaps in no small measure because they felt they could not take its validity seriously. Yet there can be no real understanding of the meaning of the Old Testament nor of the course of Israel's history without paying close attention to it, regardless of what we think about its truth." In more than one publication I have indicated that I share this point of view,[4] and I had already undertaken to deliver a course of lectures on this subject[5] before Professor Wright's article appeared. The present lectures are an expansion of those

---

[1] Cf. W. Eichrodt, *Journal of Biblical Literature*, lxv, 1946, p. 215, translated by W. F. Albright, *ibid.*, p. 207: "For biblical religion this means that one cannot pass over the central concept, that God bears a special relationship to His people, a relationship appropriately designated by the words 'covenant' and 'election'." S. A. Cook has some valuable, but very compressed, pages on this subject in his *Introduction to the Bible*, 1945, pp. 85ff.

[2] Eichrodt also observes that even where the term "election" is not used the reality is meant when the prophets speak of the deliverance from Egypt and the settlement in Canaan (*Theologie des Alten Testaments*, i, 1933, p. 196).

[3] Cf. *Theology To-day*, iii, 1946, p. 187.

[4] Cf. *Religion in Education*, xi, 1943–44, pp. 63ff. ; *The Missionary Message of the Old Testament*, 1945, pp. 14f., 25, 38, 57f., 78f. ; *The Rediscovery of the Old Testament*, 1946, English ed., pp. 60ff., 137f. (American ed., pp. 85ff., 194f.).

[5] At Bangor. This course of four lectures was delivered in December, 1946

earlier lectures, and in them I propose to examine in broad outline the grounds on which the faith of Israel in her election rested, and the nature and purpose of that election; the relation of the New Testament faith in the election of the Church to the election of Israel; and the nature and purpose of individual election as it appears in the Bible. While the study will be as objective as possible, I shall not avoid indicating how far I accept the doctrine as valid. Needless to say, it will be impossible here to examine all the passages in which the idea of election is found, and there will be aspects of the subject which will be left without treatment.

At the outset it must be made clear that I do not propose to deal with the theological question of predestination to salvation or damnation, to heaven or to hell. That is an entirely different question from the one that is before us, though it is probable that the wide prevalence of Arminian views on that question, even in churches that inherit a Calvinistic tradition, has contributed in some measure to the decay of interest in the one which is before us. It is probable, too, that the modern decay of interest in theology—yielding now to a revived interest—has contributed to the neglect of this subject. For while the Biblical doctrine of election is distinct from that which has generated so much heat among theologians, it is quite certainly a theological question.

In an article published some twenty years ago, J. M. Powis Smith stated[1] that Israel's faith in her election rested on a natural pride of nation and race, and on the Israelite faith in Yahweh, whose representative she was among the nations. If it had no deeper basis than this, it would have little validity in itself, and would possess no more than a historical interest. Powis Smith himself adduced a great deal of evidence to show that throughout the ancient Near East, kings regarded themselves as the chosen of the gods. Amongst the instances he cites is the address to the gods of Tiglath-pileser I, where they are said to be those "who have enlarged the kingdom of Tiglath-pileser, the beloved prince, the

---

[1] "The Chosen People", in *American Journal of Semitic Languages*, xlv, 1928–29, pp. 73ff.

desire of your hearts, the exalted shepherd, whom in your faithful hearts ye have chosen, whom ye have crowned with a lofty diadem, and did solemnly appoint to be king".[1] A more familiar instance is Cyrus's declaration that Marduk "in all lands everywhere searched, he looked through them and sought a righteous prince, after his own heart, whom he took by the hand. Cyrus, king of Anshan, he called by name, to lordship over the whole world he appointed him".[2] Of such instances Powis Smith observes that there was no great or essential difference between their conceptions of divine choice and mission and the Hebrew conviction of the same sort, at least until the post-exilic period.[3] He also observes that pride of race was not confined to the Near East, or to the ancient world. He therefore treats the Old Testament doctrine of Election, at least throughout the pre-exilic period, as fundamentally the same in character as the doctrine amongst the peoples that surrounded Israel, but goes on to trace its survival to the spiritual achievements of the prophets, and the unique collection of books gathered into the Old Testament, in which the doctrine is enshrined.

This seems to me to fall very far short of the truth. Some superficial similarity may be found between the utterances of eastern kings and some words that have been traditionally interpreted in a messianic sense:

> He said to me: My son art thou,
> I have to-day begotten thee;
> ([4]) And I will give thee the nations for thy heritage,
> And the ends of the earth for thy possession.[5]

But even if these were the proud words of some Israelite king, they would not dispose of the Old Testament thought of election, either of the nation or of individuals. That there were Israelites who cherished the idea that God was tied to

---

[1] Cf. D. D. Luckenbill, *Ancient Records of Assyria and Babylonia*, 1926, i, pp. 72f.
[2] Cf. R. W. Rogers, *Cuneiform Parallels to the Old Testament*, 1912, p. 381. Cf. H. Gressmann, *Altorientalische Texte zum Alten Testament*, 2nd ed., 1926, p. 369.
[3] *Loc. cit.*, p. 75.
[4] The Massoretic Text here adds: "Ask of Me." For my reasons for omitting these words, see *Journal of Theological Studies*, xlii, 1941, p. 150.
[5] Psa. 2: 7f.

Israel, and that His honour demanded her exaltation, and who prided themselves in the thought that they were the Chosen People, is undoubtedly true. But they stand rebuked in the Old Testament, whose teaching is quite other. Here it is not taught that Israel was chosen because she was better than other nations. Rather was it the miracle of Divine grace that God chose her in her weakness and worthlessness, and lavished His love upon her. If we read: "Yahweh thy God chose thee out of all the peoples on the face of the earth to be his own special people",[1] we have only to proceed to the following verse to read: "It was not because ye were the greatest among all the peoples that Yahweh set His heart on you and chose you; for ye were the least of all the peoples. It was just because Yahweh loved you."[2] Similarly prophets who were profoundly convinced that they were chosen of God for their office were not puffed up with pride at the thought, but humbled by its wonder. At the call of Jeremiah, God says to him:

> Before I formed thee in the womb I chose thee,[3]
> And before thou camest forth from thy mother I sanctified thee;
> I appointed thee to be a prophet to the nations.

But Jeremiah did not indulge in proud boasting. He cried in profound humility of spirit:

> Ah! Lord Yahweh!
> Behold, I cannot speak;
> For but a child am I.[4]

No superficial comparison of the words of oriental kings announcing their divine vocation to rule and to conquer with words which may be culled from the Old Testament should be allowed to obscure the world of difference between the essential thought of election there and here. Nor can we

---
[1] Deut. 7 : 6.
[2] Deut. 7 : 7f. Cf. Deut. 9 : 5f.
[3] The literal rendering of the Hebrew is "I knew thee". But the essential meaning is as given, as also in Am. 3 : 2.
[4] Jer. 1 : 5f.

compare such pride in her election as appears in the teaching of the Old Testament with the racial pride that has flourished among men. Nowhere is it taught in the Old Testament that God chose Israel because of her inherent greatness;[1] yet there are passages where it is held that Israel's greatness lies in the fact that God chose her. Nations shall honour her because she is His people, and therefore in honouring her they will really honour Him.[2] This is not the climax of Old Testament teaching, which is concerned only with the honour of God, and which thinks of Israel not so much as destined to receive honour from men as called to fulfil the purpose of her election in the service of men.

There are passages in the Old Testament which represent the divine choice of Israel as made in the time of the patriarchs, and especially of Abraham; there are others which represent it as made in the time of Moses. Galling has argued that the latter is the older tradition.[3] It is certain that the Exodus left its mark deep on all the thought of the Old Testament, and that for many writers the great beginning

[1] In post-Biblical Jewish literature, it is, on the contrary, frequently taught that the divine choice of Israel was due to the worth of the patriarchs or of Israel. Cf. J. Bonsirven, *Le Judaïsme palestinien*, i, 1934, p. 78; Montefiore and Loewe, *A Rabbinic Anthology*, 1938, p. 676, n. 48.

[2] Isa. 60: 11f., 61: 5f., 9.

[3] Cf. *Die Erwählungstraditionen Israels*, 1928, p. 63. Cf. J. Pedersen, *Israel III—IV*, 1940, p. 666: "All the main features of the stories about Abraham are coloured by the time of the regal period." N. Dahl (*Das Volk Gottes*, 1941, p. 16) observes that "originally the patriarchal tradition was independent, rather a parallel to the Exodus tradition". A. G. Hebert accepts the Exodus tradition as fundamental to the Old Testament, and observes that "the general view of of the Bible seems to be that the story of Abraham and the other patriarchs is a necessary prologue to the story of the nation of Israel, which begins at the Exodus" (*The Throne of David*, 1941, p. 29 n.). G. A. Danell (*Studies in the Name Israel in the Old Testament*, 1946, pp. 34f.), goes so far as to argue that Abraham was originally a cult-hero and cult-founder belonging to Hebron, who was taken over by Israel in the time of the monarchy. It will be seen below that the present writer is less sceptical of the substantial historicity of the patriarchs, and is less concerned to brush aside either of the two traditions of the election than to understand how they arose and what truth they enshrine. W. A. Irwin (*The Intellectual Adventure of Ancient Man*, 1946, pp. 329f.) thinks that the original statement of the doctrine of election may stand in the story of the call of Abraham, but he attaches little historical value either to the election in Abraham or to the election through Moses. For he holds that the idea only came into existence after the settlement in Canaan, and offers no suggestion as to what brought it into existence. He says: "Somewhere along this line of development of the pagan national god into the ethical doctrine of the covenant, there entered the concept of the divine choice of Israel that was destined to become the distinctive feature of the nation's thought of itself."

of things was with Moses.¹ On the other hand the representation of the choice as made with Abraham stands in passages that belong to the oldest of the main strands of the Pentateuch, itself usually dated earlier than the earliest of the canonical prophets. For the moment we may note the two points of view, without comparing the antiquity or the validity which belongs to them.

Hosea says:

> When Israel was a child I came to love him,
> And out of Egypt I called my son.²

Similarly Jeremiah:

> I remember your early devotion,
> The love of your bridal days;
> How through the wolds you followed me,
> Through lands unsown.³

Both of these represent the beginnings of the relation between Yahweh and Israel as belonging to the time of the Exodus. Similarly Ezekiel says:

> Thus said the Lord Yahweh:
> In the day when I made choice of Israel,
> And raised my hand to the seed of the house of Jacob,

---

[1] Cf. E. Jacob, *La tradition historique en Israël*, 1946, p. 148: "Jeremiah does not ignore the patriarchal traditions, but he does not regard them as belonging to the story of salvation; the history of Israel begins with Moses." Cf. *ibid.*, p. 152: "The election does not go back to the patriarchal period, but to the Exodus from Egypt; it is there that Yahweh chose Israel in stretching out His hand over her." Also S. Hanson, *The Unity of the Church in the New Testament*, 1946, p. 11: "By delivering Israel out of Egypt, JHWH ... elected Israel His people." Cf. too, C. R. North, *The Old Testament Interpretation of History*, 1946, p. 50: "If the prophets knew of any covenant with Abraham they do not mention it. Indeed, their allusions to any covenant at all are fewer than might have been expected." Similarly W. A. Irwin (*The Intellectual Adventure of Ancient Man*, 1946, p. 327): "Since the old narrative documents incorporated in the Pentateuch, commonly designated J and E, according to orthodox criticism were already in existence before the age of the prophets, it is strange that these writers should pass over the impressive account of Abraham's call and the promise to him." C. G. Montefiore (*The Old Testament and After*, 1923, p. 76) says: "It is very generally now believed either that Yahweh only became Israel's God in the Mosaic age, and then by an act of deliberate choice, or that, even if Yahweh was known in Israel before Moses, He was, as it were, chosen and accepted afresh after the escape from Egypt."

[2] Hos. 11 : 1.

[3] Jer. 2 : 2 (Moffatt's rendering).

And made myself known to them in the land of Egypt,
And raised aloft my hand to them, saying:
I am Yahweh your God.[1]

Moreover, it is well known that there are passages in the Pentateuch which state that the worship of Yahweh in Israel began in the time of Moses. The most important of these passages is Ex. 6 : 2f., which says: "God spake unto Moses and said unto him: I am Yahweh; but I appeared unto Abraham, unto Isaac and unto Jacob as El Shaddai, and by my name Yahweh was I not known to them." In the passage just cited Ezekiel follows this view, and declares that Yahweh made Himself known to Israel in the land of Egypt. So, too, Hosea says: "I am Yahweh thy God from the land of Egypt."[2]

As against this we have the passages in Genesis which represent God as saying to the patriarchs: "I am Yahweh",[3] and which represent Him as blessing the patriarchs and declaring His election of their descendants. At some of these passages we shall have to look more closely, and they may be left for the moment uncited. Here we may observe merely that these passages left some echoes in other parts of the Old Testament, though they are later than the passages already cited, which present the other view. Thus in Deutero-Isaiah we find:

> Look unto Abraham your father,
> And unto Sarah who bore you;
> For one was he when I called him,
> And I blessed him and made him many.[4]

Or again:

> But thou, Israel, my servant,
> Jacob, whom I have chosen,
> The seed of Abraham, my friend,
> Of whom I have laid hold from the ends of the earth,
> And called from the corners thereof,
> And said to thee: Thou art my servant,
> I have chosen thee and have not rejected thee.[5]

---

[1] Ezk. 20 : 5.
[2] Hos. 12 : 9 (Heb. 10). Cf. 13 : 4.
[3] Gen. 15 : 7, 28 : 13.
[4] Isa. 51 : 2.
[5] Isa. 41: 8f.

Similarly, in the concluding verse of the book of Micah, which is commonly ascribed to the post-exilic period,[1] we find the election in the patriarchs referred to:

> Thou wilt show faithfulness to Jacob,
> Devotion[2] to Abraham,
> As thou didst swear to our fathers
> From the days of old.[3]

Or again, in Psalm 105, which also belongs to the post-exilic period,[4] we read:

> Remember his wonders which he hath wrought,
> His signal acts and the judgements of his mouth,
> O seed of Abraham, his servant,
> Ye elect ones, the children of Jacob.

---

[1] Cf. W. Nowack, *Die kleinen Propheten* (HK), 1897, pp. 221f.; K. Marti, *Dodekapropheten* (KHC), 1904, p. 298; J. M. P. Smith, *Micah, Zephaniah and Nahum* (ICC), 1912, p. 152; H. Guthe, *Micha* (HSAT), ii, 1923, p. 64; G. W. Wade, *Micah, Obadiah, Joel and Jonah* (WC), 1925, p. 63; E. Sellin, *Zwölfprophetenbuch* (KAT), 1929, p. 349; and T. H. Robinson, *Die zwölf kleinen Propheten* (HAT), 1938, pp. 151f. Against this, however, cf. A. Van Hoonacker, *Les douze petits prophètes* (EB), 1908, pp. 347–353.

[2] A. R. Johnson argues (in a forthcoming monograph; cf. *Journal of Biblical Literature*, lxvi, 1947, p. xxx) that the word *ḥesedh*, which is variously rendered *loving-kindness, mercy, kindness*, is fundamentally equivalent to the English word *devotion*. It involves the element of *loyalty*, and also an emotional quality. Cf. G. A. Smith: "*ḥesedh* is more than an affection; it is loyalty to a relation. To translate it but *kindness* or *mercy*, as is usually done, is wrong—*troth* is our nearest word" (*Jeremiah*, 3rd ed., 1924, p. 104). Similarly N. H. Snaith holds that the word means *covenant-love*, and that "without the prior existence of a covenant, there could never be any *chesed* at all" (*Distinctive Ideas of the Old Testament*, 1944, p. 95). So, too, G. E. Wright, *The Challenge of Israel's Faith*, 1944, pp. 73f. (English ed., 1946, pp. 90f.). This seems to be going too far and the statement of M. Burrows (*An Outline of Biblical Theology*, 1946, p. 252) seems to be preferable: "The Hebrew word commonly rendered 'kindness' or 'loving-kindness' means primarily 'loyalty', *but it often implies also a beneficence which exceeds anything the recipient has a right to expect*" (italics mine). Cf. A. Lods, *Les prophètes d'Israël*, 1935, p. 100 (English Tr. by S. H. Hooke, *The Prophets and the Rise of Judaism*, 1937, p. 89): "hèsèd, a very comprehensive word, which, for want of an adequate equivalent, we are obliged to translate, now by piety, now by mercy, love or grace: it corresponds fairly closely to the Latin *pietas*, meaning not only the feeling of a faithful believer towards God, or of a son towards his father, but also the feeling of God or of a leader towards his subordinates, and in a general way, the natural feeling which prompts a man, apart from the constraint of law, to be kind and indulgent towards the members of his family or tribe."

[3] Mic. 7 : 20.

[4] Cf. B. Duhm, *Die Psalmen* (KHC), 1899, p. 247; C. A. Briggs, *The Book of Psalms* (ICC), ii, 1909, p. 342; H. Gunkel, *Die Psalmen* (HK), 1926, p. 458; R. Kittel, *Die Psalmen* (KAT), 1929, p. 345; W. E. Barnes, *The Psalms* (WC), ii, 1931, p. 501; G. R. Berry, *The Book of Psalms*, 1934, p. 194; J. Calès, *Le Livre des Psaumes*, ii, 1936, p. 288; W. O. E. Oesterley, *The Psalms*, ii, 1939, p. 445;

He is Yahweh, our God,
In all the earth are his judgements.
He remembers his covenant for ever,
The word he commanded to a thousand generations;
Which covenant he made with Abraham,
And his oath to Isaac.
And he confirmed it to Jacob by a decree,
To Israel in an everlasting covenant.[1]

The passage already cited from the book of Deuteronomy brings the deliverance from Egypt through Moses into relation with the election in Abraham, and declares that it was in loyalty to His oath to the patriarchs that He brought them forth. It says: "It was just because Yahweh loved you, and because he kept the oath which he sware to your fathers, that Yahweh brought you forth with a strong hand, and redeemed thee from the house of bondage, from the hand of Pharaoh the king of Egypt."[2] The same bringing of these two things into relation with one another is found in Psalm 105, where we read:

For he remembered his holy word
To Abraham his servant;
And he brought forth his people with gladness,
His elect ones with a song.[3]

There was a time when the patriarchs were dismissed altogether from the stage of history, or were resolved into personifications of tribes. Thus Wellhausen declared that "we attain to no historical knowledge of the patriarchs, but only of the time when the stories about them arose in the Israelite people; this later age is here unconsciously projected, in its inner and its outward features, into hoar antiquity, and is reflected there like a glorified mirage."[4] To-day

---

A. Bentzen, *Fortolkning til de gammeltestamentlige Salmer*, 1940, p. 538. With this wide consensus of opinion cf. I. Engnell, *Studies in Divine Kingship in the Ancient Near East*, 1943, p. 176 n.: "There is merely one psalm in the whole Psalter of which I am quite convinced that it is post-exilic: No. 137." It should be added that amongst recent writers who ascribe Psalm 105 to the pre-exilic period are M. Buttenwieser, *The Psalms Chronologically Treated*, 1938, p. 805; B. D. Eerdmans, *The Hebrew Book of Psalms*, 1947, p. 478.

[1] Psa. 105 : 5–10.
[2] Deut. 7 : 8. Cf. Deut. 4 : 37, 10 : 15.
[3] Psa. 105 : 43.
[4] Cf. *Prolegomena to the History of Israel*, E. Tr., 1885, pp. 318f.

there is a greater disposition to believe that genuine historical traditions are embodied in these patriarchal stories,[1] and our growing knowledge of the age in which they are set increases our respect for the writers who embodied the traditions in their narratives.[2] So far as Abraham is concerned, it was always felt to be difficult to resolve him into a tribal personification,[3] and all probability is on the side of the view that he was a genuinely historical person. Nor is there reason to doubt that Isaac and Jacob were also actual individuals, though it may be agreed that there are cases in the Old Testament where groups are personified.[4] Nevertheless, the acceptance of the patriarchs as historical individuals does not mean that all the narratives about them are to be read literally, and the conversations in them to be treated as verbatim reports. It was centuries later than their day when the present picturesque stories of the Bible were written down, with their accounts of divine appearances in human form, and dialogue between the Deity and the patriarchs—sometimes overheard by third parties. We must therefore not conclude without more ado from the credibility of the core of the tradition that the form in which it is cast is in all details to be relied on.

On the other hand, we must beware of supposing that when we have treated the theophanies as of the form of the story, rather than as of the substance of the tradition, we have dissolved all into thin air. To accept Abraham, for instance, as a genuine historical character, about whom we know nothing, does not get us very far. The writers of the

---

[1] Cf. S. H. Hooke, *In the Beginning* (Clarendon Bible), 1947, p. 62: "The sagas of Genesis, while they throw light on the religious ideas of the writers who were using this material, also reflect in many ways the customs and social conditions of an age so far removed in time from that of the Hebrew historian who recorded them that he did not always understand what he was recording; so that we may believe him to have faithfully preserved much of the ancient tradition of his people in its early form."

[2] Cf. R. de Vaux, 'Les patriarches hébreux et les découvertes modernes", in *Revue Biblique*, liii, 1946, pp. 321-348, lv, 1948, pp. 321-347, lvi, 1949, pp. 5-36. R. Weill ("La légende des patriarches et l'histoire", in *Revue des Études Sémitiques*, 1937, pp. 145-206) would seem to allow less historical substance to the tradition.

[3] Cf. J. Skinner, *Genesis* (ICC), 1910, p. xxv. Cf. too, P. Dhorme, "Abraham dans le cadre de l'histoire", in *Revue Biblique*, xxxvii, 1928, pp. 367-385, 481-511, xl, 1931, pp. 364-374, 503-518.

[4] Cf. R. de Vaux, *loc. cit.*, p. 326; J. Skinner, *op. cit.*, pp. xii, xx.

stories of Genesis certainly worked with some ancient traditions, and there can be no reason to doubt that amongst them was the tradition that Abraham was a man of singularly exalted character. Was there substance in this tradition, or did they create it? To suppose that they created it would only lead us to wonder who was responsible for this creation in the age when the fiction must have been created, and why Abraham was represented as so much more exalted than the more immediate founder of the Israelite race, Jacob, and so much more exalted than the more remote ancestor, Noah. It seems far more reasonable to suppose that the portrait of Abraham is a substantially reliable one, and that, like the general portrayal of his age, it rests on solid foundations.

Whether Abraham ever worshipped God under the name of Yahweh is much more doubtful. On this matter there are, as has been said, two traditions in the Old Testament. According to the one, the worship of Yahweh in Israel began with Moses; according to the other, it began long before his time. While both cannot be precisely correct, there is probably a measure of truth in both. Obviously it cannot be true that God was not known to Abraham by the name Yahweh[1] and that He was known to him by that name.[2] To this extent there is a flat contradiction that cannot be resolved by any shift. But behind that contradiction there is room for some study which may yield the conclusion that in each tradition is some substance of truth. It is less profitable to expose the contradiction than to ask what truth the two writers, or traditions, purposed to guard by their statements. The contradiction arises because within the Bible we have combined in a single account traditions which arose amongst once separated groups.[3] We do not have to choose one as reliable and reject the other as unreliable, but to recognize that both are reliable, and that it is only the superficial

[1] Ex. 6 : 3.
[2] Gen. 15 : 2, 7.
[3] Cf. S. H. Hooke, *In the Beginning*, pp. 62f.: "The underlying assumption of the Moses saga is that the call of Israel dates from the time of the Egyptian bondage, while the tradition which the Jahvist is using in the Abraham saga represents the call of Israel as going back to Jahveh's call of Abraham out of Mesopotamia. . . . Now it seems to have been the purpose of the Jahvist to unify these two traditions."

impression that we have a single stream of tradition which is misleading.

It is widely recognized to be probable that the name Yahweh did not appear in history for the first time in the days of Moses. Some recent writers have claimed that this divine name is found in the Ras Shamra texts from North Syria, dating from the fourteenth century B.C.[1] This is strongly disputed by others,[2] and seems very improbable. A more probable view is one which has been held for many years, according to which Yahweh was the God whose priest Jethro, the father-in-law of Moses, was.[3] This is admittedly only a theory, and it is by no means universally accepted;[4] yet it does seem to offer a reasonable explanation of a good deal in the Old Testament.[5] At the same time it does not mean that the work of Moses is simply resolved into the mediation to Israel of the worship of his father-in-law's God. For Moses gave to Israel not merely a new name for their God, but a conception of the character of God that certainly did not derive from Jethro. But to this we must return. Here I would merely observe that if Abraham is correctly stated in the Bible never to have known God by the name Yahweh, we have to ask for what reason he is represented in other traditions as having worshipped him by that name.

Many scholars hold that not all the Israelite tribes were

[1] Cf. A. Vincent, *La religion des Judéo-araméens d'Éléphantine*, 1937, pp. 27f.; Ch. Virolleaud, *La déesse 'Anat*, 1938, p. 98; R. Dussaud, *Comptes Rendus de l'Académie des Belles Lettres*, 1940, pp. 364-370, and *Les découvertes de Ras Shamra (Ugarit) et l'Ancien Testament*, 2nd ed., 1941, pp. 171f. See also H. Bauer, *Zeitschrift für die alttestamentliche Wissenschaft*, N.F. x, 1933, pp. 92-94; A. Bea, *Biblica*, xx, 1939, pp. 440ff. J. N. Schofield (*The Religious Background of the Bible*, 1944, facing p. 25) goes so far as to suggest that a bas-relief of a god from Ras Shamra may be a representation of Yahweh. So far as I know there is no shadow of evidence for this suggestion.

[2] Cf. R. de Vaux, *Revue Biblique*, xlvi, 1937, pp. 552f.; W. F. Albright *From the Stone Age to Christianity*, 1940, pp. 197, 328; C. H. Gordon, *Ugaritic Grammar*, 1940, p. 100; W. Baumgartner, *Theologische Rundschau*, N.F. xiii, 1941, pp. 159f.; R. de Langhe, *Un dieu Yahweh à Ras Shamra?* 1942.

[3] Cf. B. Stade, *Geschichte des Volkes Israel*, i, 1887, pp. 130f., and *Biblische Theologie des Alten Testaments*, i, 1905, pp. 42f.; K. Budde, *Religion of Israel to the Exile*, 1899, pp. 17ff.; A. J. Wensinck, "De oorsprongen van het Jahwisme", in *Semietische Studiën uit de nalatenschap van A. J. Wensinck*, 1941, pp. 23-50; B. D. Eerdmans, *The Religion of Israel*, 1947, p. 15.

[4] Cf. e.g., M. Buber, *Moses*, 1947, pp. 42f., 94f., for a recent and strong objection to this view.

[5] Cf. what I have written in the *Bulletin of the John Rylands Library*, xxii, 1938, pp. 285-290.

with Moses in Egypt, and that some of them—and particularly the tribe of Judah—entered Palestine from the south by a movement quite independent of that led by Moses and Joshua.[1] It is probable that this movement was much earlier than the time of Moses,[2] and that the tribe of Judah remained largely isolated from the central tribes right up to the time of the establishment of the monarchy. Yet there is no reason to doubt that the tribe of Judah was already Yahweh-worshipping when it came into the stream of a common life with the other tribes. If it did not derive its worship of Yahweh from Moses, we are left to guess how and when it learned it. Here the theory that Yahweh was the God whom Jethro served is able to provide an answer. For while the father-in-law of Moses is called a Midianite, his brother-in-law is called a Kenite.[3] And associated with Judah in her conquest of the south of Palestine were Kenite elements.[4] If these were worshippers of Yahweh, it is possible that their religion gradually spread throughout the associated tribes, until it permeated the whole. If it were thus taken over from elements that had worshipped Yahweh from time immemorial, it would be natural for Judah to have no tradition of the moment of the beginning of this worship, but to ascribe its existence to the ancient past. Hence it ascribed it not alone to Abraham, but to remoter ancestors, and in one of the traditions we find the name of Yahweh on the lips of Eve, the first mother of mankind.[5]

---

[1] Cf. L. B. Paton, "Israel's Conquest of Canaan", in *Journal of Biblical Literature*, xxxii, 1913, pp. 1–53; C. F. Burney, *Israel's Settlement in Canaan*, 1921; G. A. Barton, "The Habiri of the El-Amarna Tablets and the Hebrew Conquest of Palestine", in *Journal of Biblical Literature*, xlviii, 1929, pp. 144–148.

[2] T. J. Meek, however, places the movement into Judah later than the occupation of the Central Highlands, and associates Moses with the entry into Judah. Cf. "A Proposed Reconstruction of Hebrew History", in *American Journal of Theology*, xxiv, 1920, pp. 209–216; "The Israelite Conquest of Ephraim", in *Bulletin of the American Schools of Oriental Research*, No. 61, February 1936, pp. 17–19; *Hebrew Origins*, 1936, Chapter 1.

[3] Judges 4 : 11.

[4] Judges 1 : 16.

[5] Gen. 4 : 1. This passage is usually referred to the J Document of the Pentateuch. O. Eissfeldt assigns it to his Lay source, L, which he regards as the oldest of the sources (*Hexateuch-Synopse*, 1922, p. 89). By R. H. Pfeiffer it is ascribed to an Edomite source, S, which is located in the age of Solomon. It is not quite clear, however, whether Pfeiffer holds this verse to belong to the original form of the source, or to its revised form, which he places in the period 600–

That Yahweh was worshipped by Kenites as anciently as the time of Abraham is thus likely enough, though it is improbable that Abraham ever worshipped God by that name. Not seldom the religion of the patriarchs is represented in modern works as a form of animism,[1] and up to a point this is undoubtedly true. They worshipped by sacred wells,[2] and trees,[3] and stones,[4] which were doubtless regarded as the habitations of the spirits. But again, when we penetrate beneath the form to the substance, we are dissatisfied with this as a sufficient and complete account. To revert to Abraham, we find that he stands out in the traditions as a man of singularly noble character, whose fundamental greatness of spirit is unaffected whatever the name of the God he worshipped, and we are left to wonder at the quality of his religion, whose fruits were visible in the loftiness of his spirit. Here is something which does not belong inherently to animism, and we have not disposed of Abraham's religion by simply labelling it as animism, or polydaemonism. It is highly probable that his religion was more exalted in its quality than any contemporary Kenite Yahwism, and it was certainly more exalted than Jacob's. He is said to have left Ur of the Chaldees for Harran with his father, Terah.[5] In recent years it has been claimed that the name of Terah is found in the Ras Shamra texts, where he figures as a lunar deity.[6] This view is, however, contested and has secured little

---

400 B.C. See his *Introduction to the Old Testament*, 1941, pp. 160f. On the general conception of this source see "A Non-Israelite Source of the Book of Genesis", in *Zeitschrift für die alttestamentliche Wissenschaft*, N.F. vii, 1930, pp. 66–73.

[1] Cf. E. Kautzsch, in Hastings' *Dictionary of the Bible*, Extra Vol., 1904, cols. 615ff.; H. P. Smith, *Religion of Israel*, 1914, Chap. 2; Oesterley and Robinson, *Hebrew Religion: Its Origin and Development*, 2nd ed., 1937, Chaps. 2–4.

[2] E.g. at Kadesh (Gen. 14 : 17), Beersheba (21 : 29ff.); cf. Beer-lahai-roi (16 : 14).

[3] E.g. at Hebron (Gen. 13 : 18, 14 : 13, 18 : 1), Beersheba (21 : 33), Shechem (35 : 4), Bethel (35 : 8).

[4] E.g. at Bethel (Gen. 28 : 11–22).

[5] Gen. 11 : 31.

[6] Cf. Ch. Virolleaud, *Syria*, xiv, 1933, p. 149, and in several other places, but especially *La Légende de Keret*, 1936, pp. 22ff.; R. Dussaud, *Les découvertes de Ras Shamra (Ugarit) et l'Ancien Testament*, 2nd ed., 1941, pp. 141, 156f. Cf. too, J. W. Jack, *The Ras Shamra Texts: their Bearing on the Old Testament*, 1935, pp. 41, 54; H. L. Ginsberg, *Journal of the Royal Asiatic Society*, 1935, p. 61, and *The Ugaritic Texts*, 1936, p. 85; E. Dhorme, *La religion des Hébreux nomades*, 1937, pp. 72f.

following.[1] It is well known that both Ur[2] and Harran were great centres of the worship of the Moon, so that migration from the one to the other is easily credible.[3] When Abraham went forth from Harran, it is probable that his migration was religiously determined. The Biblical account says: "Now Yahweh said to Abram, Go thou forth from thy land, and from thy kinsmen, and from thy father's house, unto the land which I will show thee."[4] If it were in response to a religious urge that Abraham left Harran, his greatness of character could reasonably be found to be its fruit, and his descendants were more penetrating in cherishing the memory of his greatness and thinking of him as an important figure in the story of religion than are those who are content to treat him as an animist, to be classed with animists of all ages and all races.[5]

When Ex. 6 : 2 f. declares that God was not known to the patriarchs by the name of Yahweh, it goes on to declare that the El Shaddai whom they worshipped was to be identified with Yahweh. More important than the name of the deity worshipped is the character of the religion, and the syncretism that claimed the religion of the patriarchs for Yahweh was worthier than that which later debased Yahwism to the level of Canaanite Baalism. Whether, there-

[1] Cf. R. de Vaux, *Revue Biblique*, xlvi, 1937, pp. 543f.; W. F. Albright, "Was the Patriarch Terah a Canaanite Moon-god?", in *Bulletin of the American Schools of Oriental Research*, No. 71, October 1938, pp. 35–40; R. de Langhe, *Les textes de Ras Shamra-Ugarit et leurs apports à l'histoire des origines israélites*, 1939, pp. 47–53, and *Les textes de Ras Shamra-Ugarit et leurs rapports avec le milieu biblique de l'Ancien Testament*, ii, 1945, pp. 488–519; W. Baumgartner, *Theologische Rundschau*, N.F. xiii, 1941, pp. 15ff.; J. Pedersen, *Berytus*, vi, 1941, p. 66.

[2] A. Lods advanced the theory that the Ur of the patriarchal narrative was distinct from the well-known city of Lower Mesopotamia, and was located in Upper Mesopotamia (*Israël des origines au milieu du viiie siècle*, 1930, pp. 187–189; E. Tr. *Israel*, 1932, pp. 165f.). This theory has not commended itself widely to scholars.

[3] Cf. P. Dhorme, *Revue Biblique*, xxxvii, 1928, pp. 379ff., 481ff., and *La religion des Hébreux nomades*, 1937, pp. 69ff.

[4] Gen. 12 : 1.

[5] It would carry us too far to review recent studies on the religion of the patriarchs. A. Alt has advanced the view that each of the patriarchs, Abraham, Isaac and Jacob, had a great religious experience, and that each worshipped a separate deity, around whom a cult grew (*Der Gott der Väter*, 1929). Cf. the view of J. Pedersen, who holds that the different names of gods may preserve reminiscences of diverse divine personalities in early Israel, but that, as we know them, they are all revelations of the same God of Israel (*Israel, III-IV*, 1940, p. 665). B. D. Eerdmans maintains that to the author of the book of Job Yahweh continued to be distinct from El, Eloah and Shaddai (*Studies in Job: 1. The Conceptions of God in the Book of Job*, 1939).

fore, the patriarchs are represented as worshipping Yahweh or as not worshipping Yahweh, they are treated as significant religious figures, and especially so Abraham, and the God of Israel is held to have directed their steps.[1] In this there is nothing which is theologically repugnant to our own ideas. If God is One, and beside Him there is no other, then He accepts as offered unto Him worship that is true and sincere, and guides the feet of all who will respond to His guidance.

Nor is there any irreconcilable conflict between the thought of an election made known through Moses and an election in the fathers. God was not born in the days of Moses, and He who then in grace rescued Israel from her bondage had been active amongst men in earlier days. What the Old Testament writers wished to say by declaring the election of Israel to date back to the time of Abraham was that it was not merely the tribes that were led out of Egypt by Moses that were chosen of God. The tribes that were akin to them in origin, that worshipped the same God, and that came into the stream of a common life with them, were also of the elect people. This was not a mere antedating of the election through Moses. It was a recognition of facts. In responding to that religious urge which brought him out of Harran, Abraham was not alone taking a step which brought blessing upon him and determined his subsequent course; he was also doing something which entailed blessing for his descendants and affected their history. Abraham's migration was a significant moment in the history of Israel's election, in which the hand of God was legitimately seen.[2]

---

[1] Cf. E. A. Leslie, *Old Testament Religion*, 1936, p. 76: "Abraham, Isaac and Jacob we rightly view as towering figures among the ancient Hebrews. Although shrouded with mystery they must have been personalities of great religious genius to have so permanently influenced Israel." The character of Isaac is more colourless than the others, and that of Jacob less exalted than that of Abraham. Indeed the character of Joseph is more exalted in the traditions that have survived than that of Jacob.

[2] The priestly writer who preserved the genealogies that figure in the book of Genesis clearly believed that long before the time of Abraham God was fashioning for Himself a people that should serve Him. But that rests on a tracing back from the patriarchs, and is quite different from the election in Abraham or through Moses. For here we have a personal response in conscious obedience in the first, and a corporate response mediated through the second. Of those who preceded only one here and there, such as Enoch and Noah, is noted for commendation, and there is little suggestion of an unbroken sequence of chosen men.

Yet when this is said, it should be added that with the work of Moses we come to a far more significant moment in the story of that election. Whatever Abraham may have achieved in the sphere of personal religion, he is not credited in the tradition with having achieved anything in the prophetic sphere.[1] But the work of Moses was essentially prophetic. This is declared in the Old Testament,[2] though Moses is often omitted from the list of prophetic figures of the Bible in modern works.[3] He came to men as the mouthpiece of God, announcing His word, declaring and interpreting the event of history, and finding in the interpreted event the revelation of the character of God.[4] He also established the religion of Yahweh amongst the tribes he led, and gave it a character which was new. All this was essentially prophetic work, and Marti observes that "he is only rightly understood when he is conceived as a prophet".[5] Similarly C. R. North says: "The Hebrew estimate of him was that he was a prophet, indeed the greatest of the prophets. If the function of the prophet was to act as interpreter between Yahweh and his people, that estimate does not seem exaggerated."[6]

It is well that both the election in Abraham and the election through Moses figure in the Bible. One of the consequences of the very constitution of human society is that a man may bless or curse not alone himself, but those who are associated with him and those who come after him. By the very fact of his exaltation of character, and the tradition of that exaltation which he passed on to his descendants Abraham was a blessing. No man lives to himself alone, and no man can tower above the level of his contemporaries without blessing others. Yet that blessing is not quite so

---

[1] In Gen. 20 : 7, 17 Abraham is called a prophet, and exercises the intercessory function of the prophet (cf. 1 Sam. 12 : 23, Jer. 15 : 1). He is nevertheless not represented in the tradition as a prophetic figure, mediating the word of God to his fellows.
[2] Num. 12 : 6ff., Deut. 18 : 5, 34 : 10, Hos. 12 : 13 (Heb. 14).
[3] It is to be noted, however, that P. Volz included Moses amongst his *Prophetengestalten des Alten Testaments*, 1938.
[4] Cf. H. Wheeler Robinson, *Inspiration and Revelation in the Old Testament*, 1946, pp. 43ff.
[5] Cf. *The Religion of the Old Testament*, E. Tr., 1914, pp. 63f.
[6] Cf. *The Old Testament Interpretation of History*, 1946, pp. 170f.

automatic as some passages would suggest. It may be accepted or rejected by those whose heritage it is, and they who reject it lose their heritage. But if Abraham was a blessing by what he was, Moses was a blessing rather by what he did. He came to men declaring not that they were chosen *in* him, but that their election was announced *through* him. The purpose of his election was to declare theirs, and to establish their faith in that election and all that it involved.

Israel's election in Abraham is announced in that passage that tells of his migration from Harran. There God is represented as saying to him:

> And I will make thee a great nation,
> And I will bless thee;
> And I will make thy name great,
> And it shall be[1] a blessing.
> I will bless them that bless thee,
> And thy curser will I curse;
> And all the families of the earth
> Shall invoke blessing through thee.[2]

In other passages the same thought appears. We read: "And Abraham shall surely become a great and powerful nation; and in him all the nations of the earth shall invoke blessing."[3]

Or again:

> For I will surely bless thee
> And greatly multiply thy seed,
> As the stars of the heavens,
> And as the sand by the shore of the sea;
> And thy seed shall possess the gate of its foes,
> And all the nations of the earth
> Through thy seed shall invoke blessing.[4]

No reason for the election of Abraham is offered. Yet the reader feels that though it is of God's grace that He chooses him it is not an arbitrary choice. At first sight there might

---

[1] Reading $w^eh\bar{a}y\bar{a}h$ for the Massoretic $wehy\bar{e}h$=*and be*. Cf. Skinner, *Genesis* (ICC), p. 244.
[2] Gen. 12 : 2f. For the justification of the rendering of the last line, see below in Chapter 2.
[3] Gen. 18 : 18.
[4] Gen. 22 : 17f.

seem to be some arbitrariness in it, since it involved the descendants of Abraham.¹ But, as has been said, a beneficent God has made it of the very constitution of things that a man's character and achievements are never his alone, and in this there is a principle which has worked to the enormous advantage of men, despite its reverse side in the entail of curse which a man may leave.² Moreover, that it was not really arbitrary is made clear in the sequel. For Esau was not the heir of the election. It was not quite automatic for the descendants of Abraham. It became the inheritance of Isaac, and then of Jacob alone. For it is declared to have been renewed to each of these. To Isaac God said:

> I will multiply thy seed
> As the stars of the heavens,
> And I will give to thy seed
> The whole of these lands;
> And all the nations of the earth
> Through thy seed shall invoke blessing.³

And again to Jacob He said: "And thy seed shall be as the dust of the earth, and thou shalt spread to the west and to the east and to the north, and to the south; and through thee and thy seed shall all the families of the earth invoke blessing."⁴

¹ Frequently we find a reference back to this covenant, to which no condition appears to be attached, and it is sometimes emphasized that it was everlasting and irrevocable. So J. F. Walvoord, *Bibliotheca Sacra*, cii, 1945, pp. 27–36, esp. p. 30. Cf. Ex. 32 : 13, Lev. 26 : 42, Deut. 1 : 8, 4 : 31, 6 : 10, 9 : 27, 2 Kings 13 : 23, 1 Chr. 16 : 16–18. Cf. too, Ass. Mos. 4 : 2, Pas. Sol. 9 : 16–19, 11 : 8f. Similarly the fact of the Divine election is frequently referred to as though it were unconditional and eternal. Cf. 1 Sam. 12 : 22, Psa. 33 : 12. Deut. 32 : 9 throws back the Divine election of Israel to the beginning of time, and 4 Ezra (2 Esdras) 6 : 55, 59 says that the world was made for the sake of Israel. W. O. E. Oesterley (*II Esdras*, 1933, p. xl) says: "This is certainly not the teaching of the Old Testament, where the election of Israel on the part of God is always referred to as an act of divine love, or mercy, or grace . . . the Old Testament teaches that Israel was chosen to be the instrument of the conversion of the Gentiles." While this is true of the Old Testament as a whole, it should not be forgotten that there are also the above-mentioned texts, which, taken by themselves, might seem to justify another point of view. It will be seen below that the everlasting and irrevocable character of the divine election of Israel may be maintained, provided Israel is not equated with the physical descendants of Abraham or of Jacob, but instead this thought is linked with the rest of the teaching of the Old Testament as to who are Israel.

² Cf. what I have written in *The Rediscovery of the Old Testament*, 1946, pp. 150f. (American ed., pp. 213f.).

³ Gen. 26 : 4.   ⁴ Gen. 27 : 14.

Here already there appears by implication an incipient idea which was emphasized by the prophets, and it is of importance to note that its germs are found here in documents that antedate the work of the eighth- and seventh-century prophets. The divine election and covenant is never merely automatic. It must be renewed by each generation of those that inherit it. Neither the first establishment of the covenant nor its renewal is arbitrary. For God is never arbitrary in His electing grace or in the establishment of the covenant that follows it. In so far as any reason for Abraham's election could be deduced from the book of Genesis, it would be the loftiness of the character which he shows. For while his marriage with his half-sister[1] would be condemned as incest by later law and practice,[2] and while his passing his wife off as his sister[3] does not commend him in our eyes, we cannot but acknowledge that the figure of Abraham, as he stands before us in these narratives, is a singularly exalted one, and especially when we remember the times in which he lived and the antiquity of the documents in which his story is enshrined. Yet it would be unwise to conclude that the Divine election rests on a worth which God merely recognizes, and which lies in a man's own soul. Such a thought could only lead to the self-congratulation of the elect, to whose worth God Himself pays tribute. Moreover, it begs the question how far the greatness of Abraham was the fruit of his election and his response to the grace of God.[4]

The character of Isaac is more colourless than that of Abraham, and more colourless too than that of Jacob. It has already been said that the character of Jacob is less exalted than that of Abraham, and if we were inclined to conclude from the story of the latter that God chooses them that are choice, we should be much more doubtful when we came

[1] Gen. 20 : 12.
[2] Cf. Lev. 18 : 9.
[3] Gen. 11 : 10ff., 20 : 1ff.
[4] Cf. J. O. F. Murray, in Hastings' *Dictionary of the Bible*, i, 1898, p. 679 a: "Since the root of all loveliness is in God, and since there can be no goodness apart from Him, we cannot argue as if it were possible for man to possess or develop any goodness or loveliness independent of, and so constituting a claim on, the choice of God. We ought not, therefore, to be surprised when we find Israel expressly warned in Holy Scripture to reject the flattering assumption that they had been chosen on the ground of their own inherent attractiveness."

to the story of Jacob. Sometimes God chooses those who are not particularly choice. This is not the demonstration of His arbitrariness, but of His wisdom and His grace. For underlying His choice His purpose is to be sought. Instead of looking behind for its causes, we should view it teleologically, and perceive that God was choosing an instrument fitted for His purpose. For the character that he came to attain Abraham was chosen; Isaac and Jacob less for themselves than for those who should come after them.

The election of the Israelite slaves in Egypt through Moses is something wholly different from the election of the patriarchs, and, as has been said, of far greater significance in the history of religion. In many modern works Moses is treated as one of whom we can have little knowledge.[1] That all the detailed legislation of the Pentateuch is not to be ascribed to him is generally agreed. Even the Decalogue is commonly denied him. The story of his childhood is treated as pure legend, to be paralleled by similar legends from many countries and times.[2] Whether he lived at all is sometimes doubted.[3] Even if we can believe that he lived, there are some scholars who suppose that we can scarcely credit more than that he somehow led the Israelites out of Egypt, and persuaded them to worship the Kenite God, Yahweh, while one recent writer denies that Moses ever set foot in Egypt, and makes him only the priest of Kadesh who persuaded the Israelites who came out of Egypt, after the event, to believe that his God had delivered them.[4]

Against this extreme scepticism I think it is fair to say that there is some reaction to-day, though I think we must beware of an unrestrained acceptance of all the details of the traditions. It is important that we should sift the tradi-

---

[1] Cf. H. Preserved Smith, *Old Testament History*, 1911, chapter 4, which reaches the conclusion that "there may have been an Israelite clan that sojourned in Egypt. Its exodus was not improbably due to a religious leader". These results are rightly described by the author as "meagre". Cf. J. N. Schofield, *Historical Background of the Bible*, 1938, chapter 4.

[2] For a valuable collection of parallels, cf. W. J. Gruffydd, "Moses in the Light of Comparative Folklore", in *Zeitschrift für die alttestamentliche Wissenschaft*, N.F. v, 1928, pp. 260-270.

[3] So Eduard Meyer, *Die Israeliten und ihre Nachbarstämme*, 1906, p. 451 n.

[4] Cf. C. A. Simpson, *Revelation and Response in the Old Testament*, 1947, chapter 2.

tions, both in the light of extra-Biblical materials provided by archaeology and in the light of the literary criticism of the Old Testament, in order to gain, if possible, some reasonably clear idea of the broad outlines of the historical facts that were for Israel charged with significant message.[1] For Israel found God in history, and believed that His character stood revealed in His acts on that plane. If we would understand Biblical religion, therefore, we cannot treat the history as immaterial.[2]

In a number of places I have traced the broad outlines of the facts of history, so far as I believe they can be pieced together from the scattered materials in our hands.[3] I regard Moses as a real figure of history, of Levite stock, but with some Kenite blood on his mother's side,[4] who was brought up in Egypt, but who fled to the desert to some of his relations on his mother's side, when he was compelled to leave Egypt. Here he felt the call of his father-in-law's God, Yahweh, to go in His name into Egypt and to lead out the brethren whose sufferings had aroused his indignation and been responsible for his flight. Constrained by the power of

---

[1] Cf. what I have written in "The Significance of Moses and his Work", in *Religion in Education*, xi, 1943–44, pp. 63–67, and in *The Missionary Message of the Old Testament*, 1945, chapter 1. Cf. too, N. W. Porteous, in *Theologische Aufsätze* (Karl Barth Festschrift) 1936, pp. 147f.

[2] This is true of both Testaments, for Christianity, like the religion of Israel, is rooted and grounded in history. With this contrast the view of E. Brunner, *The Mediator*, 1942, p. 81: "The Christian faith has just as little to do with the influence of Jesus on the history of the world as it has to do with His historical personality. It is not interested in the 'Founder of Christianity', nor in His influence on history."

[3] Cf. "Israel's Sojourn in Egypt", in *Bulletin of the John Rylands Library*, xxii, 1938, pp. 243–290; "The Eisodus and the Exodus", in *Expository Times*, l, 1938–39, pp. 503–508; "The Exodus and the Settlement in Canaan", in *Bulletin of the American Schools of Oriental Research*, No. 85, February 1942, pp. 27–31; "Early Levite History and the Question of the Exodus", in *Journal of Near Eastern Studies*, iii, 1944, pp. 73–78; *The Rediscovery of the Old Testament*, 1946, pp. 79ff. (American ed., pp. 111ff.). To this question I return in my Schweich Lectures, 1948.

[4] Cf. his mother's name, Jochebed, which is probably compounded of the divine name, Yahweh. This name has been sometimes supposed to be the Achilles' heel of the Kenite theory of the origin of Yahwism, and its embarrassment has been avoided by emphasizing the lateness of the evidence for the name and the possibility that it may be differently interpreted. Thus, M. Noth doubts the connexion with Yahweh (*Die israelitischen Personennamen*, 1928, p. 111). On the other hand, H. Bauer connects it with the doubtful Yw of the Ras Shamra texts (*Zeitschrift für die alttestamentliche Wissenschaft*, N.F. x, 1933, pp. 92f.). Actually it may be frankly accepted without providing any embarrassment to the Kenite theory. Cf. *Expository Times*, l, 1938–39, p. 508.

THE ELECTION OF ISRAEL

God, revealed in natural events, which responded not alone to Israel's need, but to the prior promise of Moses, who claimed that he was speaking not out of his own cleverness but as the divine mouthpiece, Pharaoh was compelled to let them go. Moses then led the people he had brought out of Egypt to the sacred mount, and there they pledged themselves in a covenant of loyalty to the God who had delivered them. Moreover, Moses gave them more than a new Divine name for their God, derived from that of his father-in-law's God. He gave a new quality to their religion, which was not to be found in Kenite Yahwism, and crystallized that new quality in a new Decalogue.[1]

That Israel was delivered from Egypt seems to me hard indeed to doubt. The memory of that deliverance was so deeply engrained in Israelite traditions that it seems inconceivable that it was mere fancy. Nor is it credible to me that Israel's sense of her election should rest on nothing more substantial than her sense of self-importance. For in that case why did she so surprisingly invent the story that at the time of her election she was living in foreign bondage? None of the credit for her deliverance is ascribed to her own activity, and no Israelite vanity is reflected in the story. She was but the passive spectator of wonders that broke the power of Pharaoh and struck the fetters from her hands. Yet if that were all, her faith in her election would not be very securely based. For all might be explained as the chance of circumstance, whereby events responded to her need, and turned to her advantage. Nor, if that were all, could any explanation be offered of Israel's pledging herself to a new God. If she just happened to find an opportunity to escape from Egypt, she would most naturally have attributed her deliverance to the God she had always worshipped. Through all her history she looked back to this as the supremely

---

[1] It should be emphatically stated that the Kenite view of the origin of the divine name does not mean the reduction of the work of Moses to no more than the mediating of the Kenite religion to the Israelites. Cf. my *Rediscovery of the Old Testament*, pp. 84ff. (American ed., pp. 119ff.). Cf. too, K. Marti, *The Religion of the Old Testament*, English Tr., 1914, p. 62: "Even though Jahwe was originally the name of the God of Sinai, it immediately received a higher significance under the Israelites than that which it had possessed as the God of the confederate tribes of Mount Sinai."

creative moment of her history, and we have already looked at the passages which regard it as the moment when Yahweh and Israel first came together as God and people.

The really vital elements in the story seem to me to lie in the fact of Moses' call, and in the covenant which was the sequel to Israel's election. In the call there was something unique in the history of religion. For here, if the view above outlined is correct, the Kenite God took under His wing a people that did not know Him as its God, and sent Moses in His name to effect its deliverance. That was surely a strange idea to occur to Moses, and he could only have acted on it if he were first profoundly convinced that it was more than his idea. And such a conviction could only come to him through some deep spiritual experience, such as that which is dramatically portrayed in the story of his call. It should be added that if we regard that story as pure fiction, the baseless creation of a later writer, we are in no better case. For it would be just as strange an idea to occur to that writer, while if we deny the historicity and the reality of the call of Moses, we leave the story of the Exodus and the mark it made on Israelite thought quite unintelligible. Nor can we resolve the story of this call into the disordered fancy of a deluded man, who just out of the womb of his own thought produced this strange idea. We have to reckon with the fact that Moses not only believed that Yahweh had sent him in His name to lead the Israelites out of Egypt, but that he announced to them his mission, and succeeded in leading them out. Events responded, therefore, not alone to the need of Israel, but to the prior promise of Moses. Yet they were such events as could not be controlled by Moses, or by any other human agency. Israel therefore believed that God had chosen her, because she was undoubtedly saved—and that by no human hand—as the sequel to the declaration of her election and her response in faith—albeit a halting faith—in the declaration.

Here is something completely other than the self-vaunting inscriptions of eastern potentates. The election here is not called forth by any quality of greatness in the nation that is chosen, yet it carries religious significance of the greatest importance. It might seem again, on a superficial view, to be quite arbitrary. If there was nothing of special worth in Israel to account for God's choice of her, and if she was really no better than peoples around her, then surely His choice must have been arbitrary. We seem, indeed, to be ever on the horns of a dilemma. If God chooses the worthy, then His grace is in question; while if He chooses the unworthy, then His justice is in question. Either He is self-interested, and man's salvation is really determined by himself; or God is arbitrary, and we are not sure whether we can respect Him. From this unreal dilemma we are saved when we view election teleologically. It is ever election for some purpose, and God ever chooses those who are best suited for His purpose.[1] His purposes are many, and He chooses many to serve Him. His greatest purpose is to reveal Himself to men, and for that purpose Israel was chosen because Israel was most suited to it. This is not to say that He has not revealed Himself to men of other nations, or that He has not chosen other nations for other purposes. He has not withheld the revelation of Himself from man anywhere, but in varying measure, according to the capacity and willingness of men to receive it, has granted it. Yet through men of Israel did He give fuller revelation than through any other, not because they were initially better than others, or because they were His favourites, but because they were more suited to this purpose. In all the realms of cultural activity—in literature, in art, in science, in philosophy—Greece far outclassed Israel. And these are not realms to be despised. We can legitimately recognize that all this is of God, and that for this purpose He chose Greece in a special measure, because she was suited to this purpose. The uniqueness of His choice of Israel was the uniqueness of the degree in which He purposed to reveal His character and His will through her, and for this she was supremely suited.[2]

---

[1] Cf. my *Rediscovery of the Old Testament*, pp. 63 ff. (American ed., pp. 89 ff.).
[2] N. W. Porteous (in *Theologische Aufsätze* [Karl Barth Festschrift], 1936, p. 163) protests against the use of the term election for anything but a religious purpose: "It involves a misunderstanding and a misuse of the term 'election' when one says God 'elected' a people for a particular task, because this people

It may be replied that there are passages in the Bible which suggest that God is arbitrary. There are, for instance, those passages which speak of Him under the metaphor of a potter, making now a vessel of honour, and now a vessel of dishonour, of the same lump of clay, or refashioning the clay at will. When Jeremiah watched the potter at work he observed that "when the vessel that he was making of the clay was spoilt in the hand of the potter, he made it up again into another vessel, just as it seemed good in the eyes of the potter to do".[1] And the prophet found here the message of Yahweh, who said: "Can I not do with you, O house of Israel, as this potter does? Behold, as clay in the hands of the potter, so are ye in my hands." And the Apostle Paul says: "Shall that which is moulded say to the moulder, Why hast thou made me thus? Has not the potter the right to make with his clay of the same lump now a vessel of honour and a vessel of dishonour?"[2]

But is the potter arbitrary in his work? Neither Jeremiah nor Paul had in mind an aimless dilettante, working in a casual and haphazard way, turning out vessels according to the chance whim of the moment, but a potter who makes vessels according to some plan, and who uses his materials under the control of his purpose. There are some materials which better suit one type of vessel and some which better suit another, and within each category of materials there are varieties of vessels which can be made. If the material does not work suitably into one form, the potter may convert it to another, but it is another for which he has some use. There is nothing morally reprehensible about it. The vessel

---

possessed some special quality. To speak in the same breath of the election of Greece or Rome and of the election of Israel betrays a complete inability to understand what election means. It is a theological, not a cultural concept." Despite this I have no wish to modify what I have said above. I differentiate between culture and religion, and do not place them on the same level, but I cannot prohibit God interest in, or access to, the world of culture, or deny Him any purpose in this sphere. And if I allow Him any desire to co-operate with man in this sphere, I can hardly deny Him the right to choose His own instruments for His purpose. If the Scriptures can use the language of election with reference to Assyria and Babylonia, elect only to be scourges, we may without impropriety use it of Greece and Rome, which served higher purposes of God.

[1] Jer. 19 : 4.
[2] Rom. 9 : 21.

that is destroyed is one for which he has no use,[1] and not one that he has made for the express purpose of destroying it. Similarly, when God destroys, He destroys because His purpose is not realized, and men are not serviceable to Him, and not because He created in order to destroy.

I have always found it hard to understand why it should be supposed that there is anything morally repugnant in God's electing one nation for one purpose and another for another, or one man for one purpose and another for another. It is probably largely because of the notion of election to heaven or hell, which men have introduced into the question. The vessel of dishonour is thought of as a child of hell.[2] But this is really irrelevant to the meaning of either prophet or apostle.[3] To suppose that a crazy potter, who made vessels with no other thought than that he would afterwards knock them to pieces, is the type and figure of God is supremely dishonouring to God. The vessel of dishonour which the potter makes is still something that he wants, and that has a definite use. Perchance he is confident that he can sell it to some customer, and thus it will be serviceable to him. He does not make it with the deliberate intention that it shall be

---

[1] Calvin observes, with reference to this passage, that "nothing is taught with Jeremiah than that Israel is in the hand of the Lord, so that for his sins he may break him in pieces, as a potter may his earthen vessel" (*Commentary upon the Epistle to the Romans*, English Tr. by H. Beveridge, 1844, p. 268). This clearly recognizes that in the teaching of Jeremiah the potter is not arbitrary.

[2] Cf. Calvin, *Institutes of the Christian Religion*, English Tr. by H. Beveridge, ii, 1869, p. 210: "Scripture clearly proves this much, that God by his eternal and immutable counsel determined once for all those whom it was his pleasure one day to admit to salvation, and those whom, on the other hand, it was his pleasure to doom to destruction."

[3] Cf. Sanday and Headlam, *The Epistle to the Romans* (ICC), 5th ed., 1920, p. 260: "The potter is represented not merely as adapting for this or that purpose a vessel already made, but as making out of a mass of shapeless material one to which he gives a character and form adapted for different uses, some honourable, some dishonourable." C. H. Dodd observes that this "is the weakest point in the whole epistle" (*The Epistle of Paul to the Romans* [MC], 1942, p. 159). Its weakness lies, as J. Denney remarks (*Expositor's Greek Testament*, ii, p. 664 a) in the fact that "the relation of God to man is not that of the potter to dead matter". This is clearly recognized by Jeremiah in the application of the parable. In Rom. 9 : 22 Paul goes on to speak of "vessels of wrath", but Denney (*loc. cit.*, p. 664 b) thinks the word "vessels" is "perhaps prompted by the previous verse, but the whole associations of the potter and the clay are not to be carried over". He says they are expressly excluded by "endured with much longsuffering". When the apostle speaks of them as "prepared for destruction", he can hardly have been thinking of a potter preparing vessels for the sport of destroying them.

injurious to his interests. The wicked, on the other hand, are rebels against God's purpose, and can in no sense be said to be elected by God to oppose Him. It is true that He can overcome their opposition, and can even make it serve His purpose against their very intention. But the metaphor of the potter can certainly not be used to support the idea that God elects any to oppose Him and rebel against Him. It implies that all the vessels, both those of honour and those of dishonour, are chosen, for all in their varying ways serve the potter's purpose, and the vessel that is destroyed is one for which the potter has no purpose or use. Whom God chooses, He chooses for service. There is variety of service, but it is all service, and it is all service for God. Whom God destroys, He finds no longer serviceable. Hence the use of this metaphor only supports the view that the Divine election concerns exclusively the Divine service.

When God chose Israel in her weakness and bondage, therefore, and sent Moses in His name to lead her forth from Egypt, it was because Israel was especially suited to the purpose of revelation which He cherished. The Divine initiative in grace was revealed, and the Divine compassion for the downtrodden and the oppressed. God's electing and His saving grace were revealed, as they could not have been by His choice of some great and powerful people. His activity in human history is seen, and the wonder of His resources to effect His will. For us who think of God as One, and who look back on many centuries of unfolding revelation that have followed the Exodus, these things seem commonplace. But they were anything but commonplace at that time. The Kenite God was not thought of as the sole God of the universe, and that He should choose a people that did not worship Him must have seemed amazing. Yet His power was equal to His purpose, and all the might of Egypt and her gods could not deflect Him from it. The forces of Nature lay within His control, and whatsoever He would that He could do. Yet even more significant than the revelation of His power was the revelation of His character as gracious and merciful and saving. The theological corollaries of the election and the Exodus were therefore of the greatest importance, and they provide the great foundation of Old Testament religion.[1] For we must never forget that these did not belong to Kenite Yahwism. To the Kenites Yahweh was their God because He always had been; to Israel He was their God because He had chosen them, and His character, as revealed in the deliverance which Moses both promised and interpreted, was understood as the Kenites did not understand it.

Nor could the matter rest there. Election is for service. And if God chose Israel, it was not alone that He might reveal Himself to her, but that He might claim her service. Hence Moses mediated the Covenant to Israel, in which she responded in gratitude to the Divine election and deliverance, and pledged her loyalty to Him who had delivered her—a loyalty as complete and as unconditional as the deliverance had been.

While, then, there is a measure of truth in the election of Abraham and in the election of Israel through Moses, it is the latter which has proved religiously so much the more fruitful. In so far as there is truth in either, it is not the truth of an abstract idea, but the truth that has been established in experience. For the religion of the Old Testament is fundamentally rooted and grounded in history and experience.[2] It is not the fruit of the speculations of the philosopher, weaving patterns out of the material of his own abstract thought, but the faith of realists who based themselves on the things through which they had lived. Yet the facts of experience are seldom so simple as we should like them to be, and they are often capable of yielding more than one deduction, and if we select our facts we can establish the conclusion that is agreeable to us, and persuade ourselves that it is the only principle on which truth rests. Yet truth is more often to be expressed in paradox than in any simple pro-

---

[1] Cf. *Religion in Education*, xi, 1943-44, pp. 63ff.; and my *Rediscovery of the Old Testament*, pp. 65f. (American ed., pp. 91ff.).
[2] Cf. G. E. Wright, *The Challenge of Israel's Faith*, p. 16 (English ed., p. 26): "The prophets know nothing of an abstract principle of truth. They know only of God's revelation in the natural and human world. Disregard the history, and we should have left in prophetic religion little but meaningless abstractions which we ourselves have made."

position, and in the tension between two apparently incompatible principles there is a greater degree of truth than in either alone.[1] Jeremiah could warn the men of his generation of the bitter suffering in which they would involve their children by the folly of their way;[2] he could also declare that it was of no use for them to blame their fathers for the suffering they experienced.[3] Neither was the whole truth, yet in each there is a measure of truth. It belongs to the complexity of our social relationships that we are carried in the stream of the life of those around us, and of those who preceded us; yet each generation and each individual may modify that stream, instead of being carried passively on its current. From the story of Abraham we may conclude that God chooses those who are, or who will become, the choice, and that His election carries consequences for generations yet unborn. Yet that is not the whole truth, and it could not of itself explain why the Jews, and only the Jews of Abraham's descendants, became the Chosen People. From the story of the Exodus and all the complex of events out of which it arose and to which it led we may conclude that His choice bears no relation to moral or spiritual worth. Yet again that would be far from the whole truth. God's choice is never to be understood save in relation to its purpose, and He chose Israel in the patriarchs and in those Israelite elements which were in bondage in Egypt, because Israel could serve His purpose. And despite all her lapses and follies, and all the things for which the prophets so castigated her, she did greatly serve that purpose, and all the world is enriched by the riches of her inheritance.

[1] Cf. my *Relevance of the Bible*, 1942, pp. 158f.
[2] Jer. 16 : 3f.
[3] Jer. 31 : 29f.

Chapter Two

THE COROLLARIES OF ISRAEL'S ELECTION

ELECTION is for service. This is not to ignore the fact that it carries with it privilege. For in the service of God is man's supreme privilege and honour. Yet, as will appear, the measure of the privilege varies widely according to the glory of the service. Some are chosen for involuntary service, and there is little honour or privilege for them. In its highest form, however—election to be the recipient of the divine revelation and the medium of revelation to others—so great a privilege is involved that all who are granted it must be filled with humble wonder in the moment of their realization of its greatness. To those who willingly and consciously accept the task to which they are called, the resources of God are open for the fulfilment of their mission, and here again is high privilege. Yet it is never primarily for the privilege but for the service that the elect are chosen.[1]

Throughout the Old Testament the first corollary of the Divine election of Israel and the deliverance of the tribes that were in Egypt is that God has a claim to Israel's service. When the people whom Moses led reached the sacred mount, he said to them in the name of God: "Ye have yourselves seen what I did to Egypt, and how I lifted you on eagles' pinions, and brought you unto myself. And now if ye will truly hearken to my voice, and keep my covenant, then shall ye be my own possession out of all the peoples."[2] König has

---

[1] Cf. S. Cave, *The Gospel of St. Paul*, 1928, p. 99: "Election is not for privilege, but for service, and God's favour is not dependent on men's birth or colour."

[2] Ex. 19 : 4f. These verses are assigned to J by S. R. Driver (*Introduction to the Literature of the Old Testament*, 9th ed., 1913, p. 31) and by Oesterley and Robinson (*Introduction to the Books of the Old Testament*, 1934, p. 37). Eissfeldt, however, assigns them to E (*Hexateuch-Synopse*, 1922, p. 146*), and G. Beer to E1 (*Exodus* [HAT], 1939, p. 97). W. H. Bennett (*Exodus* [CentB], p. 157) assigns them to R, without specifying which Redactor is intended, while A. H. McNeile (*The Book of Exodus* [WC], 2nd ed., 1917, p. 110) specifies R^D. With

observed that this verse supplies the dominating note of all Old Testament prophecy.[1] Again and again the thought is expressed that by His deliverance of Israel God had a claim on her loyalty, and that she who was His people, bound to Him by a sacred Covenant, was pledged to give Him that loyalty.

The Covenant is sometimes thought of in the somewhat sordid terms of a bargain.[2] Jacob made that sort of covenant with God at Bethel: "If God will be with me, and keep me on this journey that I am making, and will give me food to eat and clothes to wear, so that I return safely to my father's house, then Yahweh shall be my God."[3] But the Covenant of Sinai was not of that sort. It was based on the fact of what God had already achieved, and not on His conditional performances. "Ye have seen what I did." And Israel's response to God's achieved deliverance was the pledge of her undeviating loyalty. Against this it may be argued that the verse already quoted contains a condition, though this time laid down by God and not to Him. "If ye will truly

---

this last agrees C. A. Simpson (*The Early Traditions of Israel*, 1948, p. 199), following B. Baentsch (*Exodus-Leviticus* [HK], 1903, p. 172), and so *La Bible du Centenaire* (i, 1941, p. 94). That the tradition of a covenant goes back to the most ancient of the sources is, however, generally agreed. Ex. 24 : 9–11 tells how Moses and Aaron ascended the sacred mount with Nadab and Abihu and the seventy elders and "beheld God, and ate and drank". C. R. North observes that this may well be the most primitive story of the covenant between Yahweh and Israel (*The Old Testament Interpretation of History*, 1946, p. 30). Cf. M. Noth, *Die Gesetze im Pentateuch*, 1940, pp. 32f.; K. Möhlenbrink, *Zeitschrift für die alttestamentliche Wissenschaft*, N.F. xviii, 1942–43, p. 26. This passage is ascribed by Eissfeldt (*op. cit.*, p. 152*) to L (the oldest of the documents), by Driver (*loc. cit.*), Oesterley and Robinson (*loc. cit.*), Bennett (*op. cit.*, p. 198), McNeile (*op. cit.*, p. 148) and *La Bible du Centenaire* (i, p. 103) to J, and by Baentsch (*op. cit.*, p. 216) and Beer (*op. cit.*, p. 126) to E1. W. A. Irwin (*The Intellectual Adventure of Ancient Man*, pp. 328f.) argues that the idea of the covenant is absent from the early sources, but was introduced by J and E. As there are few sources of the Old Testament older than these, apart from a few poems and the Court History of David, we have insufficient basis for this view. What we can say with certainty is that the oldest documents dealing with the wilderness period which have come down to us speak of a covenant.

[1] Cf. *Das alttestamentliche Prophetentum und die moderne Geschichtsforschung*, 1910, pp. 63f.

[2] G. E. Wright (*The Challenge of Israel's Faith*, p. 73; English ed., p. 90) speaks of the Covenant in terms of a contract. He says: "A special contractual relationship was therefore felt to exist between the two parties, a relationship carrying with it certain obligations." Cf. with this R. B. Y. Scott (*The Relevance of the Prophets*, 1944, p. 121): "The covenant required a real sharing of life, and could not be thought of simply as a formal contract, conferring on Israel a special status and a claim upon her God."   [3] Gen. 28 : 20f.

hearken to my voice, and keep my covenant, then ye shall be my own possession." This might seem at first sight to be precisely like Jacob's covenant, but from God's side. The difference, however, is that here Israel was already under a deep obligation to God, whereas in the other case Jacob had not already put God in his debt. Here God has delivered Israel, and Israel pledges herself to Him, while God undertakes that her election shall continue so long as she wishes it to continue. Israel is not compelled to enter into the Covenant; she is not compelled to remain in it. It is her free response to His grace.[1] If she then chooses to violate her Covenant, God will not hold her to it, even though it is an unconditional Covenant which she is making. But if she repudiates the Covenant, then she will repudiate it. It will be terminated, because she terminates it. And in terminating the Covenant she will declare that she no longer wishes to be His people, and therefore she will not be His people.[2]

It could not be made clearer that here there is no conception of God being tied to Israel willy-nilly, so that whatever Israel cared to do He was bound to back her. Her election was not something automatic that made her His people for all time by mere physical generation. She entered into the Covenant voluntarily, and each generation must renew it by accepting for itself its obligations, or it would

---

[1] Cf. C. H. Dodd, *Études théologiques et religieuses*, xxiii, 1948, Nos. 2–3, pp. 11f.: "God's Covenant is a *diathēkē*, and not a *synthēkē*; that is to say, God fixes the terms of the Covenant and offers it to man that he may accept it: the acceptance is also essential."

[2] With what I have written in the foregoing paragraph cf. E. Lohmeyer, *Diatheke*, 1913, p. 54: "The berith of Sinai was for Israel not the solemn confirmation of a natural relationship, such as that between a father and his son, nor yet an agreement to which the parties had pledged themselves under all circumstances, but something that had been brought about on the ground of an overwhelming event in the history of the people, in which they recognized the free activity of God. Hence it always contained the thought that Yahweh of His free grace had made Israel His people ... and that Yahweh was a God of history and that this was a witness of his active love for His people." I have not entered into the question of the derivation of the word $b^e r\hat{\imath}th$ (on which cf. G. Quell, *Theologisches Wörterbuch zum Neuen Testament*, ii, 1935, pp. 107ff.), partly because it would be out of place here, and partly because, as Lohmeyer observes (*op. cit.*, p. 42): "The etymology of a word does not always provide an unquestionable indication of its original meaning, but only a probable clue."

place itself outside the Covenant.[1] The fundamental essence of the Covenant was that it was man's response to the Divine grace,[2] and only those who were heirs of the response could therefore be heirs of the Covenant. The book of Deuteronomy represents Moses as saying to Israel: "Yahweh our God made a covenant with us in Horeb. It was not with our fathers that Yahweh made this covenant, but with us, even with us, all of us who are alive here to-day."[3] It is there implied that the Covenant with the patriarchs was not valid for the generation of the Exodus, but that only the Covenant into which they themselves entered could have validity and meaning for them. And by the same token their Covenant could not have automatic validity for the generations that followed.

This does not mean that God had no claim on their loyalty any longer than they cared to give it. He had delivered them, and in so doing had placed not alone the generation of the Exodus, but all succeeding generations under an obligation to Him. In the act of deliverance He had given a revelation of Himself, which was the inheritance of succeeding generations. The Covenant of Sinai was the response of gratitude; but if any succeeding generation repudiated it, it would be displaying ingratitude, and showing its unworthiness of the privileges to which it was

[1] It is by no accident that the book of Deuteronomy, which insists on the fact of Israel's election in an especial degree, and which calls Israel the personal possession of Yahweh, and which continually reminds Israel of the bondage in Egypt from which she was rescued by Yahweh, most insists on the duty of obedience to the statutes and ordinances of God, and on the demand for gracious service of the helpless and the needy, and is under no illusions about the irrevocable and automatic character of the election, but with vivid force sets forth the consequences of faithlessness. G. von Rad observes that "The verb *bāḥar*, with subject God and object the people, is an original deuteronomic coinage" (*Das Gottesvolk im Deuteronomium*, 1929, p. 28). It is equally to be observed that to the Deuteronomist, the love of God as manifested in his choice of Israel laid upon Israel the sacred obligation to respond to that love by love, and to express her love in obedience.

[2] H. P. Smith (*The Religion of Israel*, 1914, p. 186) observes that the Deuteronomists dwell on the idea of the Covenant with almost wearisome iteration, but regard it as an act of free grace on the part of Yahweh. Cf. N. W. Porteous, *Theologische Aufsätze* (Karl Barth Festschrift), 1936, p. 153, where it is observed that the Covenant is first and foremost the work of God and not of man. It rests on the Divine election and is therefore born of His grace.

[3] Deut. 5 : 2f.

heir. It would be repudiating a moral bond which lay upon it.

It is sometimes observed that the Covenant was bilateral. It was not bilateral in the sense that it laid obligations on both parties; nor in the sense that it was terminable by either party on due notice being given.[1] It laid no obligations upon God. He had already taken upon Himself His obligations before the Covenant was made, for they were the fruit of His grace and not of the Covenant.[2] It offered no right of termination to either party.[3] It declared that God from His side would never terminate it, but it recognized that Israel from her side might terminate it, and if she did God would not hold her to it. By its very nature He could not hold her to it if she wished to terminate it; for loyalty cannot be compelled.[4] But it is made clear that if she terminated it, it would not be because by its terms the Covenant gave her the right to terminate it, but because she dishonourably repudiated it.

All through the Old Testament it is implied that Israel's Covenant is an unconditional one, and not one that she is morally free to withdraw from at any time she wishes. When

---

[1] Cf. J. Bonsirven, *Le judaïsme palestinien*, i, 1934, p. 39: "The covenant was not entirely bilateral. It is so nevertheless in its object, and in its end. God chooses Israel for His people, and he undertakes to preserve her national existence, to develop it and to shower His blessings upon her; on her side the people promise to keep the law of God."

[2] Cf. H. Wheeler Robinson, *Redemption and Revelation*, 1942, p. 226: "When God enters into a covenant, this relation is necessarily the expression of His grace, and springs from the initiative of His own nature and purpose." On the meaning of the word $b^e rîth$ cf. L. Köhler, *Theologie des Alten Testaments*, 1936, pp. 43ff.

[3] H. Wheeler Robinson (*Judaism and Christianity: III. Law and Religion*, ed. E. I. J. Rosenthal, 1938, p. 62) says: "Lord Macmillan, writing on 'Law and Religion', says of the Old Testament that 'the whole conception of the relationship between God and man is legal' (*Law and Other Things*, p. 64). His misconception is due to his taking 'Covenant' to mean 'contract', which is a very misleading rendering of the Hebrew term, *berith*. It would be much truer to say that *berith* is the external expression of one of the richest religous words in the Old Testament, viz. *ḥesed*, which we know as 'loving-kindness', though it includes the sense of loyalty as well as of love." H. F. Hamilton (*The People of God*, i, 1912, p. 42) speaks of the Covenant in the terms of a contract, laying mutual obligations on the contracting parties.

[4] P. Ducros (*La Bible et la méthode historique*, 1945, p. 67) observes that "this 'moralization' of the notion of covenant, opposed to the automatism of the primitive notion, is the essential content of the prophetic message, and even more of that of the Gospel".

she ceases to accept its obligations, she acts treacherously. Hosea says:

> But they transgressed the covenant like Adam;[1]
> There they dealt treacherously with me.[2]

Or again:

> Because they have transgressed my covenant,
> And against my law have rebelled.[3]

Similarly Isaiah says:

> Hear, O heavens! And give ear, O earth!
> For Yahweh hath spoken:
> Sons have I reared and brought up,
> And they have rebelled against me.[4]

And immediately after we read:

> Ah! sinful nation!
> People burdened with guilt!
> Seed of evil-doers!
> Sons that deal corruptly!
> They have forsaken Yahweh;
> They have spurned the Holy One of Israel;
> They have turned back in estrangement.[5]

---

[1] The meaning of this expression is very doubtful, and many editors resort to emendation. Marti (*Dodekapropheten* [KHC], p. 57; similarly J. Lindblom, *Hosea literarisch untersucht*, 1928, p. 86) thinks the word k^e'$ādhām$=*like Adam* conceals a place name, but does not attempt to decide what it was. That a place name is concealed is suggested by *there* in the following line. Nowack (*Die kleinen Propheten* [HK], p. 44) inclines to favour b^e'$adhmāh$=*in Admah* (cf. xi: 8), and this is followed by Powis Smith in the American translation of the Bible. T. H. Robinson (*Die zwölf kleinen Propheten* [HAT], pp. 26f.) prefers to read b^e'$ādhām$=*in Adam*, and to connect with the place name Adam. W. R. Harper (*Amos and Hosea* [ICC], 1910, p. 288) retains the Massoretic text, and renders *like men*, and so Van Hoonacker (*Les douze petits prophètes* [EB], 1908, p. 64), who then renders *basely*. Nyberg (*Studien zum Hoseabuche*, 1935, p. 42) also retains the Massoretic text, and in the following line he takes *shām* to be not an adverb of place, but the equivalent of the Arabic *thumma*=*therefore*.

[2] Hos. 6 : 7.

[3] Hos. 8 : 1.

[4] Isa. 1 : 2.

[5] Isa. 1 : 4. The last line is omitted by the LXX, and by some modern editors. Others do not like the pregnant construction, since the literal rendering would be "they are estranged backwards", and so read *nāsōghū*="they have turned backwards", instead of *nāzōrū*. But there is much play on the root *zwr* in this chapter, and we may have collected here oracles that contain it.

In yet another passage we read:

> For they have rejected the law of Yahweh of hosts;
> And the word of the Holy One of Israel have they despised.[1]

And in similar strain Jeremiah says:

> Surely as a woman is faithless to her lover,
> So were ye faithless to me, O house of Israel![2]

He continues:

> A sound is heard on the heights,
> The suppliant wail of the children of Israel;
> For they have perverted their way,
> Have forgotten Yahweh their God.
> Return, O apostate children!
> I will heal your backslidings.[3]

From these and many other passages which stand in the prophets it is clear that Israel's repudiation of the Covenant is regarded as morally reprehensible, a response in disloyalty to One who was supremely loyal to her, an act of base ingratitude towards One whose gracious gifts she had so freely received. It is also clear that in repudiating the Covenant she was repudiating her election.[4] If she ceased to acknowledge Yahweh to be her God, then she declared that she no longer wished to be His people. This is well brought out in Jeremiah's parable of the potter.[5] The vessel that fails to realize the intention of the potter is refashioned into another vessel; and in the same way the people that by reason of the defective stuff of its moral and spiritual make-up, by reason of the intractability of its substance, will not fulfil the purpose of God, cannot hope to abide.

It is made abundantly clear, in passages too numerous to cite, that the repudiation of the Covenant is thought of, not as the renunciation of Yahweh in name, but as the failure to give Him service. Jeremiah says in the name of God:

[1] Isa. 5 : 24.
[2] Jer. 3 : 20.
[3] Jer. 3 : 21.
[4] Cf. J. Morgenstern, *Amos Studies*, i, 1941, pp. 401–428 (=*Hebrew Union College Annual*, xv, 1940, pp. 277–304).
[5] Jer. 18 : 1f.

"This is the word which I commanded them, saying, Obey ye my voice, and I will be your God, and ye shall be my people."[1] The purpose of the election is service, and when the service is withheld the election loses its meaning, and therefore fails.

This must not be understood to mean that the moment the Covenant is broken from Israel's side the election is repudiated from God's side. Far from it indeed! In that moment Israel ceases to have any claim on God, and repudiates her election. But the grace of God pursues her, and seeks to renew His claim upon her loyalty. He will not lightly give her up. Just as His grace preceded her response in her deliverance from Egypt, so it persists after the failure of her response. Yet it is never indifferent to her response. Its continuance after her failure to respond is a claim to the renewal of her response, and a claim which continues so long as there is any hope of that renewal.

No prophet more poignantly expressed the reluctance of God to give up His Chosen People, even when they repudiated Him and their own election, than Hosea:

> How shall I give thee up, O Ephraim!
> How surrender thee, O Israel!
> How can I make thee like Admah,
> Or treat thee as Zeboim,
> My heart is turned within me;
> My compassions are stirred together.
> I will not execute the fierceness of my wrath;
> I will not destroy Ephraim again.[2]

The same thought is found in Jeremiah, who returned to it again and again, speaking of God with moving anthropomorphism as "rising early" to speak to Israel or "rising early and sending the prophets" to call them back to His way. "I have repeatedly spoken to you, rising early and speaking, but ye have not hearkened unto me. And I sent unto you all my servants the prophets, rising early and sending, saying, Return now every one from his evil way, and amend your deeds, and go not after other gods to serve them, that ye

[1] Jer. 7 : 23.
[2] Hos. 11 : 8f.

may dwell in the land which I gave to you and to your fathers; but ye inclined not your ear, nor hearkened unto me."[1] The anthropomorphism did not belong to the theology of the prophet, but merely provided the metaphor whereby he expressed the tender love of God for His people, and the patience and persistence with which He sought to renew the bond between Israel and Himself, even when Israel had broken it.

Nevertheless, the prophets continually gave warning of the discipline wherewith God would discipline Israel. This is thought of in various ways. Sometimes it is thought of as the punishment of Israel for her disloyalty, and sometimes as the suffering she brings upon herself by the folly of her way. But more characteristic of the Old Testament, and more profoundly true, is the treatment of this discipline as the fruit of God's love for His people, designed to awaken her to the evil of her way and to bring her back to the response in loyalty to His grace. Cried Amos in God's name:

> You alone have I chosen[2]
> From all the families of the earth.
> Wherefore I will visit upon you
> All your iniquitous deeds.[3]

Here the discipline is the corollary of the election, and the proof of the divine love. It is not simply because God is just that He punishes Israel's sins; it is rather because He is gracious that He seeks to chasten her for her profit. It is not due to His variability, but to His unchanging love. He showed His love when Israel was suffering under Egyptian taskmasters by rescuing her from her plight; but He shows His love no less by delivering her to suffering when her rebellious heart yields Him no allegiance.

All of this springs from the fundamental conception of Israel's election. It was election for service; and the render-

---

[1] Jer. 35 : 14f. The thought recurs in a whole series of passages in Jeremiah—7 : 13, 25; 11 : 7; 25 : 4; 26 : 5; 29 : 19; 32 : 33; 44 : 4.
[2] Lit. "have I known", where the sense is clearly not merely "recognized", but "recognized as mine", or "chosen". Sellin (*Das Zwölfprophetenbuch*, p. 250) says that "Amos did not think of an election of Israel". This seems to me to be incorrect, and to ignore this text.
[3] Amos 3 : 2.

ing of that service was the supreme honour for which she was chosen. Not for His own sake, but for hers, that she might attain the goal of her high calling, God desired her to yield that service, and His love was frustrated until she yielded it.

As to the nature of the service, it is first of all to receive and to treasure the revelation of God given to her in the crucial experience of the Exodus and the uniquely significant events that preceded and followed that deliverance. "Yahweh, Yahweh, a God compassionate and merciful, slow to anger and abundant in loyalty and faithfulness; maintaining his devotion to thousands, forgiving iniquity and transgression and sin, yet not holding guiltless the guilty, visiting the iniquity of the fathers upon children, and upon children's children, unto the third and fourth generation."[1] But the receiving and the treasuring of the revelation of God was not the whole of the purpose of Israel's election. It was then to obey His voice and to walk in the way of His will. "If you will truly hearken to my voice, and keep my covenant."[2] "Observe well the commandments of Yahweh your God, and his testimonies, and his statutes which he hath commanded you; and do that which is upright and good in the eyes of Yahweh."[3] Only gradually was the way of His will unfolded to her, but from the first some things were clear. To Him was owed the undivided loyalty and allegiance of Israel. He was to be her only God, and whether other gods were real or not was of no moment to her.[4] They were not for her, and their ways were not to be her ways. Moreover, in the great Decalogue of Exodus 20 and Deuteronomy 5, in the original form which lay behind both of the forms in

[1] Ex. 34 : 6f. This passage is assigned to J by S. R. Driver (*The Book of Exodus* [CambB], 1918, p. 367). McNeile (*The Book of Exodus* [WC], p. 217), and Oesterley and Robinson (*Introduction to the Books of the Old Testament*, p. 37). It is assigned to the hand of a Redactor by Bennett (*Exodus* [CentB], pp. 256f.), Eissfeldt (*Hexateuch-Synopse*, pp. 54-57, 158*), Beer (*Exodus* [HAT], p. 160), and Simpson (*Early Traditions of Israel*, p. 215).
[2] Ex. 19 : 5.
[3] Deut. 6 : 17f.
[4] Ex. 34 : 14; 20 : 3. The former passage is assigned to J by Driver (*op. cit.*, p. 369), Eissfeldt (*op. cit.*, p. 158*), Oesterley and Robinson (*loc. cit.*), and Beer (*op. cit.*, p. 160)—the last-named specifying J2; while Bennett (*op. cit.*, p. 258) and McNeile (*op. cit.*, p. 218) refer it to a Redactor. The latter passage is ascribed to E by all these writers (McNeile E2), except Beer, who ascribes it to a Redactor (*op. cit.*, p. 98).

which it now stands,[1] Israel had the summons to a moral way of life.

It is often argued that the Ritual Decalogue[2] of Exodus 34 —now expanded to thirteen commands—was earlier than the Ethical Decalogue of Exodus 20, yet was itself clearly later than the settlement in Canaan, since it contains provisions for the agricultural festivals. Hence it is argued that later than the time of Moses, Yahwism had only reached the relatively primitive level of the Ritual Decalogue, and therefore the heights of the Ethical Decalogue must have been first reached long after his time.[3]

This argument seems to me to be fallacious, and to assume that Yahwism developed in a single line. But if all of the tribes were not with Moses at Sinai, and some of them acquired their Yahwism independently of him by gradual permeation by Kenite religious influence, those tribes would have taken over their Yahwism at the Kenite level, and could have adapted the Kenite Decalogue to their new conditions without seriously modifying its level. There is no ground to assume that this Decalogue would issue of itself, by the mere lapse of time, in something higher. It is far more likely that under the influence of a creative personality and a notable experience some vital change would be made. And

---

[1] That this Decalogue is not in its original form is indicated by the different expansions that mark the fourth commandment in Exodus and Deuteronomy. It is probable that all the commandments were originally short.

[2] On this Decalogue cf. R. H. Pfeiffer, "The Oldest Decalogue", in *Journal of Biblical Literature*, xliii, 1924, pp. 294-310; G. R. Berry, "The Ritual Decalogue", *ibid.*, xliv, 1925, pp. 39-43; J. Morgenstern, in *Hebrew Union College Annual*, iv, 1927, pp. 54-98.

[3] Cf. J. Meinhold, *Der Dekalog*, 1927, where it is argued that it originated in the Exile; and S. Mowinckel, *Le Décalogue*, 1927, where it is ascribed to prophetic circles, perhaps the disciples of Isaiah. Cf. too, J. Morgenstern, "Decalogue", in *Universal Jewish Encyclopedia*, iii, 1941, pp. 506-513, where it is held that the Decalogue of Ex. 34 was the Kenite code, dating from 899 B.C., while a northern Decalogue, closely akin to this and dating from the time of Jehu's revolution, stands in Ex. 30 : 23-26, 23 : 10-19; the Decalogue of Ex. 20 and Deut. 5 is held to have been composed either in the time of Hezekiah or of Josiah and to have been first promulgated at the time of Josiah's reform, while yet another Decalogue, that of H, stands in Lev. 19 : 2b-18. L. W. Batten (Hastings' *Encyclopaedia of Religion and Ethics*, iv, 1911, pp. 513-517), while holding that all the commandments of the Decalogue of Ex. 20, in its original short form, with the possible exception of the first and the almost certain exception of the second, may be Mosaic, yet inclines to think that it was the growth of some centuries, and will only commit himself to say that it was complete by 621 B.C.

it seems to me that the experience of the Exodus and Sinai, and the personality of Moses, as reflected in the Biblical traditions, can supply a fully credible setting for the change. The Israelite elements that were not with Moses at Sinai could have continued on the lower level long after his time, but for the group that was with him the demands of God for ethical standards of conduct stood revealed from his day. Those demands went beyond men's acts to their springs. In other passages of the Old Testament we find the call for that love for God with every fibre of a man's being,[1] and that love for his neighbour as himself,[2] which our Lord found to express the chief demands of the Law.[3] Yet here in the Decalogue we find the same demands incipiently set forth. The first of its commands is "Thou shalt have no other gods before me", and the last is a prohibition of any kind of envy of one's neighbour's possessions. From the sole recognition of Yahweh as God and from undeviating loyalty to Him, it was not a long step to a devotion towards Him that could only be described as love. And in the expansion of the original Decalogue, in which all the commands were probably brief and without annotation, we already find a reference to "them that love me and keep my commandments".[4] Similarly, from the eschewing of any thought that was potentially inimical to one's neighbour, it was not a long step to a positive desire for his well-being that could be described as love for him, and in due course that step was taken.

What loving and serving God involved became clearer as He unfolded through the prophets the fuller revelation of His character. For if the first message of the election was that Israel was called to receive the revelation of God, it became increasingly clear that she was called to reflect the character of the God who was revealed to her. When Amos called for justice, it was not because the concept of justice was a grand one, and its application could be justified by argument, as making for the greatest happiness of the greatest number,

---

[1] Deut. 6 : 5.
[2] Lev. 19 : 18.
[3] Mark 12 : 29ff. and parallels.
[4] Ex. 20 : 6.

or conducive to the strength and prosperity of the state. It was because God was just, and because they who worshipped Him must be like Him. God's will was born of His character. The gods and goddesses of Greece gave themselves dispensations to act in ways that would have brought a blush of shame to the face of any decent citizen, and that would certainly have brought severe condemnation upon any Greek caught following them. Yahweh was not like that. The standards laid down for men were set by the character of God Himself. That is why the religion of the Old Testament is described as an ethical religion. Other religions prescribe codes of ethical conduct for men. But here the code springs out of the character of God Himself. So when Hosea calls for loyalty and devotion to God and to one another, it is because God is Himself of that character. His tender grace was revealed to Israel in the childhood of the nation, and never had He turned from that spirit. By what He was He called Israel to respond in loyalty unto Him, and to manifest towards one another the same spirit of grace and devotion. Similarly when the prophet, whether Micah or another, whose great saying stands preserved in the book of Micah, defined the vital demands of God, he said:

> He hath told thee, O man! what is good;[1]
> And what doth Yahweh demand of thee,
> Save only to execute justice,
> To love the quality of ḥesedh,[2]
> And humbly to walk with thy God.[3]

[1] S. Daiches has suggested that this line should be rendered "The man hath shewed thee what is good", where "the man" is to be understood of Moses (*Bulletin of the Bible Readers' Union*, iii, 1942, pp. 62–64). More usually it is understood to declare God's demands on man *qua* man, and not merely on the Israelite. Cf. A. Van Hoonacker, *Les douze petits prophètes* (EB), 1908, p. 398: "The moral duties such as the observance of justice, the practice of kindness, and humble conduct in relation to God, are inscribed in the code of natural law; their transgression can the less be made up for, or compensated for, by ritual practices, since they themselves do not depend on a constitution or on positive ordinances proper to the Israelite people in particular, but are imposed on man as such. It is this which Micah implies in giving to his interlocutor in this connexion the quality of *man*."

[2] I find it impossible to translate ḥesedh by any one word here. It involves the mutual loyalty of man to man and of man to God, and an initiative in the service of one's fellow-men comparable with the divine initiative in the service of men.

[3] Mic. 6 : 8.

The character of God can only be reflected in those who humbly walk with Him. But they must then become just since He is just, and must show *ḥesedh* because that is the quality of His heart.

No prophet, however, presented the exhaustive demands of God. Each could emphasize only the particular aspect of God's Being which stood out most clearly for him, and point to the corollary of that aspect in demand upon men. To Isaiah God was "the Holy One of Israel", and the corollary of this was a demand for holiness in men. Social righteousness and mutual loyalty amongst men and between man and God needed to be supplemented by a holiness which consisted in what a man was rather than in what he did. Isaiah was not the first to apply the term "holy" to God, or to think of it as an epithet for men. There were "holy men" and "holy women" in the shrines of Israel, set apart from common life to the service of the god, devoted to a life of sacred prostitution. And God's holiness was thought to lie in His separation from men. But that was not Isaiah's conception of holiness. In the moment of his call he saw Yahweh high and lifted up. And when the Seraphim cried one to another:

> Holy, holy, holy is Yahweh of hosts:
> All the earth is full of his glory[1]

the prophet trembled exceedingly and cried "Woe is me!" But it was not the consciousness that he was a man, separated from God by the fact of his humanity, that filled him with terror; it was the fact that he was a sinner, separated from that moral holiness which was God by the moral failure of his own life. He cried:

> Woe is me! for I am undone!
> For a man unclean of lips am I,
> And in the midst of folk unclean of lips
> I have my habitation;
> Yet the King, Yahweh of hosts,
> Mine eyes have seen.[2]

[1] Isa. 6 : 3.
[2] Isa. 6 : 5.

To Jeremiah it was the humble walk with God that loomed largest in his thought of the essence of religion. He explored the riches of prayer to a degree that is without parallel amongst the records of other Old Testament characters, and prayer was fellowship rather than merely thanksgiving and petition. He did not conceive of religion as primarily worship in the shrine, but as the soul's intercourse with God—an intercourse that was open to it at all times and in all places. By that intercourse the soul could be so attuned to the spirit of God that His law should become inscribed on the very heart, instead of on external tables of stone. And Jeremiah looked forward to the day when all Israel should know that sort of religion, and should know God in the immediacy of experience and should therefore have their personality in perfect harmony with His.

> I will put my law in their inward parts,
> And upon their hearts will I write it;
> And I will be their God,
> And they shall be my people.
> And they shall teach no more every man his neighbour,
> And each his brother, saying:
> Know ye Yahweh;
> For all of them shall know me,
> From the least of them to the greatest.[1]

In all of these there is the unwavering implication that Israel is called to reflect the character of God and to do His will. Her high calling to be the Chosen People was not the mark of the Divine indulgence or favouritism, but a summons to a task exacting and unceasing, and election and task were so closely bound together that she could not have the one without the other.[2]

Moreover, Israel's election was not merely for herself and God. It was not simply that she might reflect the will of God in all her own life and delight His heart by so doing. Her

[1] Jer. 31 : 33f.
[2] Cf. C. H. Dodd, *The Bible To-day*, 1946, p. 107: "God's choice, however, is (as the prophets are at pains to point out) not an act of favouritism, conferring privileges arbitrarily denied to other peoples. It is election to special responsibility. To be God's chosen people means to be immediately exposed to His Word, with all the momentous consequences that flow from hearing it."

election was for service to the world. For she had a mission to the nations. There is a reviving tendency to find monotheism in the religion of Moses.[1] While I would not go so far as this, I do find an incipient monotheism there.[2] Yahweh alone amongst the gods counts, and all other gods are negligible. That is far from speculative monotheism, but its seed can be found there. It is true that the Assyrian kings claimed that their gods alone counted, and required their recognition as the suzerains of the gods of the conquered peoples; but this was merely the reflection of the self-glorification of the Assyrian kings. There could be no incipient monotheism in a religion which was itself essentially polytheistic, in the sense that it not alone recognized the existence of many gods, but offered them worship. And when the Rabshakeh came to Jerusalem in the days of Hezekiah, he boasted that none of the gods of the nations had been able to deliver their people out of *his master's hand*.[3] But in the story of the Exodus there is no suggestion of the prestige of Yahweh being enhanced by the exploits of His people. Here it is uniquely the case that Yahweh alone counts. His people are utterly without prestige or power, but Yahweh does as He wills in Egypt or anywhere else. Further, in claiming for Himself a people that did not worship Him, and gathering into Himself the God they had hitherto worshipped, He is again pointing towards monotheism.

In all syncretism there is the seed of monotheism, though often it has not proceeded to germinate. In Israel it proceeded to full speculative monotheism. And in any case this syncretism, which identified Yahweh with El Shaddai, is not quite like the syncretism that has been so common amongst men. After the Settlement in Canaan the Israelites lived alongside the Canaanites, and came to identify the God they worshipped with the god their neighbours worshipped. But in the time of the Exodus this is not what happened. There

---

[1] Cf. W. F. Albright, *From the Stone Age to Christianity*, 1940, pp. 196–207; *Archaeology and the Religion of Israel*, 1942, p. 116. Cf. too, G. E. Wright, *Theology To-day*, iii, 1946, pp. 185–191.
[2] Cf. *The Missionary Message of the Old Testament*, pp. 21f., 27; *The Rediscovery of the Old Testament*, pp. 87f. (American ed., pp. 123f.).
[3] Isa. 36 : 19f.

Yahweh adopted Israel and sent Moses to claim them for Him. The God they had hitherto worshipped ceased to count as against Yahweh; He could continue to count only if He was recognized to be Yahweh. A full monotheism that recognizes but one God of all men finds no difficulty here, but in proportion to the initial recognition of the otherness of the gods identified difficulty is created by syncretism. The syncretism that identified Yahweh and Baal was never smooth and unchallenged. In any time of national feeling Yahweh was recognized to be other than Baal. When Gideon came forward to lead Israel, the first thing he did was to break down a Baal altar and build a Yahweh altar.[1] But there is no trace of a conflict between Yahweh and the God of the patriarchs. Problems arise in the Wilderness, giving rise to questions and complaints, and neither Yahweh nor Moses escapes criticism, but there is no violent return to El Shaddai.[2]

I do not want to exaggerate the incipient monotheism of this period, however, and I recognize that it was not until much later that monotheism reached its clear expression in Israel. To the eighth-century prophets Yahweh was supreme amongst the gods. While it is doubtful if they would have denied the reality or existence of other gods, Yahweh was regarded as the God who controlled all the forces of Nature, and whose will prevailed over all the earth. Only a thin line separated them from clearly formulated monotheism, such as we find in Deutero-Isaiah:

> I am Yahweh, and there is no other;
> Beside me there is no god.[3]
>
> Is there a God beside me,
> Or a Rock of whom I know not.[4]

---

[1] Judges 6 : 25.
[2] The story of the Golden Calf in Ex. 32 is not represented as a return to El Shaddai, though it is regarded as defection from Yahweh.
[3] Isa. 45 : 5.
[4] Isa. 44 : 8. For the second line R.V. has "yea, there is no Rock; I know not any." Many modern editors read the correlative interrogative *we'im* for the negative *we'ēn*. The text then yields the rendering given above, the relative particle being omitted, as very commonly in poetry.

To these many other passages could be added, showing that with Deutero-Isaiah monotheism was fundamental to his whole theology, and explicitly set forth.

Monotheism necessarily implies universalism.[1] If God is One and there is no other, then He must be the God of all men, and if men are to have any true religion He it is that they must worship. If, then, they are to worship rightly, they must come to know Him and His will. Hence they to whom knowledge has been mediated are called to share their their treasures with all men. Deutero-Isaiah draws these consequences quite explicitly from monotheism:

> Look unto me and be ye saved,
> All the ends of the earth!
> For I am God and there is none else.
> By myself have I sworn,
> From my mouth there has gone forth in righteousness
> A word that shall not return;
> For to me every knee shall bow,
> Every tongue swear.[2]

It is by no accident that it is the prophet who most stresses monotheism and its corollary of universalism who also most stresses the thought of Israel's election and the corollary of that election in her world mission:

> And thou, Israel, my servant,
> Jacob whom I have chosen,
> The seed of Abraham, my friend.[3]

> And I said, My servant art thou,
> I have chosen thee and have not rejected thee.[4]

> And now hear, O Jacob, my servant!
> And Israel, whom I have chosen![5]

---

[1] . Cf. H. G. May, "Theological Universalism in the Old Testament", in *Journal of Bible and Religion*, xvi, 1948, pp. 100–107.

[2] Isa. 45 : 22f. R. Levy (*Deutero-Isaiah*, 1925, p. 195) calls the first of these verses "the grandest verse in the prophet's scroll".

[3] Isa. 41 : 8.

[4] Isa. 41 : 9.

[5] Isa. 44 : 1.

Ye are my witnesses, saith Yahweh,
And my servant, whom I have chosen.[1]

I Yahweh have called you in righteousness,
And I have taken you by the hand,
I have kept you and given you for a covenant of the people,[2]
To be a light of the Gentiles;[3]
To open blinded eyes,
To bring forth the prisoner from the dungeon,
From the prison house them that sit in darkness.
I am Yahweh, that is my name,
And my glory to another I will not give,
Nor my praise to idols.[4]

It is to be observed that for Deutero-Isaiah universalism did not spell the rejection of the thought of Israel's election. An election that was merely favouritism would have little in common with universalism, but an election that is conceived in terms of purpose is entirely consistent with universalism. And Deutero-Isaiah, who thinks of election in terms of purpose, and that the purpose of a world-wide mission, emphasizes as no other prophet the thought that Israel is the Chosen People of God.[5] Not in self-satisfaction but in challenge does he stress this thought, and election is not divorced from the solemn responsibility it entails.

Deutero-Isaiah was not the first to think in these terms, and it is not to be supposed that there were no preparations for his teaching amongst his predecessors. It has already been noted that in the great saying which stands in the book of

[1] Isa. 43 : 10.
[2] R. Levy (*op. cit.*, p. 147) renders this phrase "a universal covenant", and justifies by reference to the Arabic '*āmm=general, universal*. C. C. Torrey (*The Second Isaiah*, 1928, pp. 231, 327) renders "my pledge to the peoples", and argues that elsewhere we find in poetry a singular form for the plural. The absence of the article with a definite noun is exceedingly common in poetry. G. Quell (in Kittel's *Theologisches Wörterbuch zum Neuen Testament*, i, 1933, p. 34 n.) renders "a covenant of humanity". Cf. W. Staerk, *Zeitschrift für die alttestamentliche Wissenschaft*, N.F. xiv, 1937, p. 13.
[3] This line is lacking in some manuscripts of the LXX, and in consequence is omitted by some modern authors. So M. J. Lagrange, *Le judaïsme avant Jésus-Christ*, 1931, p. 369; C. R. North, *The Old Testament Interpretation of History*, 1946, p. 177 n. [4] Isa. 42 : 6–8. [5] W. Staerk (*loc. cit.*, p. 3) observes that outside Deutero-Isaiah the Hebrew verb *bāḥar=choose* is found but three times with Israel as object. This is misleading, however, unless the use with pronominal object standing for Israel is remembered.

Micah, commonly ascribed to the beginning of the seventh century B.C., God's demands are expressed in terms of a requirement of man, and not merely of Israel.[1] There is here already, therefore, a suggestion of universalism.

In a floating oracle which is ascribed independently to both Isaiah and Micah[2] we read:

> It shall come to pass in the days to be
> The mount of Yahweh's house shall be established
> As the chiefest of the mountains,[3]
> And exalted above the hills.
> And all nations unto it shall stream,
> And many nations shall go up and shall say:
> Come! let us go up to the mount of Yahweh,
> To the house of the God of Jacob!
> That he may teach us of his ways,
> And that we may walk in his paths.
> For from Zion shall go forth instruction,
> And the word of Yahweh from Jerusalem.[4]

While the authorship of this oracle cannot be determined, the fact that it is ascribed to two contemporary prophets may be some indication of its approximate age. It clearly implies that the religion of Israel is not for her alone, but is for all nations, and therefore her election was ultimately to be the medium of blessing to all men. Of the nature of that blessing the sequel goes on to speak. War shall cease and men shall live in peace and brotherhood, and even in the economic sphere they shall be profited.

> And they shall beat their swords into ploughshares,
> And their spears into pruning hooks;
> Nation shall not lift sword against nation,
> And the art of war they shall no more learn.
> Every man shall sit under his own vine,
> And under his fig-tree, with none to make him afraid.[5]

---

[1] Mic. 6 : 8.
[2] Isa. 2 : 2-4; Mic. 4 : 1-4.
[3] Cf. M. L. Margolis, *Micah with Commentary*, 1943, p. 43: "In view of Ezek. 40 : 2 and Zech. 14 : 10 it is conceivable that the prophet has in mind physical elevation."
[4] Isa. 2 : 2f.
[5] Mic. 4 : 3f.

THE COROLLARIES OF ISRAEL'S ELECTION

The general picture here is not dissimilar to that of the Golden Age described in other passages, as resulting from the rule of the Scion of David, when enduring peace and perfect justice shall prevail,[1] and when even the brute creation shall be transformed to match changed men and women.[2] It is of importance to note that the Hebrew writers were realists, who did not expect the fruits of peace and of universal bliss to be gathered save from the tree whereon alone they can grow. They realized that man cannot reach the goal of his manhood until his life and character reflects the will of God, and they therefore placed the repair to the house of God and the humble learning of His ways before the beating of swords into ploughshares.[3] But in their belief that it was to the God of Israel that all men would repair ere the Golden Age dawned they reflected their implicit consciousness that the revelation of God's grace to Israel was something that concerned all men, and that the service of God for which she was chosen could only be fully rendered in mediating that revelation to the world.

There is to-day a disposition to regard all these oracles as older than some earlier scholars did, and to accept the messianic element in prophecy as very ancient.[4] Into the question of their age we need not go here, however, since it can scarcely be denied that even before the eighth century B.C. there was some perception of the universal significance of Israel's election. In the earliest of the main documents of the Pentateuch, commonly dated in the middle of the ninth century B.C., we find the account of Israel's election in Abraham, to which reference was made in the preceding lecture. Here we find the words which are rendered in the Revised Version: "in thee shall all the families of the earth be blessed".[5] Whilst this is a possible translation of the words, it is probable that it goes somewhat beyond its meaning. The verb is in the Niph'al, which is normally used with a passive meaning in Biblical Hebrew, but which was origin-

---

[1] Isa. 9 : 6. [2] Isa. 11 : 6-8. [3] Cf. Isa. 56 : 7: "My house shall be called a house of prayer for all peoples." Cf. also Isa. 19 : 16-25.
[4] Cf. G. Widengren, *Literary and Psychological Aspects of the Hebrew Prophets*, 1948, p. 90 : "To blot out from the revelations of the pre-exilic prophets these expectations of a future Messianic state under the rulership of the Anointed of Yahweh is a maltreating of the prophets." [5] Gen. 12 : 3. This comes from the J document.

ally a reflexive conjugation, and which sometimes has a reflexive meaning in the Old Testament. If this were the only occurrence of this expression we should most naturally translate it as in the R.V. But the thought is repeated in other passages in Genesis, and while in two[1] the same verbal form is used, in two others[2] the Hithpa'el is used. This is regularly used in Biblical Hebrew as a reflexive conjugation, so that the meaning here would most naturally be expressed in English by "shall bless themselves in thee". Since this is a possible translation of all the five passages, and since it is probable that they are all to be understood alike, this is the meaning given to them all in most modern works.[3] Moreover, this is in harmony with the general thought of them all.

In the case of the first passage, that relates the call of Abram, it is expressly stated that upon some he would bring a curse rather than a blessing. "Thy curser will I curse." The general sense of the passage is that the patriarch and his descendants will be so blessed by God, that all men will wonder at their blessing, and will think of no higher blessing to invoke upon themselves than to know a like blessing. It is the honour of Abram and his decendants that is here in mind, rather than any sense of a mission to spread blessing among the nations. In that sense the word has not been fulfilled, and there have been few ages when the Jews have so excited the admiring wonder of the world that men have thought of nothing higher than to share their honour.

Nevertheless we have not disposed of the significance of this word when we have resolved it into an expression of the national pride to which Powis Smith traces the whole concept of the election of Israel. If it was in response to a

---

[1] Gen. 18 : 18, 28 : 14. Both of these verses belong to the J document.
[2] Gen. 22 : 18, 26 : 4. Both of these verses are ascribed to a Redactor by S. R. Driver (*The Book of Genesis* [WC], 1904, pp. 220, 250), W. H. Bennett (*Genesis* [CentB], pp. 241, 267); J. Skinner (*Genesis* [ICC], 1910, pp. 331, 364), and H. E. Ryle (*The Book of Genesis* [CambB], 1921, pp. 239, 274). Eissfeldt, however, ascribes them both to E (*op. cit.*, pp. 36*, 46*), while Oesterley and Robinson ascribe the first to E and the second to J (*op. cit.*, p. 35).
[3] Cf. C. G. Montefiore, *The Old Testament and After*, 1923, p. 85: "Not 'in thee shall all the families of the earth be blessed,' but 'with thee' (or 'by means of thee') 'shall all families of the earth bless themselves' is the correct translation. The meaning is that everybody shall wish for themselves the happiness and the blessing which have been, or shall be, granted to Abraham and to his seed."

religious urge that Abraham went forth from Harran, then this greatness that should arouse the wonder of men was thought of as something that did not inhere in Israel, but that rested on a religious foundation. It was because of his response to the guidance of God that Abraham and his descendants should become of significance to all men. Here already in germ we have the perception of something of greater significance than the thought of the visible greatness and prosperity of a nation. There is not yet the thought of others sharing the springs of her blessing in the sharing of her faith, but there is the consciousness that ultimately it is her faith which gives her whatever significance she has for men, and, as C. R. North says, "something like the note of universalism is already struck in these words".[1]

From this faint gleam we may trace the growing light through the passages at which we have looked, and others which cannot be here examined, to the full perception of Deutero-Isaiah that by her election Israel is called to a conscious mission to the world, and that she can only fulfil the purpose of her election in the execution of the mission. This thought is taken up in the book of Jonah, and emphasized as it is emphasized nowhere else in the Old Testament. When Jonah refuses the mission to which he is called, he is swallowed by the fish for his discipline, and thus chastened sets out to fulfil the task assigned him. That task is to summon to repentance those who are not the heirs of the Covenant. Just as God had adopted Israel in Egypt and sent Moses to lead her out of her bondage, so He desired to claim for Himself others, and to lead them out of a worse bondage into obedience to His will. And He needed His people to be His messengers. That is the message of the book of Jonah, conveyed through a story which has the character of a parable. Jonah's reluctance to undertake his mission and his disappointment at the repentance of Nineveh probably reflect the author's reluctance to believe the great message with which he was charged. It is probable that in his thought Jonah stood for the nation, and his mission to Nineveh for Israel's mission to the world. And if so, then unless and until

[1] Cf. *The Old Testament Interpretation of History*, 1946, p. 26.

she undertook that mission, she was denying the very purpose of her election, as Jonah was when he turned from Nineveh towards Tarshish.

If this be taken in conjunction with that other thought which we have seen to lie at the heart of so much of the work of the prophets, it becomes of startling significance. For we have seen that they taught that in rejecting the purpose of her election she was repudiating her election. If the purpose of that election was not alone that she might receive the revelation of God's grace and reflect His character in her life and His will in her society, but also that she might carry His name to all men and share with them the treasures mediated to her, then she might repudiate her election no less surely by insularity than by the individual selfishness and sin so strongly condemned by the prophets. The election and the Covenant belonged together, so that loyalty to the Covenant was essential to the continuance of the election, and loyalty to the Covenant required obedience to the will of God. The growing perception of the nature and content of that will was itself an enrichment of Israel's inheritance, but brought a growing sacred obligation upon her. The election was only to be interpreted in terms of purpose and service, and the unfolding of the Divine purpose through prophets who were the mouthpiece of God to Israel brought to her expanding horizons from which she could not turn without turning from the Covenant and repudiating her election.

Chapter Three

THE LIMITATION AND EXTENSION OF ISRAEL'S ELECTION

RUNNING through all the thought of Israel's election in the Old Testament is the recognition that it involved obligations for Israel, and that the repudiation of those obligations was tantamount to the repudiation of the election. Yet God is no Shylock, watchful to catch Israel in a breach of her obligations in order to find an excuse for her repudiation. With tender patience He renews His claim on her even when she is false to Him, for His election was born of His love, and love is not lightly defeated. Yet speaking generally, the pre-exilic canonical prophets, with the exception of Nahum, were prophets of doom upon Israel, rebuking her for her faithlessness, and announcing the discipline with which God would visit her in His love, but cherishing little hope that she would respond to that discipline and return to faithfulness, that the purposes of her election might be realized.[1]

It was not that the pre-exilic prophets never prophesied good, but only ill. There are many passages in the prophetic books which speak of restoration. Most of these passages have been held to be additions by later hands, though it is improbable that they are all rightly to be so treated, and there is to-day a greater disposition to find some of them to be genuinely from the prophets to whom they are ascribed. Moreover, Isaiah certainly prophesied good of Jerusalem when the army of Sennacherib stood before the gates. Further, there are the messianic prophecies of the good time

[1] Cf. N. A. Dahl, *Das Volk Gottes*, 1941, pp. 30f., in summarizing elements of the message of Amos and Hosea: "JHWH *can* destroy the people, He *must* do so, since the people is completely corrupted by sin. JHWH has chosen the people for Himself, in order to accomplish His will in the world by this means. ... JHWH will no more have mercy on the people, Israel is no longer the people of God, and so the life of the people is at an end ... JHWH has in His freedom chosen Israel; He can also in His freedom reject her."

coming in the more distant future, on the horizons of time, "in the latter end of the days". There is no sufficient reason to doubt that some of these came from the pre-exilic period. Nevertheless it is true that by and large the pre-exilic prophets were charged first and foremost with a message of warning and of doom for their fellow-men.

We must not set them down as pessimists, however, who thought that God's purpose could be finally defeated, or that His election of Israel would end in dismal failure. Their despair of the nation was coupled with a faith in the Israel within Israel, and in the Israel that should be. For running through the prophets, and indeed through all the Old Testament, is the thought of the Remnant, who were still the heirs of the promises through all the ills that should befall the nation, and who should convey the heritage of the election and the tasks it entailed to those who should follow.[1] Though the nation as a whole repudiated the will of God, and therefore their election, and though through the prophets He pleaded with them to return, but with little response, it was always recognized that there was an element that should persist. "The Remnant", says R. de Vaux,[2] "is the portion of the Chosen People that escapes the chastisement of God." It was this element alone which was perceived to be the heirs of Israel's election, sometimes because they alone renewed for themselves the covenant and accepted the obligations of service which belonged to their election, and sometimes of the pure grace of God, that they might convey the heritage of the election to those who would respond more fully than themselves. "The Remnant is always presented" says de Vaux again,[3] "as a mark of the mercy of God." Just as the initial election preceded the response, though it demanded it, so now God's mercy may continue it where there is no response, but always with a view to a response. For election is never divorced from its purpose.

It has been already said that if Abraham and Isaac were

---

[1] M. N. Eisendrath (*Bulletin of the Canadian Society of Biblical Studies*, i, 1935, p. 15) rightly notes that in the doctrine of the Remnant a step is taken by Israel on the path leading to universalism.
[2] Cf. *Revue Biblique*, xlii, 1933, p. 528.
[3] *Ibid.*, p. 538.

chosen, of the children of Isaac one inherited the election and the other did not. Here, so early, was the seed of the doctrine of the Remnant.¹ The heritage of the promises was not automatic, but something that needed to be accepted. And only one of these two inherited it. Again it is easy to find reflected here the self-esteem of Israel, and her depreciation of the neighbouring people. But it should not be forgotten that history has justified her. For the indisputable fact is that Israel has mediated to the world a great spiritual heritage and Edom has not. The character of Jacob is not set forth in very exalted terms, and we know too little of the character of Esau to justify with any confidence the choice of the one rather than the other in terms of character. But if we rightly find in election not the reward of character so much as the summons to service, then the election of Israel and not Edom is justified. For Israel, with all her failures, did through her Remnant render that service, and Edom assuredly did not. There is here, therefore, something deeper than Israelite self-esteem. There is a vindicated faith.

To trace the doctrine of the Remnant within Israel all through the Old Testament would carry us too far, and it must suffice to cite some familiar passages in which the idea is expressed.² That it should be formulated at all is evidence of the existence of circles in Israel that were not filled with national self-esteem. For who could accuse the greater prophets, who thundered against the sins of their day, and announced the coming judgement on the nation, of any mere pride of race. Yet they still cherished the thought of Israel's election, and thus offered the clearest evidence of a deeper conception of that election than national pride.

In the time of Ahab there was a great religious crisis in Israel. At the time of the contest on Mount Carmel, Elijah appears as a lone figure standing against the hosts of Baal

---

¹ H. Dittmann (*Theologische Studien und Kritiken*, lxxxvii, 1914, pp. 605f.) emphasizes the fact that the notion of the Remnant was older than the prophets, who but established it more deeply.

² On the Remnant cf. R. de Vaux, "Le 'reste d'Israël' d'après les prophètes", *Revue Biblique*, xlii, 1933, pp. 526-539. Cf. also S. Mowinckel, *Profeten Jesaja*, 1925, pp. 66-71; H. Gressmann, *Der Ursprung der israelitisch-jüdischen Eschatologie*, 1905, pp. 229-238; H. Dittmann, "Der heilige Rest im Alten Testament", in *Theologische Studien und Kritiken*, lxxxvii, 1914, pp. 603-618.

prophets, behind whom was the sinister figure of the queen,[1] and the following chapter tells how he went to Horeb, and there bemoaned in depression of spirit that he alone was left loyal to his God.[2] That this was not the whole story is made clear apart from the reassuring answer that came to cheer him. For we are told that when Jezebel cut off the prophets of Yahweh, a hundred of them escaped through the good offices of Obadiah.[3] Moreover, at the end of Ahab's reign four hundred prophets are found at his court, and while Micaiah holds them to be false prophets, and the event proves them to be so, they are yet prophets of Yahweh.[4] But of more interest to us at the moment is it that when Elijah is commissioned to anoint Hazael and Jehu,[5] both of whom are to wield the sword of destruction, he is assured that a righteous Remnant, consisting of seven thousand loyal souls that had not bowed the knee to Baal, should escape.[6]

This thought thereafter appears frequently in the prophets. Not always is it described as a righteous Remnant. Amos, the earliest of the canonical prophets, describes it as a torn and bruised Remnant, which God in His mercy spares:

> Thus saith Yahweh of hosts:
> As a shepherd delivers from the lion's mouth
> Two legs or a piece of an ear,
> So shall the children of Israel be delivered.[7]

Or again:

> I have overthrown some among you
> As God overthrew Sodom and Gomorrah;
> And ye were as a brand saved from the burning,
> Yet ye returned not to me, saith Yahweh.[8]

---

[1] 1 Kgs 18 : 19.
[2] 1 Kgs. 19 : 10. A. S. Peake thought that this scene must really have stood earlier in the career of Elijah than the contest on Mount Carmel (*The Servant of Yahweh*, 1931, pp. 134f.).
[3] 1 Kgs. 18 : 4.
[4] 1 Kgs. 22 : 6.
[5] There is no record of Elijah's anointing of either Hazael or Jehu. Elisha anointed Jehu through the hand of one of his disciples (2 Kgs. 9 : 6), and also encouraged Hazael to murder his master and seize the throne (2 Kgs. 8 : 13). Eissfeldt (*Einleitung in das Alte Testament*, 1934, p. 331) holds that the relation of the Elisha saga to the Elijah saga is comparable to the relation of J to E. More often it is held that the Elisha stories are based on those of Elijah.
[6] 1 Kgs. 19 : 18.   [7] Amos 3 : 12.   [8] Amos 4 : 11.

In neither of these passages is there any suggestion of a righteous Remnant, and in the second it is made quite clear that it is an unrepentant Remnant. It reminds us of a familiar word of Isaiah's:

> Were it not that Yahweh of hosts
> Had left us a few survivors,[1]
> We had been like Sodom,
> We had resembled Gomorrah.[2]

The doctrine of the Remnant is more closely associated with Isaiah's name than with that of any other prophet.[3] How early in his career he cherished this thought cannot be known with certainty. The final verse of the chapter that records his call seems to contain some hint of it, though the concluding words "the holy seed is the stock thereof" are absent from the best manuscript of the Septuagint, and are accordingly omitted by some editors.[4] This seems an inadequate ground for omitting the words, when their omission in that Greek manuscript can be so much more simply explained than their insertion in the Hebrew and in all other authorities,[5] and antecedently it would not be surprising for some hint of a characteristic doctrine to be contained in the experience of the prophet's call. At the same time it must be confessed that the interpretation of the verse is very doubtful.[6]

However that may be, we know that Isaiah named his

---

[1] The usual word for Remnant does not stand here, though the general thought is closely similar. Cf. A. S. Kapelrud, *Joel Studies*, 1948, pp. 142f.   [2] Isa. 1 : 9.

[3] Cf. G. A. Danell, *Studies in the Name Israel in the Old Testament*, 1946, pp. 162f.

[4] So some older editors, and many moderns, including K. Marti (*Das Buch Jesaja* [KHC]. 1900, p. 69), B. Duhm (*Das Buch Jesaia* [HK], 1902, p. 46), G. B. Gray (*The Book of Isaiah* [ICC], 1912, p. 111), G. H. Box (*The Book of Isaiah*, 1916, p. 45), G. W. Wade (*The Book of the Prophet Isaiah* [WC], 1911, p. 43), H. Guthe (in Kautzsch-Bertholet, HSAT, i, 1922, p. 600) and O. Procksch (*Jesaia I* [KAT], 1930, p. 52).

[5] It is quite simple to explain the omission in LXX by homoioteleuton. The words are retained by J. Fischer (*Das Buch Isaias* [HSATes], i, 1937, p. 64), R. Kittel (*Biblia Hebraica*, 3rd. ed., 1931, p. 9), and E. J. Kissane (*The Book of Isaiah*, i, 1941, p. 76). Kissane observes that "without it the comparison would be incomplete". Similarly I. Engnell (*The Call of Isaiah*, 1949, pp. 14f.) maintains with emphasis the originality of the words. Cf. too, I. L. Seeligmann, *The Septuagint Version of Isaiah*, 1948, pp. 63f.

[6] The first part of the verse appears to say that if anything survives, it shall only be destined for destruction; while the second part appears to promise fresh life from the lopped tree. Some scholars have emended the first half to harmonize with the second (cf. E. Robertson, *American Journal of Semitic Languages*, xlix, 1932–33, pp. 313–315). Cf. Engnell, *op. cit.*, pp. 18f.

son Shear-Jashub,[1] which means "A Remnant shall return", and he declared that the name was symbolic.[2] In that name he indicated his faith that a Remnant should be spared, and probably also his faith that they should justify their survival. For the name could equally well be rendered "A Remnant shall repent". Certainly Isaiah is not here thinking of a return from exile, though possibly of a return to their homes of survivors who had scattered in terror to hide.[3]

That Isaiah did not think merely of a spared Remnant, but of one that should justify its survival by profiting from the discipline through which it came, he makes quite clear. He says:

> Never again shall the Remnant of Israel
> And the fugitives of the house of Jacob
> Stay themselves on him that smote them,
> But shall stay themselves upon Yahweh,
> The Holy One of Israel, in truth.
>
> A Remnant shall return, the Remnant of Jacob,
> Unto the mighty God.
> For though thy people, O Israel, should be[4]
> As the sand of the sea,
> Only a Remnant of them shall return.[5]

Here he emphasizes the smallness of the Remnant, but also declares that it shall consist of those who shall be chastened into a new loyalty.[6] And since we find here in the words "A Remnant shall return" the name of his son, it is probable that this passage indicates the significance of the sign given in that name.

[1] Isa. 7 : 3.
[2] Isa. 8 : 18.
[3] Cf. S. H. Hooke, *Prophets and Priests*, 1938, p. 32: "Unlike Amos and Hosea, Isaiah did not contemplate a captivity, and the symbolic name of his son, Shear-Jashub, does not mean 'The remnant shall return', that is, from captivity, but 'The remnant shall turn', that is, to Jahweh."
[4] E. G. Hirsch (*Jewish Enclyclopedia*, x, 1905, p. 375 b), with a very slight change of the Hebrew, reads: "If Yahweh is with thee, O Israel", but this does not seem to be a very likely reading.
[5] Isa. 10 : 20–22.
[6] For a comparison of Isaiah's thought of the Remnant and Micah's thought of the true people of God, cf. J. Lindblom, *Micha literarisch untersucht*, 1929, pp. 176f.

THE LIMITATION AND EXTENSION OF ISRAEL'S ELECTION

More than once Isaiah returns to the thought of the deeper loyalty that should mark the saved Remnant:

> And it shall be that he that remains in Zion
> And he that is left in Jerusalem,
> Holy shall he be called,
> Even everyone destined for life[1] in Jerusalem.[2]

Or again:

> In that day Yahweh of hosts shall be
> For a crown of glory and a diadem of beauty
> Unto the Remnant of his people.[3]

It is clear, therefore, that the Remnant will not be spared by accident, but saved by God for His own purposes. This is made even clearer when he says:

> And the Remnant from the house of Judah that survives
> Shall again take root downwards
> And shall bear fruit upwards.
> For from Jerusalem shall go forth a Remnant,
> And a survival from the mountain of Zion,
> The ardour of Yahweh of hosts shall perform this.[4]

In another passage we read of the discipline that is coming upon Israel under the figure of a reaper gathering sheaves, yet leaving gleanings in the fields, or one gathering olives from an olive tree, yet leaving a few stray berries out of reach. Here the figure might seem to imply that it is chance rather than design that lets any be spared, but it is probable that it is really chosen to emphasize the fewness of the Remnant. For the sequel declares that the Remnant will justify its survival:

> In that day will a man look to his Maker,
> And his eyes shall seek the Holy One of Israel.[5]

Nor should we fail to note that Amos expresses the thought of a Remnant that is spared not by accident, as the passages

---

[1] Literally, *written for life*, or *written as belonging to the living.*
[2] Isa. 4 : 3.
[3] Isa. 27 : 5.
[4] Isa. 37 : 31f.
[5] Isa. 17 : 7.

already quoted from him might suggest, but because by its repentance it is returning to a faithfulness that makes it the heir of the promises:

> Hate evil and love good,
> And set up justice in the gate.
> Perchance Yahweh will have mercy,
> Even the God of hosts on the Remnant of Joseph.[1]

With this we may compare the word of Zephaniah:

> Seek Yahweh, all ye meek ones of the earth,
> Who do his will;
> Seek righteousness, seek humility;
> Perchance ye may be hidden
> In the day of Yahweh's wrath.[2]

There are passages in Jeremiah which suggest that he looked for a complete and utter destruction of Judah. If a single righteous man would suffice to save Jerusalem, yet would it not be saved.[3] Or again the prophet is likened to an assayer of silver, and the nation to the lump of ore to be refined. Yet for all his efforts no silver is obtained, for all is dross.[4] Or yet again we have the terrible yet brilliant poem in which Jeremiah describes the coming terror:

> I looked to the earth, and lo! chaos;[5]
> To the heavens, and their light was gone.
> I looked to the mountains, and lo! they were quaking;
> And all the hills were a-quiver.
> I looked, and lo! not a man!
> And all the birds of the air had fled.[6]

Yet if this were all his message, his greatest word would have had no meaning. For there he prophesied of the day when God's law should be inscribed on men's hearts, and when He would renew His covenant with Israel in a richer

---

[1] Am. 5 : 15.
[2] Zeph. 2 : 3. With this cf. Psa. Sol. 12 : 7, 13 : 9-11, 14 : 2, 7.
[3] Jer. 5 : 1.
[4] Jer. 6 : 27-30.
[5] The Massoretic text has two words here, '*tōhū wābhōhū*, which stand together in Gen. 1 : 2, where R.V. renders "waste and void". The LXX renders but one word here, however, and since one is all that the rhythm requires, some modern editors follow that version.
[6] Jer. 4 : 23-25.

and worthier form.[1] Clearly he thought of some Remnant who should survive the dark days of the immediate future, and who should convey to those who should follow a heritage greater than they had possessed for themselves. Moreover, in one passage which some editors deny to Jeremiah for reasons which seem to me insufficient he says: "And I will gather the Remnant of my flock out of all the lands whither I have scattered them, and will bring them back to their folds; and they shall be fruitful and multiply. And I will raise up over them shepherds who shall shepherd them; and they shall not be afraid any more, neither shall they be dismayed or be lacking, saith Yahweh."[2]

To Ezekiel the Remnant was rather the Israel that should arise from the death of the exile, when the dry bones should once more come together and flesh should grow upon them, and the breath of God should infuse them with new life.[3] He prophesied of the day when

> I will give them another[4] heart,
> And a new spirit will I put in their midst;
> I will remove the heart of stone from their flesh,
> And will give them a heart of flesh;
> That they may walk in my statutes,
> And keep my commandments and do them,
> And may be to me for a people,
> And I will be their God.[5]

To this prophet, therefore, as to Jeremiah, the Remnant was not the unsullied faithful who should maintain their

---

[1] Jer. 31 : 31–34. Many modern editors deny this passage to Jeremiah, while others as firmly retain it for the prophet. It will be seen from what stands above that the present writer ranges himself with the latter. On this question cf. A. S. Peake, *Jeremiah and Lamentations* (CentB) ii, pp. 101–103; J. Skinner, *Prophecy and Religion*, 1922, pp. 320–334; G. A. Smith, *Jeremiah*, 3rd ed., 1924, pp. 374–380.
[2] Jer. 23 : 3f. On the authenticity cf. Peake, *op. cit.*, i, pp. 259f., Skinner, *op. cit.*, pp. 312f., *note*.
[3] Ezk. 37 : 11–14.
[4] The Massoretic Text has here "one heart", which can hardly be correct. Since the Syriac has "a new heart", and since this stands in the repetition of this verse in 36 : 26, some editors so read here. The LXX, however, has here "another heart", which seems a preferable reading. Graphically it differs but slightly from the Massoretic text, and if the thought were repeated, there is no need to assume an absolutely verbatim repetition in this verse any more than in the one that follows.
[5] Ezk. 11 : 19f.

purity through the general disaster, but the new Israel that should be born again, and that should fulfil its mission in a new devotion to its God. Sometimes he expresses the thought that this is the fruit less of God's love for Israel than of His love for His own glory:

> It is not for your sake that I am acting,
> O house of Israel!
> But for my holy name which ye have profaned
> Amongst the nations whither ye came.
> And I will hallow my holy name,
> Now profaned among the nations,
> In whose midst ye profaned it;
> And the nations shall know that I am Yahweh—
> This is the oracle of the Lord Yahweh—
> When I hallow myself in you before their eyes.
> For I will take you out from the nations,
> And will gather you from all the lands,
> And will bring you unto your land.
> And I will pour pure waters upon you,
> And ye shall be pure from all your uncleannesses,
> And from all your idols will I cleanse you.[1]

Here the election and the purification of the saved Remnant are firmly insisted on, and equally the fact that the election is called forth by nothing in Israel, but is directed to service. It is because Israel by her election can serve God that she is elect, and that her children shall be gathered again. Moreover, it is a service that is directed towards the nations, though less to convert than to impress them with the greatness and the power of God, and a service that is rendered not by conscious effort on the part of Israel, but simply by enjoying in faithfulness the blessings which God showers upon her.

In contrast with this stands Deutero-Isaiah's thought of the saved community. Israel had received of the Lord's hand double for all her sins,[2] and should come forth chastened and purified, restored to the Divine favour, but restored also to the Divine service:

> Fear not, for I have redeemed thee;
> I have called thee by name, thou art mine . . .

[1] Ezk. 36 : 22-25. [2] Isa. 40 : 2.

THE LIMITATION AND EXTENSION OF ISRAEL'S ELECTION

> Because thou art precious in mine eyes,
> Art honoured, and I have loved thee . . .
> Fear not, for I am with thee;
> From the east will I bring thy seed,
> And from the west will I gather thee.[1]

Here the restoration to favour is expressed, and if this were all, there would be nothing that went beyond the teaching of Ezekiel. But we have already seen how the restoration to service, wider in its range and more exuberant in its spirit, is expressed. Both find frequent expression in this prophet, who is filled with rapture at the thought of the restoration to favour, but who is profoundly anxious that the purpose of the Divine favour shall not again be forgotten. That purpose is the conscious and eager leading of the nations to Israel's God that He may be their God. As T. W. Manson says: "They are to conquer the world, not by force of arms, but by spiritual power; not to establish an earthly empire after the manner of Assyria and Babylon but to bring men under the sway of Jehovah; not to compel the unwilling submission of vassal states to themselves, but to attract individual men and women to voluntary acceptance of Israel's King as their King."[2]

An oracle preserved in the book of Micah is more in harmony with the spirit of Ezekiel than with that of Deutero-Isaiah:

> And the Remnant of Jacob shall be
> In the midst of many peoples,
> As the dew from beside Yahweh,
> As the showers upon the grass,
> Which tarrieth not for man,
> Nor waiteth for the sons of men.
> And the Remnant of Jacob shall be[3]

---

[1] Isa. 42 : 1, 4f.
[2] Cf. *The Teaching of Jesus*, 2nd ed., 1935, p. 180.
[3] The Massoretic text adds "among the nations", but this is omitted by some modern editors, on the ground that it overloads the metre, and spoils the apparently designed repetition of the opening of verse 6. In such a case some variation of one of the terms in the repeated line would occasion less surprise than a variation of the rhythmical balance of the line. It should be noted, however, that the LXX unifies the two lines by adding "among the nations" in verse 6, and T. H. Robinson follows this (*Die zwölf kleinen Propheten* (HAT), p. 144), restoring the rhythmical balance by treating "and shall be" in both vv. 6 and 7 as anacrusis.

In the midst of many peoples,
As the lion among the beasts of the forest,
As the young lion among the flocks of sheep,
Which, if he passes through, tramples down,
And tears, with none to deliver.
Your hand shall be high over your foes,
And all your enemies shall be cut off.[1]

It is commonly held that this oracle is not from the hand of Micah, though there is less agreement as to when it should be dated.[2] Of more consequence to us than its date is its conception of a conquering Remnant, filling the peoples with terror by its military prowess. This links the thought of the saved Remnant with that in some of the passages that speak of the coming Davidic leader, where the might of that leader is emphasized, though it should not be forgotten that it is never the thought of ruthless might, but always of might that is exercised in accordance with righteousness. It has, indeed, been suggested that the concept of the Remnant belongs to the terminology of eschatology,[3] in which case it had a common origin with the whole messianic thought. While this seems doubtful,[4] it is not surprising that in some of its forms it merges into the messianic idea. For it is apparent that if sometimes the Remnant is thought of as a

[1] Mic. 5 : 7–9 (Heb. 6–8). Some modern writers think the last of these verses does not belong to this oracle, but should be transferred to follow 4 : 13. So, e.g., J. Lindblom, *Micha literarisch untersucht*, 1929, pp. 89, 95.
[2] By some it is dated as late as the Maccabæan period (so K. Marti, *Dodekapropheton* [KHC], p. 288; H. Guthe, in Kautzsch-Bertholet, HSAT, ii, 1923, p. 61; cf. Oesterley and Robinson, *Introduction to the Books of the Old Testament*, pp. 384f.); by others in the Persian period (so J. M. Powis Smith, *Micah, Zephaniah and Nahum* [ICC], 1912, pp. 110f.; R. H. Pfeiffer, *Introduction to the Old Testament*, p. 593—Persian or Early Greek period, 500–200 B.C.; T. H. Robinson, *Die zwölf kleinen Propheten* [HAT], p. 144—not before the exile, and perhaps considerably later); by some during the twenty years preceding the destruction of the Temple by Nebuchadrezzar (so G. W. Wade, *Micah, Obadiah, Joel and Jonah* [WC], pp. 38f.). It should be noted that E. Sellin ascribes the verses to Micah, and suggests that they may date from the period of Sennacherib's invasion of 701 B.C. (*Das Zwölfprophetenbuch* [KAT], p. 308), while O. Eissfeldt, while inclining to deny them to Micah, does so "with all reserve" (*Einleitung in das Alte Testament*, 1934, p. 457).
[3] Cf. H. Gressmann, *Der Ursprung der israelitisch-jüdischen Eschatologie*, 1905, pp. 229–238, 242f. J. Skinner (*Isaiah* [CB], i, Revised ed., 1915, p. lxiv) observes that in the teaching of Isaiah the doctrine of the Remnant is on the one hand a purely eschatological idea, and on the other a practical principle.
[4] Cf. S. Mowinckel, *Psalmenstudien II. Das Thronbesteigungsfest Jahwäs und der Ursprung der Eschatologie*, 1922, pp. 276–282.

contemporary loyal group, spared for its loyalty, and at others as a contemporary group, spared not so much for its loyalty as by Divine grace that succeeding generations may be blessed, there are times when the future Remnant, the heirs of the contemporary Remnant, who will inherit the election and its tasks and who will bring a fuller faithfulness to their discharge, are in mind. And that would be on the far horizons of time, in the messianic age, since the messianic age was in essence the age when God's will should be perfectly done.[1]

In treating of Ezekiel and Deutero-Isaiah, T. W. Manson says: "The Remnant doctrine bifurcates at this point: and in all later religious teaching, where it is present, it takes the form either of a *saved* Remnant or a *saving* Remnant: and the religion becomes accordingly either Pharisaic, in the proper sense of that much-abused word, or Apostolic."[2] Amongst the collection of prophecies that goes under the name of Trito-Isaiah in modern works—a collection that probably comes from the hands of more than one author[3]—there is a passage that appears to combine these two conceptions of the Remnant:

---

[1] R. de Vaux (*Revue Biblique*, xlii, 1933, p. 539) concludes his study of the Remnant by saying: "In every age the Remnant is first of all that which will escape the danger of the present. But back of this first plane on which the contemporary events are more sharply drawn in the mind of the prophet, a second may be discerned, dominated by the person of the Messiah: the Remnant is there identified with the New Israel; established in the Promised Land, it there forms a holy community which lives in the love and fear of Yahweh and receives His blessings. Yet this is not all, for a yet more distant and vaster plane is to be seen: it spreads to the horizon of time, when the Remnant, not alone the New Israel, but the spiritual Israel, having gathered at once all the dispersed of the people and all the converted of the nations, will alone remain before Yahweh in the final annihilation of the wicked."

[2] Cf. *The Teaching of Jesus*, 2nd ed., p. 181.

[3] Against this, however, cf. K. Elliger, *Die Einheit der Tritojesaia* (BWANT, 3 F., ix), 1928, who holds that Isa. 56–66 come from the hand of a disciple of Deutero-Isaiah in the last quarter of the sixth century B.C., and H. Odeberg, *Trito-Isaiah: a Literary and Linguistic Analysis*, 1931. W. S. McCullough (*Journal of Biblical Literature*, lxvii, 1948, pp. 27–36) maintains that Isa. 56–66 comes from a single Palestinian source, and is to be dated before Deutero-Isaiah— circa 587–562 B.C. C. C. Torrey (*The Second Isaiah*, 1928) ascribed the whole of Isa. 40–66, together with 34f., to a single author who lived circa 400 B.C. He therefore eliminated every reference to Cyrus, Babylon, or the Chaldaeans. In this he has been followed by W. A. L. Elmslie (*How Came our Faith*, 1948, pp. 341ff.), save that the latter separates Isa. 47 and attaches it to Isa. 13f., and also removes Isa. 46 : 1f. as secondary.

For I am coming[1] to gather
All the nations and tongues;
And they shall come and behold my glory,
And I will set amongst them a sign.
And I will send those that escape from amongst them
Unto nations[2] and isles afar,
That have not heard of my fame,
And have not seen my glory.
And they shall declare my glory among the nations,
And all your brethren shall they bring
From all nations as an offering to Yahweh,[3]
Unto my holy hill Jerusalem—
It is Yahweh who speaks—
As the children of Israel bring an offering
In a pure vessel to the house of Yahweh.[4]

The Remnant is here first saved and then sent on a mission to the world. The thought does not rise to the height of Deutero-Isaiah's, in that it is the glory of Israel rather than the service of the nations that is uppermost in the writer's mind.[5] The nations are conceived of as restoring the scattered Israelites as an offering to God. Yet in that they are thought of as making an offering to Yahweh, there is a recognition of the principle of universalism. The nations are thought of, not as being trampled on by Israel, or even merely as behold-

[1] The Hebrew here reads: "And I their works and their thoughts it is coming." This is almost certainly corrupt, and many editors transfer the words "their works and their thoughts" to the preceding verse, and then for $bā'āh=it$ is coming, read $bā'$, yielding the above translation.

[2] In the Hebrew a list of nations is inserted here. This list is probably an interpretative note, either by the author or by another, interrupting the course of the oracle. The whole passage is usually treated as prose, yet when this prosaic list and the similarly prosaic list in verse 20 are removed, the remainder is in unexceptionable verse. Cf. L. Glahn and L. Köhler, *Der Prophet der Heimkehr*, 1934, pp. 238f.

[3] Here again the Hebrew inserts a catalogue of the means of transport, which is best treated as secondary.

[4] Isa. 66 : 18–20.

[5] J. Morgenstern (*Universal Jewish Encyclopedia*, x, p. 356) holds that there was a combination of universalism and nationalism circa 490–485 B.C., which culminated in a rebellion which was crushed in 485 B.C. This movement had as its programme "voluntary submission to Israel's dominion and conversion to Yahveh's worship", while "should the conquered nation or city not accept these terms, then all its males were to be massacred and the women and children reduced to slavery. In this way all the world would be brought to the worship of Yahveh, and Israel's world-dominion would be established." Cf. S. H. Blank, "Studies in Post-exilic Universalism", in *Hebrew Union College Annual*, xi, 1936, pp. 159–191.

ing with wonder the glory of God and the exaltation of His people, but as presenting themselves before Him in worship.

While it is beyond my purpose in these lectures to go outside the thought and teaching of the Bible, I may perhaps note that attention has been drawn to the fact that the doctrine of the Remnant figures in Babylonian thought.[1] The differences are, however, as significant as the resemblances. In one of the examples cited we read: "As Irra was angry and turned his face to the overwhelming of the countries and the annihilation of the people, Išum, his counsellor, appeased him so that they left a remnant."[2] Here the visitation of the peoples was due to the anger of the god, whereas in the Old Testament while the Divine anger with Israel is sometimes expressed, more fundamental is the thought that the Divine visitation is born of God's love for His people and His desire to awaken them to the folly of their way; here, too, the leaving of the Remnant is not born of the mercy of the god, but is due to the intervention of his counsellor, whereas in the Old Testament it is always the issue of God's grace; here the leaving of the Remnant is not related to any Divine and beneficent purpose which the Remnant will serve, whereas in the Old Testament such a thought is of the essence of the doctrine. We must, of course, beware of comparing only the best in the Bible with the worst that can be found elsewhere; but on the other hand we must beware of emphasizing similarities without reference to all else. In the Old Testament there is variety of thought and not all reaches the same level. But here, in so far as there is community of thought between Babylonian and Biblical teaching, it lies far below the higher levels of Biblical thought, for which no parallels are cited from the Babylonian. In Biblical thought the Remnant is not merely the company of those who survive disaster, but the heirs of Israel's election. To them the heritage is limited, and through them it is transmitted, either because they responded to the obligations of the Covenant by the loyalty to which

---

[1] Cf. A. Haldar, *Associations of Cult Prophets among the Ancient Semites*, 1945, pp. 70–73; and *id.*, *Studies in the Book of Nahum*, 1947, pp. 107f.
[2] Translation cited from Haldar, *Associations of Cult Prophets*, p. 72.

it pledged them, or because they were at least serviceable to convey the heritage to those who would more largely possess it because they would bring to the Covenant a fuller loyalty.

In this latter sense the exiles in Babylon are sometimes regarded as the Remnant. Jeremiah described the people of the first captivity as the good figs, while those who had been left behind were the bad figs.[1] It is very improbable that he thought of the good figs as wholly loyal and worthy of their high calling. For these were the people he had denounced in earlier days for their disloyalty and iniquity. Hence it is likely that what he now meant was that with all their faults they were better than those who were left in Jerusalem, and that there was hope that they would profit from the discipline of their experience and preserve their spiritual inheritance for those who should come after them.

Similarly Ezekiel, in a passage already cited, rebuked the self-satisfaction of those who remained in Palestine, and announced that the hope of the future lay with the exiles, to whom a new heart should be given.[2] Though they were imperfectly loyal, they were not beyond hope and had not finally renounced their election.

This faith of Jeremiah and Ezekiel was vindicated, for post-exilic Judaism took its rise among the exiles. It was from them that Deutero-Isaiah arose[3] with his summons to a larger conception of the implications of election and a larger response to its obligations. Later it was from them that Nehemiah and Ezra[4] brought the new impetus which

[1] Jer. 24.
[2] Ezk. 11 : 14-20.
[3] I am aware that J. A. Maynard (*Journal of Biblical Literature*, xxxvi, 1917, pp. 213-224) argues that the home of Deutero-Isaiah was in Palestine and not in Babylon, and that some other recent scholars take the same view. Cf. W. H. Cobb, *ibid.*, xxvii, 1908, pp. 48-64, M. Buttenwieser, *ibid.*, xxxviii, 1919, pp. 94-112, and C. C. Torrey, *The Second Isaiah*, 1928. Similarly L. Seinecke (*Der Evangelist des Alten Testaments*, 1870, pp. 1-16), who held that Isa. 40-66 were composed in Palestine *circa* 536 B.C. Despite their arguments I still feel, with most modern scholars, that the Babylonian background of these chapters is to be seen, and that the author had looked on Babylonian life at close range.
[4] I have offered my reasons for accepting the view of the chronological order of these two leaders which Van Hoonacker advanced nearly sixty years ago, and which has been followed by a whole series of modern scholars, in a paper which I have contributed to the *Goldziher Memorial Volume*, i, 1948, pp. 117-149, on "The Chronological Order of Ezra and Nehemiah".

gave to Judaism the character and quality it continued to have. Some flicker of life had continued in the Palestinian community, but there was no strong and exuberant life, as we can see from the prophecies of Haggai and Zechariah at the end of the sixth century B.C., and of Malachi in the fifth. In Babylonia, while probably some of the exiles had finally renounced their loyalty and ceased to have any regard for the faith of their fathers, others had cherished that faith and developed a loyalty greater than their fathers had known. They preserved their faith and their loyalty by isolating themselves as far as possible from the life of the community within which they lived, and maintaining their separateness. And that was the spirit which Nehemiah and Ezra brought into Palestinian Judaism, so that it might survive and not be overwhelmed by the influences that pressed in upon it. Thereafter Judaism became marked by a rigidity and an exclusiveness that did much to preserve it through days when far greater perils threatened it. It is easy to belittle that spirit, and to contrast the emphasis on the ritual that characterized Judaism with the scant regard for the ritual of their day that marked the pre-exilic prophets.[1] Yet we should never forget how great is our debt to post-exilic Judaism and its creators. They collected the prophetic writings, and collected, if they did not compose, the Psalms; they also gradually formed the Canon of Old Testament Scriptures.[2] Nor should we forget that they developed the organization of the synagogue, though that institution prob-

[1] Cf. what I have written in "The Unity of the Old Testament," 1946 (reprinted from the *Bulletin of the John Rylands Library*, xxix, 1945-46, pp. 326-358).

[2] Amongst the uncertainties that surround the question of the growth of the Canon of the Old Testament a few things are sure: (1) the Pentateuch must have been accepted as sacred and authoritative before the Samaritan schism (of uncertain date, but probably in the fourth century B.C.), since it is accepted by Jews and Samaritans; (2) a threefold collection of sacred books was in existence before the end of the second century B.C., since the grandson of Ben Sira in the Prologue to Ecclesiasticus refers to "the law, and the prophets, and the other books of our fathers"; (3) the third collection closed with the books of Chronicles already in New Testament times, as is shown by Luke 11 : 51; (4) there had been no formal act of canonization by an authoritative decision, since the Rabbis who were gathered at Jamnia at the end of the first century A.D. still discussed amongst themselves whether certain books were rightly regarded as sacred. For a recent summary of what is known on the question, cf. A. Bentzen, *Introduction to the Old Testament*, i, 1948, pp. 20-41.

ably took its rise in the exiled Remnant.[1] Their great ideal was loyalty, and for that ideal and all they did to attain it, they are worthy of honour.

Nevertheless, it cannot be denied that they did not rise to the full height of the mission for which Israel was elect, according to the teaching of those who had gone before them. There was no passionate eagerness to carry to all men the sacred treasure of their inheritance. For them it sufficed that they cherished in their hearts the revelation of God given unto them, and rendered Him the loyalty and obedience of their hearts in the place where they were set. It must not be forgotten, however, that Judaism conveyed the recognition of the fuller mission to those who should come after. It preserved the teaching of Deutero-Isaiah and Jonah, and it did not cease to dream of the day when all men should worship its God. If in the Remnant there was the limitation of the election of Israel to but a part of the Israel according to the flesh, there was the conception of the expansion of that election beyond the bounds of Israel according to the flesh. Not all Israel was elect, and not all the elect were of Israel. There was thus the transition from the conception of a nation to that of a church, from the thought of a body of people held together by their common descent to that

[1] The origin of the synagogue is also veiled in obscurity. It is commonly held to be probable that its first beginnings were in Babylonia amongst the exiles who were cut off from the worship of the Temple, and who began in a simple and informal way to gather together for prayer and meditation (cf. W. Bacher, *Jewish Encyclopedia*, xi, 1905, p. 619 b; G. F. Moore, *Judaism*, i, 1927, p. 283; A. Menes, "Tempel und Synagoge," in *Zeitschrift für die alttestamentliche Wissenschaft*, N.F. ix, 1932, pp. 268-276). Of this there is no tangible evidence, however. The earliest tangible evidence for the existence of the synagogue comes from Elath, if Torrey's reading *bêth k°nîshāh* (cf. *Bulletin of American Schools of Oriental Research*, No. 84, Dec. 1941, pp. 4f.) on an ostracon which Albright dates from the sixth century B.C. (*ibid.*, No. 82, April 1941, pp. 11-15) is correct. L. Finkelstein (*Proceedings of American Academy of Jewish Research*, i, 1930, pp. 49-59) argues that the Synagogue was pre-exilic, claiming that Rebecca must have gone to a prophetic oracle (Gen. 25 : 22) and that the Midrash of Iddo the Seer (2 Chron. 13 : 22) was a Synagogue, and not a literary work. On the other hand S. Zeitlin (*ibid.*, ii, 1931, pp. 69-81) holds that the Synagogue did not take its rise until after the Return from the exile and that it was originally a secular meeting place. It should be added that C. C. Torrey (*Ezra Studies*, 1910, p. 317) has suggested that there may have been Jewish temples in Babylonia, and L. E. Browne ("A Jewish Sanctuary in Babylonia", in *Journal of Theological Studies*, xvii, 1916, pp. 400f., and *Early Judaism*, 1920, p. 53) has argued that Ezra 8 : 17 may contain a reference to such a temple, where Ezra's brother was priest. But this is precarious.

of a body of people held together by a common faith.[1] Nor did Judaism wholly turn its back on the purpose of its calling. If it did not engage in any world-wide mission and developed a spirit of exclusiveness, that did not mean that it was unwilling to admit others to share the treasure of its faith. It but meant that it was more concerned to prevent alien influences from strangling that faith, and we are wise if we seek rather to understand its perils than to condemn from our safe distance.

Post-exilic Judaism, the faith of the Remnant, was always prepared to share its inheritance with individuals who came to share its faith. It was ever ready to receive proselytes.[2] Already, before the days of Nehemiah and Ezra, Zechariah had said:

> And many Gentiles shall be joined
> Unto Yahweh in that great day;
> And they shall be to Him for a people,
> And in thy midst shall they dwell.[3]
> And thou shalt know that Yahweh of hosts
> Hath sent me unto thee.[4]

Here it is of interest to note that while the process of election is reversed, the result is the same. In the time of Moses God first chose Israel to be His people, and then Israel in response chose Him to be her God; here the Gentiles are thought of as choosing Him to be their God, and then God choosing them to be His people. In either case God and people belong together in mutual loyalty, and the proselytes are thought of as sharing the inheritance of Israel.

[1] For a wider study of this transition cf. A. Causse, *Du groupe ethnique à la communauté religieuse*, 1937; N. A. Dahl, *Das Volk Gottes*, 1941. For a brief treatment, cf. O. Eissfeldt, *Geschichtliches und Uebergeschichtliches im Alten Testament*, 1947, pp. 9–23.
[2] The term used for proselyte was used earlier for the protected foreigner living in Israel, but the development of meaning is not to be mistaken. J. Pedersen (*Israel* III–IV, 1940, p. 603) observes: "The *gēr* of the old days joined the community in order to share in its benefits. Now a *gēr* becomes a proselyte, drawn to the congregation by its law."
[3] The Massoretic text has "and they shall be to me for a people, and in thy midst shall I dwell". The change of person whereby the prophet first speaks of God in the third person and then delivers part of his message in the first person is common enough in the prophets, and occasions no difficulty in itself. Here, however, the reading of the LXX, which is followed above, seems preferable, especially in the fourth line.
[4] Zech. 2 : 11 (Heb. 15).

In another passage Zechariah thinks of the initiative in proselytism as coming from the Gentiles, instead of their being claimed for God by Israel in the fulfilment of the purpose of her election:

> Thus saith Yahweh of hosts:
> It shall yet be that peoples shall come,
> And the dwellers in many cities;
> And they who dwell in one shall go to another,
> Saying, Let us go up forthwith
> To entreat the favour of Yahweh,
> And to seek Yahweh of hosts;
> I for one am going.
> And many peoples shall come,
> And populous nations,
> To seek Yahweh of hosts in Jerusalem,
> And to entreat the favour of Yahweh.
> Thus saith Yahweh of hosts:
> In those days it shall be
> That ten men shall lay hold—
> From all the tongues of the Gentiles—
> Shall lay hold of the cloak of a Jew,
> Saying, we will come up with you;
> For we have heard that God is with you.[1]

With this we may compare:

> Yahweh will have compassion on Jacob,
> And will again choose Israel,
> And will put them in their own land;
> And the foreigner shall join himself unto them;
> And they shall attach themselves to the house
>   of Jacob.[2]

The most familiar instance of a proselyte in the Old Testament is Ruth, the Moabitess. Deserting her own land she followed Naomi on her return to Israel, committing herself in loyalty not alone to Naomi and her people, but to Naomi's God:

> Whither thou goest will I go,
> And where thou dwellest I will dwell;
> Thy people shall be my people,

[1] Zech. 8 : 20–23. [2] Isa. 14 : 1.

THE LIMITATION AND EXTENSION OF ISRAEL'S ELECTION

And thy God my God;
Where thou diest will I die,
And there will I be buried.[1]

By this yielding of herself to the faith of Israel, she became grafted on to its life, sharing in the privileges of its inheritance, and becoming even the ancestress of David, and therefore of the great Scion of David in whom so many hopes culminated.

Proselytes of this kind must have been rare. For few are likely to have left their land and gone to live in Israel because they had already decided to accept her religion. It is probable that the great majority of the proselytes were men and women who continued to live in their own land, and who were so impressed with the quality of life of the Jews of the Dispersion that they sought to know and share something of their religious life. Wherever Paul went on his missionary journeys he found not alone companies of Jews keeping alive their own faith, but Gentiles alongside them. Some of them were interested Gentiles, God-fearers, who had not yet thrown in their lot definitely with the Jews; others were full proselytes, who had committed themselves unreservedly to the faith of Israel. Here it has to be remembered that Judaism never wholly emancipated itself from the thought of a nation even when it began to embrace the idea of a church. The proselytes had to associate themselves with the Jewish nation as well as with the Jewish faith. Moreover, many of the God-fearers who would have been prepared for this may have been restrained from becoming formal proselytes by the fact that they would have been required to pay a visit to Jerusalem. For every male proselyte was required to be circumcised, and both male and female proselytes were required to be baptized and to offer a sacrifice. And since the only altar recognized by Judaism was in Jerusalem, a journey to Jerusalem was entailed. This fact alone must have severely limited the number of proselytes. We learn from the New Testament of visits paid to Jerusalem by proselytes,[2] and these may well have been second or later visits by some

---

[1] Ruth 1 : 16f.   [2] Acts 3 : 10.

whose interest in their adopted faith was so deep that they desired to revisit the Temple and share in the aspects of the life of Judaism that could not be experienced outside Jerusalem. These proselytes were accepted as children of the election of Israel, and the same loyalty to God was demanded of them as of the Jew by birth. If they were heirs of privilege, they were also heirs of the duty and task of Israel.

It is improbable that Judaism was ever notably active in seeking proselytes, or that it could ever be described as a keenly missionary faith, and most of those who became proselytes must have been drawn by the loftiness of the lives of the Jews they met to inquire into the secret of their faith.[1] Nevertheless there were some individuals who engaged in active propaganda for their faith, and who accepted the missionary obligation of their election, and we ought not to minimize their significance.[2] Julian Morgenstern holds that during the quarter of a century following the work of Zechariah there was considerable missionary activity in Judaism, until it was brought to an end by the drastic legislation of Ezk. 44 : 6-9 *circa* 458 B.C.[3] Moreover, our Lord could speak of those who were prepared to compass sea and land to make one convert.[4] Many Jewish writers have maintained that

[1] Cf. C. G. Montefiore, *The Old Testament and After*, 1923, pp. 362f.: "Though there are some fine and excellent things said about proselytes ... the *making* of proselytes is very rarely stated to be the business or purpose of Israel—its *raison d'être* ... Israel is, as it were, to sit tight and do nothing, and truth, by its own native force, is at long last to prevail." Cf. *ibid.*, p. 453: "Once in the Talmud it is stated that the object of Israel's dispersion was, or is, the making of proselytes. Yet the idea of Israel's mission occurs very rarely, and the great thoughts of Isaiah 40-55 suffer comparative neglect"; also *ibid.*, p. 455: "Any sign of a desire or of a duty to *go out* and *seek* proselytes soon became wanting."

[2] Cf. G. F. Moore, *Judaism in the First Centuries of the Christian Era*, i, 1927, pp. 323-353; J. Bonsirven, *Le judaïsme palestinien*, i, 1934, pp. 22-34. Also Bousset-Gressmann, *Die Religion des Judentums im späthellenistischen Zeitalter*, 1926, pp. 76-86; A. Causse, *Israël et la vision de l'humanité*, 1924, pp. 129-149. H. G. May (*Journal of Bible and Religion*, xvi, 1948, p. 103 a) observes that "the emphasis on proselytes in the post exilic period was something more than mere tolerance of them".

[3] Cf. *Universal Jewish Encyclopedia*, x, 1943, p. 356 a. It will be noted that Morgenstern ascribes this section of the book of Ezekiel to the century following its traditional date. So many views on the book of Ezekiel have been advanced in recent years that there can scarcely be said to be any accepted view, and it is almost a case of *quot homines tot sententiae*. Morgenstern has frequently indicated his view on the proselytism of this period. Cf. *Nation, People, Religion: What are we?* 1943, pp. 7f., *Hebrew Union College Annual*, xvi, 1941, pp. 42ff., *Journal of Biblical Literature*, lxiv, 1945, pp. 27ff.

[4] Matt. 23 : 15.

this was a complete misrepresentation of Judaism, which did not seek converts,[1] and A. Jellinek went so far as to argue that a single proselyte was made each year.[2] As against this, B. J. Bamberger, who confesses that he began his study with the preconceived notion that Judaism was always opposed to proselytism,[3] holds that the Gospel text correctly represents the attitude of contemporary Judaism,[4] though there was popular prejudice against converts.[5] It is probable that there was much cleavage of opinion on this question,[6] not merely as between the people and their leaders, but amongst the leaders of the Jews,[7] and while some were indifferent to efforts to make proselytes or hostile to them, others favoured such efforts, and large numbers of proselytes were won. G. F. Moore says: "There is no way of estimating statistically the results of Jewish propaganda in the centuries that fall within the limits of our inquiry, but they were indisputably very large."[8] But so far as is known, Judaism was never a

---

[1] Cf. J. Derenbourg, *Essai sur l'histoire et la géographie de la Palestine*, i, 1867, pp. 227f.; H. Graetz, "Der Vers im Matthäus-Evangelium: einen Proselyten machen", in *Monatsschrift für Geschichte und Wissenschaft des Judenthums*, xviii, 1869, pp. 169f.; E. G. Hirsch, in *Jewish Encyclopedia*, x, 1905, p. 221; M. Friedländer, *Die religiösen Bewegungen innerhalb des Judentums im Zeitalter Jesu*, 1905, pp. 31ff. C. G. Montefiore, *The Synoptic Gospels*, ii, 1909, p. 728, says: "The charge is exaggerated and unhistorical. The Palestinian Rabbis were, on the whole, not particularly favourable to proselytes."

[2] Cf. *Beth ha-Midrasch*, 2nd ed., v, 1938, pp. xlvi f.

[3] Cf. *Proselytism in the Talmudic Period*, 1939, p. 297.

[4] *Ibid.*, pp. 267-273. Bamberger presents a good deal of evidence to show that in many quarters the active winning of converts was regarded with approval. Cf. *ibid.*, pp. 21-24; 149-169; also Strack-Billerbeck, *Kommentar zum Neuen Testament aus Talmud und Midrasch*, i, 1922, pp. 924-931. Here it is noted that the fact that we find nothing comparable with Matt. 23 : 15 in Rabbinical sources is not surprising since the materials for the time of Jesus are so scanty (p. 926).

[5] *Ibid.*, p. 277.

[6] H. de Lubac (*Le fondement théologique des missions*, 1946, pp. 25f.) notes the inner contradiction within Judaism, which could not be resolved until it passed beyond itself. He says: "Hence the Jewish people, with the double treasure—its cult, ever more national, and its God ever more universal—became a living contradiction. It is not merely a question of two currents which opposed one another, and between which it was permissible to choose. The conflict is deeper. All this religion is gathered up in two requirements which appear incompatible. How should it renounce its universal mission, which is its whole *raison d'être* and which alone explains it to itself? But how should it deliver itself to that without denying itself, with its structure so rigorously and narrowly determined?"

[7] Cf. Derenbourg, *op. cit.*, p. 229, and L. Finkelstein, *The Pharisees*, ii, 1938, p. 516.

[8] Cf. *op. cit.*, i, p. 348.

missionary faith in the sense that organized efforts were made by the Jews as a whole to win others. We have no evidence that Jews were sent from Palestine with the express purpose of winning converts to Judaism, or that the Jews of Palestine felt any personal responsibility for this work. It was left to the individuals who made contacts with non-Jews in the lands to which they were scattered to make converts or not as they felt inclined.[1]

But to whatever extent proselytism marked Judaism before the rise of the Christian Church, it ceased to be an active missionary faith to any appreciable extent after that rise.[2] Bamberger maintains that it was an essentially missionary faith until Christianity and Islam combined to force it to abandon this activity,[3] but there are so many objections to proselytism attributed to Tannaitic leaders,[4] and there is so much probability that the whole school of Shammai was opposed to the making of proselytes,[5] that it is doubtful how far Judaism can ever be said to have been an "essentially missionary" faith. Further, during the first three centuries of its existence the Christian Church was far more subject to the pressure of persecution to force it to abandon proselytism than was Judaism, yet it is certain that it was far more actively missionary than Judaism ever was, and if Judaism had taken its missionary vocation as seriously as the Church

---

[1] I. Lévi (*Revue des études juives*, li, 1906, p. 28) says: "It is indubitable that there were always two tendencies in Judaism on the question of proselytes. It can no longer be contested that the tendency favourable to propaganda was always powerful outside Palestine. It is probable that the voluntary missionaries of the Diaspora were not recruited amongst the Rabbis." See further the whole article, "Le prosélytisme juif", *ibid.*, l, 1905, pp. 1-9, li, 1906, pp. 1-31, liii, 1907, pp. 56-61.

[2] Cf. C. J. Cadoux, *The Historic Mission of Jesus*, 1941, p. 150: "Certain it is that this main line of Jewish life represented by Rabbinism paid very little regard to the universalistic ideals represented in the Old Testament, and became eventually so self-centred that even the zeal for proselytism faded away."

[3] Cf. *Liberal Jewish Monthly*, xvii, 1946, p. 21, and *Proselytism in the Talmudic Period*, pp. 287-290.

[4] Cf. Friedländer, *op. cit.*, p. 30.

[5] Derenbourg (*op. cit.*, p. 229) observes that "Shammai and his school were always opposed to these proclamations of the Jewish faith among the Gentiles". Similarly L. Finkelstein (*op. cit.*, ii, p. 516) maintains that the school of Shammai was opposed to the acceptance of proselytes. Bamberger, however (*op. cit.*, p. 225) holds that this view rests on a misunderstanding of the passages relied on.

did, no combination of forces could ever have compelled it to abandon this activity.¹

Another Jewish writer, L. I. Newman, maintains that the Jews did not entirely cease to make proselytes during the Middle Ages,² though Jewish opinion as a whole did not favour the making of such proselytes, doubtless largely owing to the dangers for both the converts and their converters,³ and he says there are instances when the Rabbis denounced would-be converts to Judaism to the Christian authorities.⁴

Here, then, we see Judaism steadily turning its back on one of the corollaries of its election, and instead of going on to the active mission to the Gentiles frowning on the admission of converts and only sporadically seeking them. It is probably by no accident that as the extension of the election to those of non-Israelite birth commanded less interest, pride in Israelite birth as itself guaranteeing Divine privilege assumed a larger place, and the limitation of the election to the Remnant that responded in loyalty to the obligations to the Covenant was less emphasized. The Fourth Gospel presents the adversaries and critics of Jesus as proudly saying "Our father is Abraham",⁵ and in the Assumption of Moses, which is probably to be dated within the lifetime of our Lord,⁶ we find the proud thought that God created the world for the sake of His people,⁷ by which the Jews are meant. How far this is from the thought of Deutero-Isaiah that the election of Israel was for the sake of the world! Frequently in Rabbinical sources we find the emphasis on the merits of Abraham as guaranteeing all his descendants, and the inalienable glory of Israel as the Chosen People.⁸ All this is far from the charac-

---

¹ R. H. Pfeiffer (*Zion's Herald*, cxxvi, 1948, p. 629) observes that "all reputable Jewish historians recognize that Jews were never persecuted either by pagan or by Christian emperors before the year 600, except by the heathen at Alexandria in the time of Caligula", yet during this time "a religion which was on the way to become universal fell back into a national and racial boundary, and normative Judaism arose in the second century of our era out of the Jewish polemic against paganism, gnosticism, and Christianity".
² Cf. *Jewish Influence on Christian Reform Movements*, 1925, pp. 394ff.
³ *Ibid.*, p. 395.
⁴ *Ibid.*, p. 396.
⁵ John 8 : 39.
⁶ Cf. my *Relevance of Apocalyptic*, 2nd ed., 1947, pp. 91ff.
⁷ Ass. Mos. 1 : 12. Similarly 4 Ezra (2 Esdras) 6 :55, 59.
⁸ Cf. Bonsirven, *Le judaïsme palestinien*, i, 1934, p. 78.

teristic thought of the Old Testament, and especially from the heights it reached.[1] For from our survey of that thought on the corollaries of election, and on the limitation and extension of the election, it is abundantly clear that here is something far greater than a people's pride in itself, or that self-vaunting of oriental kings with which Powis Smith associated it. In the thought of the Old Testament it is always election to service, and it is held to be forfeited when it has no relation to that service. The service is varied, and different writers bring out different elements of its character, but in the totality of the mission of Israel to receive the revelation of God, to reflect His will in all its life, and to mediate to all men the knowledge of God, there is a grandeur of conception that would alone entitle the Old Testament to an enduring place in the esteem of men. Nowhere do we find a nation that rises to the height of this ideal; yet the Old Testament cannot be described as a book that rests satisfied with failure to attain the ideal. It is ever held before men, who are urged to find in disaster the chastening hand of God, calling them afresh to His service. And the very prophets of doom are men of faith and vision, who find here a faithful Remnant, and there one that will respond to chastening and become faithful, and who look to the day when a community that is reborn shall arise to render in a larger faithfulness the service to God and the world to which Israel is called. It looks beyond Israel to the world that needs its faith and that God would seek through Israel, and within Israel it reckons as the elect only the faithful who accept the corollaries of their election. And of those corollaries the world-wide mission cannot be left out. The only God is the God of all men, and the Israel that truly beholds His glory must proclaim His glory to all men, that He may worthily be praised until the earth is filled with that glory as the waters cover the sea.[2]

---

[1] Cf. J. Jocz, "The Jewish-Christian Controversy", in *International Review of Missions*, xxxvii, 1948, pp. 382–392, esp. p. 384: "When we turn from the Bible to Rabbinic literature, we find ourselves in a different atmosphere. Here the dialectic of Israel's position before God is replaced by a pious conviction that God and *His people* are irrevocably committed to one another. God and Israel become so inseparable that the Midrash does not hesitate to call them twins."

[2] Isa. 11 : 9; Hab. 2 : 14.

Chapter Four

THE ELECTION OF INDIVIDUALS

WE have considered so far the Old Testament thought of Israel as the Chosen People, and we have seen how the election could be forfeited by disloyalty to the Covenant which was the response to the election, or how it could be limited to the Remnant of Israel when by her disloyalty Israel had forfeited her claim on God. Here, as we have said, there is frequently the thought that it is of the amazing grace of God that the whole people is not consumed and that a Remnant continues to inherit the election. We have also seen that the election was for service and that one element of that service was a universal mission to the world, and while there is no pretence that Israel ever seriously addressed herself to that mission she did admit individuals from the nations into the heritage of her faith so that they became fellow-heirs of the election. Within Israel itself, however, our thought so far has been only in collective terms, either of the whole people or of the group that constituted the Remnant.

We must now turn to observe that within the elect nation individuals are often thought of as specially chosen by God, and here again we soon perceive that they are always chosen for service. Not seldom they are said to have been chosen before they were born, and in this way it is emphasized that their election is not the reward of their worth. They are not chosen for what they are, or even primarily for what they shall be, but for the specific task that is assigned them and for the service God requires of them. For that service they are equipped by God, and all that is required of them is humble obedience to His will and the surrender of themselves to His power.

Some are chosen to be judges and kings, to be God's vicegerents amongst His people, to deliver them from their foes and to rule them in His name. Gideon was chosen to deliver

Israel from the Midianites,[1] and Samson, even before his birth, was chosen that he might be a thorn in the side of the Philistines.[2] Barak was chosen to lead his people in their fight against the growing Canaanite power, and because of his halting response and desire to lean on a woman rather than on God forfeited part of the honour he might have had.[3] Here already we perceive that the privilege of election and its tasks belong together, and that the one cannot be enjoyed when the other is rejected. The same pattern comes out in the thought here which we have found in relation to the people as a whole.

In the story of the establishment of the monarchy the same thing appears. Saul was chosen by God to enable Israel to throw off the yoke of the Philistines. It is well known that there are two accounts of the setting up of the monarchy combined in the Biblical story.[4] According to the later account the institution had its origin in nothing more exalted than a popular desire to imitate foreign nations, and it was in itself an act of disloyalty to Yahweh and rebellion against Him.[5] According to the earlier account the initiative was with Yahweh, who said to Samuel: "About this time tomorrow I will send unto thee a man from the land of Benjamin, and thou shalt anoint him to be a leader over my people Israel; and he shall save my people from the hand of the Philistines, because I have seen the affliction[6] of my people, for their cry has come unto me."[7] Acting on these Divine instructions, Samuel privately anoints Saul, who then takes the lead in the rescue of Jabesh Gilead and is in consequence hailed as king by all the people.

Subsequently we read that it was by Divine initiative that David was chosen to replace Saul.[8] That initiative here, as

---

[1] Judges 6 : 15.   [2] Judges 13 : 3-5.   [3] Judges 4 : 6-9.
[4] E. Robertson has challenged this view in his paper *Samuel and Saul*, 1944 (reprinted from *Bulletin of the John Rylands Library*, xxviii, 1944, pp. 175-206), but the evidence seems to me much too strong to be explained away.
[5] 1 Sam. 8 : 4-9.
[6] The Massoretic text has "because I have seen my people". The rendering given above rests on the LXX and Targumic texts. The Hebrew word for affliction is so similar to the word for *my people* that it could easily have fallen out before the latter.
[7] 1 Sam. 9 : 16.
[8] 1 Sam 16 : 1-13.

commonly, came through a prophetic channel. Samuel was sent to anoint him privately, as he had earlier anointed Saul privately. Of the rejection of Saul we have two accounts. The one attributes it to his impatience in not waiting for Samuel at Gilgal,[1] while the other attributes it to his failure to annihilate the Amalekites.[2] To the modern reader neither seems impressive, and in particular it is hard to suppose that God did really reject Saul because he was not sufficiently blood-thirsty. Yet it should be noted that Saul's failure to annihilate the Amalekites sprang from a defect of character, and if we penetrate beneath the occasion that revealed it to the defect revealed, we shall perceive that the rejection was not quite so dishonouring as we are inclined to suppose. It was not because Saul rose to a higher view of God and found it against his conscience to execute so revolting an order. He accepted the commission of Samuel as the command of God, and yet failed to carry it out, because he set his own will above the will of God.[3] The other story reveals an impatience of spirit, while in all the story of Saul there is apparent an instability of character that marred his achievement. But here in this story of the Amalekites there is a revealed a deeper defect of spirit, and a rejection of God's will as final for him. If then election is for service, and its first corollary is loyalty of spirit to God, and if the abandonment of that loyalty of spirit is tantamount to the renunciation of the election, Saul had indeed renounced his election. It was not merely that he had refused to carry out a particular order, which his own conscience no more condemned than did the conscience of his contemporaries. He had revealed the attitude of his heart towards God, and it was no longer serviceable.

Again and again the same thing comes out in relation to the monarchy. Ahijah assures Jeroboam that God has given him ten of the tribes,[4] yet it is not long after Jeroboam is on the throne that Ahijah turns against him.[5] Just as we found

---

[1] 1 Sam. 13 : 8–14.
[2] 1 Sam. 15.
[3] Cf. what I have written in *The Relevance of the Bible*, 1942, pp.
[4] 1 Kgs. 11 : 29–31.
[5] 1 Kgs. 14 : 7–11.

that not every generation of Israel fulfilled the purpose of its election, so here we find the same thing. Ahijah had promised Jeroboam that if he would truly walk in the ways of God he should have an enduring house.[1] Because he would not so walk, his house was a passing one. For in all election there is an implied condition. In the election of Israel that had been explicitly specified in the Covenant. But here the Covenant was an implicit one, yet none the less vital, and the acceptance of the election committed the elect to obedience.

It is probable that Baasha was elevated to the throne through prophetic activity, though we are not told this. We are told, however, that he had not been on the throne long before a prophet was announcing his rejection because he was unserviceable.[2] Again and again the prophets take a hand in king-making and in king-breaking. To them the function of the king is to be God's vicegerent among His people. Since Israel is God's people He is their final Lord, and through the king His will should prevail.

The election of the house of David would seem to go somewhat further than this. It is recorded that the prophet Nathan opened a Divine oracle to David with the words: "Thus saith Yahweh of hosts: I took thee from the meadowland, from following the sheep, to be a leader of my people Israel; and I have been with thee wherever thou hast gone, and I have cut off all thy foes from before thee."[3] The passage goes on to promise David that not only was he chosen to be king, but his descendants should follow him on the throne: "When thy days are fulfilled, and thou dost lie with thy fathers, I will raise up thy seed after thee, which shall issue from thy loins; and I will establish his kingdom. He shall build a house for my name, and I will establish the throne of his kingdom for ever."[4]

Just as Abraham had been chosen, and in him all his descendants, to be the people of God, according to the tradition at which we have already looked, so David is here declared to have been chosen, and in him the line of his

[1] 1 Kgs. 11 : 38.   [2] 1 Kgs. 16 : 1-4.   [3] 2 Sam. 7 : 8f.
[4] 2 Sam. 7 : 12f.

successors, to be the rulers of that people. Yet here, as there, the election is not quite so automatic as it appears. Just as the line of election ran through Jacob and not through Esau, so here it runs through Solomon and not through Adonijah. The eldest living son of David at the time of his death was Adonijah, who not unnaturally assumed that the succession would be his. That assumption was defeated through the activity of the prophet Nathan, who ensured that Solomon should succeed.[1] And when Solomon proved less serviceable than could have been wished, and imposed a heavy yoke of tyranny upon his people, and fell into an easy disloyalty to the God of Israel, Ahijah was responsible for the splitting of the kingdom. To the house of David one tribe was left, "that David my servant may always have a lamp before me in Jerusalem".[2] The election of the Davidic line was not wholly annulled, but it was greatly modified.

Here we find the same essential principles that have appeared in the Old Testament teaching about the election of the nation. The generations that repudiated the responsibilities that election brought, and that refused to validate for themselves the Covenant by the willing acceptance of its obligations, declared that they no longer desired to be God's Chosen People. Yet they were never immediately abandoned by God. He sought to bring them back to faithfulness to Himself, and for the sake of the loyal Remnant preserved them to convey to a future generation that should be more serviceable to Him the inheritance of grace. And in the same way the Davidic house was preserved in the tribe of Judah against the day when a nobler scion of that house should arise to fulfil in greater glory the purpose of the election. Nor should we forget that even over Judah the house of David ceased to rule. The condition implied in the election was repudiated by Judah and its kings, and the dynasty of David ceased to reign in Jerusalem. It is true that the promise to David was transmuted into the terms of a hope for the revival of his house, but it is idle to suppose that Nathan's promise to David that his house should be established for

---

[1] 1 Kgs. 1 : 10–39.   1 Kgs. 11 : 36.

ever, or Ahijah's assurance that David would always have a lamp in Jerusalem, has been fulfilled. The long centuries of the discontinuance of the dynasty of David could not be obliterated by its revival. The lamp long since went out, not because God was faithless to His word, but because the house of David was faithless to Him, and in repudiating Him repudiated its election. And integral to the hope of its rekindling was the need for loyalty to His will.

Even during the period that the house remained, individual kings were condemned and doom was pronounced upon them. Thus Jeremiah pronounced doom on Jehoiakim[1] and Jehoiachin.[2] Nowhere is there any idea that because they belong to the house of David they are God's favourites, and can do as they please and be sure of His indulgence. Such a corollary of election was not dreamed of by the Biblical writers. The house of David was chosen to be the instrument of the Divine rule, and though for long periods it failed, in the prophetic view, to be worthy of its high calling or to fulfil its vocation, the justification for its preservation was the hope that it would yet fulfil it. In all the pictures of the age of glory when the great scion of David's house should arise and hold the sceptre, it is fundamental that his rule should be in perfect accord with the will of God. That was the purpose of the election of David, which looked beyond itself to this nobler fulfilment on the far horizon of time.

Into the vexed and obscure question of the history of the Israelite priesthood it is impossible to go here. Suffice it to say that in the thought of the Old Testament the priesthood, too, was chosen by God. It is well known that to the Deuteronomist all members of the tribe of Levi were eligible to discharge priestly functions at the one legitimate shrine which he recognized,[3] but that at the time of Josiah's reform it was found impossible to implement this[4]—doubtless owing to the strength of the opposition of the Jerusalem priesthood. Later we find that in his plan of reconstruction Ezekiel rationalizes this situation, and argues that the Zadokites alone should

[1] Jer. 22 : 18f.   [2] Jer. 22 : 28-30.   [3] Deut. 18 : 6f.
[4] 2 Kgs. 23 : 9.

have the full priestly status, while the rest should have a lower status. The Zadokites are the Jerusalem priests, and the ground on which Ezekiel distinguishes them from the others is that they had charge of Yahweh's sanctuary when the others were ministering to idols.[1] In view of Ezekiel's description in chapter 8 of the practices that went on in the Jerusalem Temple this rings somewhat hollow, and we find that the post-exilic priestly law extends the bounds of the priesthood to include more than the Zadokites. The priests are now the descendants of Aaron, of whom the Zadokites are reckoned as one family,[2] but Ezekiel's principle of differentiation is accepted, and the rest of the Levites are put on a lower footing.[3] This was the accepted arrangement of Judaism as it existed at the close of the Old Testament period.

It is probable that behind this story there was a good deal of intrigue and controversy. For one item of the story we have some of the details. We read in 1 Sam. 2 of the man of God who came to Eli to announce the supersession of his house, and the raising up of a faithful priest, whose house, in contrast to Eli's, should be enduring.[4] It is probable that the faithful priest here in mind is Zadok, and the passage points to the replacement of Abiathar by Zadok more than half a century after the death of Eli. That replacement came, however, as the sequel to the intrigue over the succession at the time of David's death. Abiathar was on the losing side of Adonijah, and his supersession was more directly related to

---

[1] Ezk. 44 : 10-14. Never has there been a greater variety of view on the date and authorship of the book of Ezekiel than during the last two decades. Particularly has there been difference of opinion as to the authorship of Ezk. 40-48 in relation to that of the preceding chapters. G. Hölscher (*Hesekiel der Dichter und das Buch*, 1924), V. Herntrich (*Ezechielprobleme*, 1932), Oesterley and Robinson (*Introduction to the Books of the Old Testament*, 1934, pp. 320-329), J. Battersby Harford (*Studies in the Book of Ezekiel*, 1938), and W. A. Irwin (*The Problem of Ezekiel*, 1943), all deny these chapters to the prophet Ezekiel, though not agreeing with one another as to their date and authorship. A. Bertholet (*Hesekiel* [HAT], 1936) and G. A. Cooke (*The Book of Ezekiel* [ICC], 1936) find secondary expansions to a varying degree in these chapters, which have in their view a genuine nucleus. Cf. also N. Messel, *Ezechielfragen*, 1945; P. Auvray, *Ezéchiel*, 1947; and A. van den Born, *De historische situatie van Ezechiels prophetie*, 1947.
[2] Num. 18 : 1ff., 3 : 2; 1 Chron. 6 : 4ff.
[3] Note Num. 18 : 23: "they shall bear their iniquity".
[4] 1 Sam. 2 : 27-36.

that than to any defects of Eli or his sons. Indeed most of the house of Eli had perished because they had rendered a service to David[1]—a service which was regarded as meritorious —while Abiathar himself had rendered constant service to David. For the validity of the alleged connexion between the sins of Eli and his sons and the removal of Abiathar there is little to be said. Nor should it pass unnoticed that the house of Ithamar, to which Eli belonged, was later restored to its position alongside the Zadokites,[2] and that Zechariah, the father of John the Baptist, was of that house.[3]

What is of greater importance for our purpose is the fact that, whatever intrigues marked the course of the history of the priesthood, in the thought of the Old Testament writers the priests were chosen by God, and were chosen for service; and the priestly office could be forfeited by the non-performance of that service. Election confers no irrevocable title on men independent of their response. When the functions of the priests are defined in Deut. 33 : 10 we read:

> They shall teach thy judgements to Jacob,
> And thy law to Israel;
> They shall put the smoke of sacrifice in thy nostrils,
> And whole burnt-offering on thine altar.

The priest was thus not merely the custodian of the altar, to ensure that the due ritual was performed in all its service; he was the custodian of the sacred tradition, whose duty it was to guide men in the way of God's will. A sacred responsibility rested on him in virtue of the privilege of his office, and the privilege and the responsibility could not be divorced

---

[1] 1 Sam. 21 : 1–9, 22 : 9–19.

[2] 1 Chron. 24. While this chapter deals ostensibly with the time of David it is generally recognized that it reflects the conditions of the Chronicler's own day. But even without this evidence, the fact that Zechariah was of the house of Ithamar would assure us that it had been restored at some time.

[3] Luke 1 : 5 says that Zechariah was of the course of Abijah, and 1 Chron. 24 : 10 indicates that Abijah was of the house of Ithamar, since the lots were alternately drawn from the houses of Eleazar and Ithamar (1 Chron. 24 : 6)—presumably for the first sixteen of the courses. As Ezra 2 : 36–39 states that only four priestly families were represented amongst the returning exiles—Jedaiah, Immer, Pashhur and Harim—it may perhaps have been by a fiction that all the twenty-four families were reconstructed.

from one another. Frequently in the Prophets the priests are condemned because they disregard the duties of their office, and fail to give to men the teaching with which they are charged. That the priesthood was hereditary no more involved the conclusion that it conferred an irrevocable privilege on a man than Israel's election conferred irrevocable privilege on every Israelite. There was always the initial privilege and opportunity of the inheritance, but if responsibility and opportunity were cast aside, the privilege was turned into a burden of guilt. Whatever may be said about the rationalizing of history in the matter of the priesthood, there can be little complaint of the principles to which appeal was made, or of their relevance to the general teaching on election found in the Old Testament, and especially in the prophets, who brought those principles into clearer focus.

Again, we find that the prophets were divinely elected to their office. Here I am limiting my thought to those prophets whose noblest representatives are found in the greater prophetic figures of the Old Testament. We do not know how all the prophets were recruited in Israel, and it is vain to speculate. Recent study has made it probable that there were Cultic Prophets, who stood beside the priests in a regulated relation to the cultus.[1] It is not necessary to equate them with Babylonian priestly groups,[2] or to suppose that they based their oracles on the study of the liver of the sacrificed animals, though we should on the other hand beware of thinking of all the prophets in terms of such men as Elijah and Isaiah. Nor can we simply equate the Cultic Prophets with the false prophets and so differentiate them from the true prophets.[3] There was apparently no manifest difference

[1] Cf. S. Mowinckel, *Psalmenstudien III. Kultprophetie und prophetische Psalmen*, 1923; A. R. Johnson, *The Cultic Prophet in Ancient Israel*, 1944; A. Haldar, *Associations of Cult Prophets among the Ancient Semites*, 1945; and the literature cited in these works.
[2] Cf. Haldar, *op. cit.*, pp. 108-126.
[3] H. Knight, in the course of a study of prophecy (*The Hebrew Prophetic Consciousness*, 1947) reaches the facile conclusion that the canonical prophets are to be differentiated sharply from the official prophets, who are again to be differentiated from the priest-prophets, and that the official prophets and the priest-prophets together made up the false prophets. This is much too easy to be satisfying.

of function between false prophets and true, and no easily definable marks whereby the true and the false could be distinguished.[1] Easy lines of division can nowhere be drawn and all that we can say with confidence is that there were many varieties of prophet in Israel. Some appear to have been private prophetic chaplains to kings,[2] and some to have exercised their prophetic ministry at home,[3] or on the highway,[4] or wherever the spirit moved them.[5] The greater prophets seem at times to have gone to the shrines to exercise their vocation, as Amos went to Bethel[6] and Jeremiah to Jerusalem.[7] But neither of these could be thought of as Cultic Prophets in the incidents referred to. That all the prophets were subject to control within the shrine is apparent from Jer. 29 : 27, and is not surprising. For the authorities of the shrine could hardly fail to be responsible for the maintenance of proper conduct within its precincts. But that is only a negative control, to be exercised when prophets went beyond bounds that were to be recognized as tolerable. Cultic Prophets were probably more closely related to the cultus, and may have had an assigned place in the service of the shrine. It is suggested that some of the psalms may have been composed by them.[8]

How such prophets were recruited we have no means of knowing. Nor can we know how the prophetic chaplains of kings came to be prophets. What we do know is that of several of the greater prophets we have some record of their Divine call to their office.[9] They were not prophets because they were born to the office, or because they fancied the life, but because they felt a constraint which they believed to

---

[1] Cf. what I have written in *Harvard Theological Review*, xxxviii, 1945, pp. 16-19.
[2] 2 Sam. 24 : 11.
[3] 1 Kgs. 14 : 1ff., 2 Kgs. 5 : 9ff.
[4] 2 Sam. 12 : 1, 1 Kgs. 20 : 38, 21 : 17ff.
[5] 1 Sam. 10 : 5, 10, 19 : 18ff., 1 Kgs. 13 : 20f.
[6] Amos 7 : 13.
[7] Jer. 26 : 2.
[8] Cf. Mowinckel, *op. cit.*
[9] R. B. Y. Scott (*The Relevance of the Prophets*, 1944, p. 88) says: "The assurance of having a divine call and commission was a primary element in the prophetic consciousness."

be of God. This may well have been true also of other prophets. Indeed, if it were not so, it would be surprising that this was not referred to as a criterion for detecting the true prophet. It is frankly recognized in the Old Testament that to tell a true prophet from a false one was no easy matter. Deuteronomy deals twice with the question, and in neither case very satisfactorily,[1] while Jeremiah, who denounces the false prophets of his day, has no simple test to detect the true from the false.[2] It is therefore likely that many, at any rate, of the false prophets had experienced the constraint which they believed to be of God, and were prophets because they sincerely believed they were called to the office. The depth of the experience of vocation would inevitably vary in different men, and it could never be easy in dealing with the things of the spirit to draw a line and say that all who were on one side of the line were true prophets and all who were on the other side were false prophets. And even the same prophet was not always equally deserving of the name of a true prophet.[3] Hence it is probable that those who are denounced as false prophets claimed, and indeed had, an experience of vocation.[4] If this were not so, it is hard to understand the denunciations of the canonical prophets. In their denunciations it is implied that the false prophets are false to their true responsibility to speak the word of God, and therefore that the true oracles of God were available to them. Yet the oracles of God are for those on whom His spirit rests, and who are thus claimed by Him.

Of the call of Moses in the wilderness,[5] of Samuel in his childhood in the shrine of Shiloh,[6] of Amos when pursuing

---

[1] Deut.13 : 1–3, 18 : 20–22.
[2] Jer. 23 : 9–40.
[3] Cf. 1 Kgs. 13 : 18, 21. In the former verse the old prophet was a lying prophet, though the other had no means of knowing it, and clearly believed him; in the latter verse he was a true prophet delivering a word of God to his companion that the event vindicated.
[4] Cf. H. W. Robinson, *Redemption and Revelation*, 1942, pp. 143f.: "It is not likely that a prophet of the classical period would have dared to prophesy without an inaugural vision such as Isaiah's in the temple, or an audition such as Jeremiah's, or such a characteristically peculiar experience as that of Ezekiel."
[5] Ex. 3.
[6] 1 Sam. 3.

his daily work,[1] of Hosea in the tragedy of his domestic life,[2] of Isaiah in the Temple,[3] of Jeremiah in his youth,[4] and of Ezekiel in the bizarre vision that came to him,[5] we have familiar record. All of these became prophets because the hand of God was laid upon them. Some tried to resist the call, only to find that it could not be resisted.

> The lion hath roared, who can but fear?
> The Lord Yahweh hath spoken; who can but prophesy?[6]

said Amos, who had felt the imperiousness of the constraint put upon him. Of all the prophets, it was Jeremiah who most felt that imperiousness. Despite his efforts to maintain silence and refrain from prophesying he could not.

> If I said, I will not remember him,
> Or speak again in his name;
> There was in my heart a burning fire,
> Shut up in my bones,
> And I was worn out with holding it in,
> And could not bear it.[7]

---

[1] Amos 7 : 14f.
[2] Of the actual call of Hosea we have brief record. In Hos. 1 : 2 we are told that it first came in the Divine leading to take a wife of whoredom. Many believe that this represents a reading back into his experience of what only became clear later, and that it was only when Gomer's infidelity became known and the prophet through the agony which he suffered came to understand more deeply the heart of God that he realized that he had been divinely led into this tragic situation. I find no reason to cavil at the idea that Hosea, acting consciously under what he believed to be Divine influence, married a temple prostitute (so T. H. Robinson, *Prophecy and the Prophets*, 1923, pp. 75f., and "Die Ehe des Hosea", in *Theologische Studien und Kritiken*, cvi, 1934–35, pp. 301–313; H. Schmidt, "Die Ehe des Hosea", in *Zeitschrift für die alttestamentliche Wissenschaft*, N.F. i, 1924, pp. 245–272; O. R. Sellers, "Hosea's Motives", in *American Journal of Semitic Languages*, xli, 1924–25, pp. 243–247), although he loathed the sacred prostitution from which he took her. The full content of his message was mediated to him through the things which he suffered, but these were not just misfortunes which came out of the lottery of marriage, and which he learned to transmute by the spirit in which he faced them, but the issue of an act of consecration to the will of God.
[3] Isa. 6.
[4] Jer. 1 : 4–10.
[5] Ezk. 1.
[6] Amos 3 : 8.
[7] Jer. 20 : 9. Cf. W. Rudolph, *Jeremia* (HAT), 1947, p. 113: "For the understanding of the prophetic inspiration these words are of the greatest significance . . . the prophet cannot speak as he will, but as he must, even unwillingly."

THE ELECTION OF INDIVIDUALS

Moreover, Jeremiah felt that he was called to his office before he was born:

> The word of Yahweh came unto me, saying:
> Before I formed thee in the womb I chose thee,[1]
> And before thou camest forth from thy mother I sanctified thee;
> I appointed thee to be a prophet to the nations.[2]

All this would seem to imply that the call of the prophet was the arbitrary act of God, and especially if he were called before he was born. Yet there is much in the Old Testament to indicate that it was neither arbitrary, nor so irresistible as the experience of the greater prophets would suggest. There were prophets who did not fulfil the purpose of their call, and who stand under sharp condemnation. The edge of their spirit's sensitiveness became blunted, and no longer did they feel the imperiousness of the constraint of God's hand. More are called for service than truly respond to the call. In the paradox of experience it is in the measure of the prophet's response to the call that he feels the irresistibility of the constraint, and he who most justifies the call and fulfils its purpose is most conscious of the Divine element and least conscious of the human element in his commissioning. The same paradox is found in all religious experience. Paul could feel himself to be "the chief of sinners",[3] and it has ever been the case that the nearer a man comes to God the nearer he wants to come, for it is only he who is very close to God who can feel the gulf that separates him from God. We must not therefore underestimate the importance of the prophet's response to the call, however much he may belittle its significance. Though he may seek to evade it, he responds to it not merely because the hand of God is laid upon him, but because he is what he is, a man of sensitive spirit who is alive to the touch

---

[1] The Hebrew literally means "I knew thee", but with the clearly implied meaning of "I chose thee".
[2] Jer. 1 : 5.
[3] 1 Tim. 1 : 15. C. Spicq (*Les Épitres Pastorales*, (EB) 1947, p. 43) observes: "This is the cry of a conscience which preserves the lively memory of its failures and to which the remembrance of the guilty past always makes the extraordinary power of Christ's salvation feel the more wonderful."

of God and willing to respond. This is not to deny the reality of his election, or to suggest that it is his election of the vocation of prophet which makes him a prophet. He is a prophet because he is chosen of God, and responds to the choice.

Here is something once more which is wholly comparable with the election of Israel. She was first chosen by God and then responded to His choice in the Covenant; and the prophet is similarly chosen by God, and then responds in consecration. It is in the call of Isaiah that this is most explicit, but it is implicit in many others. To Isaiah there was first given the vision of God in the Temple. The initiative was not with him but with God, and he was both overwhelmed and exalted at the experience:

> Woe is me! for I am undone!
> For a man of unclean lips am I!
> And in the midst of a people of unclean lips
> I have my habitation!
> Yet the King, Yahweh of hosts,
> Mine eyes have seen![1]

When, shortly after, he says "Here am I! send me!" it is not that he spontaneously offers himself to the God he has seen. His first feeling is of his own sinfulness, and of the impossibility of one so unclean as he continuing to live in the light of that Presence. And then one of the Seraphim flew to him and touched his lips with a live coal from the altar, and said:

> Lo! this hath touched thy lips,
> And thine iniquity is removed, and thy sin cleansed.[2]

He is first the recipient of the Divine grace in the vision and the cleansing, before he responds to the Divine call for service; just as Israel was first the recipient of the Divine grace in the mission of Moses and the deliverance from Egypt, before she responded in consecration.

Here, too, the consecration is for service; for the purpose of the choice of the prophet is service. He is never chosen

[1] Isa. 6 : 5. [2] Isa. 6 : 7.

merely to receive visions, and moments of exaltation in the presence of God. He receives, indeed, but he receives that he may give; for the end of his vocation is that he may be the mouthpiece of God to man. "Go, and say to this people" was the first commission to Isaiah.[1] "Lo, I have put my words in thy mouth" was the word that came to Jeremiah.[2] Great indeed was the honour of the true prophet, and the supreme distinction of Israel was the noble succession of such men who mediated to her the word of God; but the honour had no meaning save in relation to the service, whereby the vocation was realized.

It is not without interest to observe how the prophet received the word which formed the burden of his message. I do not mean here to embark on the discussion of the question as to how far the prophet received his message in what has come to be called the ecstatic state.[3] I am more concerned with the source of the message than with his psychological condition in the moment of his receiving it. By whatever experience it reached him, it was valid only if it came from God. It was never conceived as a word which he found by his own earnest reflection on the condition of affairs. Indeed, one of Jeremiah's counts against the false prophets is just that they find their message in their own hearts:

> Hearken not to the words of the prophets;[4]
> They fill you with vain hopes.
> An observation of their own hearts they speak,
> And not from the mouth of Yahweh.[5]

The true prophet's message, on the other hand, comes from God, and it is mediated to him through close and intimate fellowship with God:

---

[1] Isa. 6 : 9.
[2] Jer. 1 : 9.
[3] Cf. my paper "The Nature of Prophecy in the Light of Recent Study", in *Harvard Theological Review*, xxxviii, 1945, pp. 1-38; also I. P. Seierstad, *Die Offenbarungserlebnisse der Propheten Amos, Jesaja und Jeremia*, 1946.
[4] The Hebrew text adds "who prophesy unto you", but these words are missing from the LXX and Old Latin texts and add nothing material, and they are accordingly omitted by many modern editors.
[5] Jer. 23 : 16; cf. 14 : 14.

> Hearken ye unto my words!
> If your prophet be from Yahweh,[1]
> In vision am I known unto him;
> In dream do I speak with him.
> Not so my servant Moses;
> In all my house he is faithful.
> Mouth to mouth do I speak with him,
> Clearly[2] and not in riddles;
> And the form of Yahweh he beholds.[3]

Jeremiah expresses this as standing in the council of God.[4] He asks:

> Who has stood in the council of Yahweh,
> That he might see and hear his word?[5]

He continues:

> If only they had stood in my council,
> To hear my words unto my people,
> They would have turned them from their evil way,
> And from the wickedness of their deeds.[6]

The same thought of the prophet as one who stands in the council of God is found in Amos, who uses the same Hebrew

---

[1] The Hebrew text reads "If your prophet be Yahweh". The rendering of R.V., "If there be a prophet among you, I the Lord . . .", involves a tacit emendation of the text. Most modern editors follow this emendation and go on to omit the word *Yahweh* as no longer translatable, save by the syntactical inelegance presupposed by R.V. The result is unnecessary violence to the text and a reading which can claim no real support from the versions, and one which is not patently satisfactory. It is preferable to add a single letter to the Hebrew text, and one which could easily have fallen out by haplography, and attain the above translated result (cf. A. R. Johnson, *The Cultic Prophet*, p. 41 n.). The text does not promise that every prophet will be inspired of Yahweh, but only that every true prophet, whom He sends, will be so inspired.

[2] The Hebrew is here ambiguous, meaning "and an appearance". Many claim the support of the versions for changing a single letter to yield "in appearance", but the word may just as well be read as an adverbial accusative, similar to "mouth to mouth" in the preceding line. In either case the ambiguity remains as to whether the reference is to the speaker's personal manifestation, as in the following line, or to the clarity of the message, which is as clear as something that meets the eye, and not obscure like a riddle. On the whole the latter seems the more likely.

[3] Num. 12 : 6f.

[4] Cf. H. Wheeler Robinson, "The Council of Yahweh", in *Journal of Theological Studies*, xlv, 1944, pp. 151-157.

[5] Jer. 23 : 18.

[6] Jer. 23 : 22.

word, which can be rendered in English by both *council* and *counsel* (or *secret*). He says:

> Surely the Lord Yahweh
> Will not perform a thing,
> Except he have revealed his secret
> Unto his servants the prophets.[1]

In these passages it is apparent that the true prophet is thought of as one who stands in so close and intimate a relationship with God that his personality becomes the vehicle of God's word. In a real sense he becomes one with God, or an extension of God's personality.[2] When he speaks he can pass easily and naturally from using the third person of God, to using the first person in delivering the Divine word. It is not his own word, but the word of God in his mouth, and for the time being he is as God Himself. This is not because the prophets ever lost the sense of the otherness of God. Nowhere are they thought of as one with God in essence, in power, or in holiness. They are one with God only in so far as they are the spokesmen of His word, illuminated in their hearts by having stood in His council, and yielding their mouths in consecration unto Him. It is only then that they fulfil the purpose of their election to their holy office. Their election is for service, and it is only valid in so far as, and so long as, they fulfil that purpose. And their service is to receive and to communicate the word of God, a word that ever has a revelation of the character and will of God as its essential content.

Finally, we must consider the election of the Servant of Yahweh in Deutero-Isaiah.[3] It would carry us much too far to discuss all the problems that gather round this figure. Nor is it necessary for our purpose. We may limit ourselves to the four songs which have been for more than half a century generally recognized as belonging together,[4] though some

---
[1] Amos 3 : 7.
[2] Cf. A. R. Johnson, *The One and the Many in the Israelite Conception of God*, 1942, pp. 36-40.
[3] For an excellent and well-documented survey of the work devoted to the book of Isaiah during the past hundred years, cf. E. J. Young, "The Study of Isaiah since the time of Joseph Addison Alexander", in *Westminster Theological Journal*, ix, 1946, pp. 1-30, x, 1947-48, pp. 23-56, 139-167.
[4] Isa. 42 : 1-4, 49 : 1-6, 50 : 4-9, 52 : 13-53 : 12.

writers have added others to them or have somewhat differently delimited the songs.¹ Nor would it be profitable here to discuss the question whether these songs come from the pen of Deutero-Isaiah, or are older or younger than their context,² since we are concerned with the thought, and not with the authorship or date of the poems. Even here it would require a book to examine the infinite variety of views that have been advanced and to establish the interpretation of their significance which I adopt, and if I leave all such questions aside it is not because I desire to dismiss every view but my own,³ or suppose that my own view is patently sound and every other is patently unsound, but because monographs on the whole question exist in plenty,⁴ and a full dis-

---

¹ Some have delimited the first three as Isa. 42 : 1-7, 49 : 1-9, and 50 : 4-11, while additional songs both in Deutero-Isaiah and in Trito-Isaiah have been brought into the series by some writers. Thus, e.g., H. Gressmann (*Der Messias*, 1929, pp. 287ff.) finds the following seven songs: Isa. 42 : 1-4, 42 : 5-9, 49 : 1-6, 49 : 7, 49 : 8-13, 50 : 4-10, 52 : 13-53 : 12, while A. Bentzen (*Indledning til det Gamle Testamente*, I i, 1941, p. 100) adds 51 : 9-16, and many have added 61 : 1-4 to the series (so G. H. Box, *The Book of Isaiah*, 1916, pp. 317f.), or 61 : 1-3 (so W. A. L. Elmslie, *How Came our Faith*, 1948, p. 354 n.). The *Westminster Study Bible*, 1948, p. 1030, observes: "Ch. 61 shows the influence of the songs of the Servant of the Lord, but the speaker can hardly be identified with the Servant. In distinction from the Servant of the Lord, the prophet is the joyous messenger, not the mediator of salvation; furthermore he is interested in Zion rather than in having a message for the whole world." N. H. Snaith, (*Expository Times*, lvi, 1944-45, pp. 79-81) protests against the segregation of these songs from the rest of Deutero-Isaiah, and maintains that "the Servant of the Songs is the Servant of the rest of the oracles."

² In addition to the views on these questions which will be found assembled in the monographs on the Servant, it may be noted that J. Morgenstern (*Universal Jewish Encyclopedia*, x, 1943, p. 356 b) ascribes them to an anonymous "disciple in spirit" of Deutero-Isaiah *circa* 460 B.C. Morgenstern also delimits the songs in an original way: Isa. 42 : 1-4, 49 : 5-7, 50 : 4-10, 53 : 1-12. The latest scholar to deny these songs to the author of the rest of Isa. 40-55 is W. F. Lofthouse ("Some Reflections on the 'Servant Songs' ", in *Journal of Theological Studies*, xlviii, 1947, pp. 169-176).

³ I have briefly stated my general view of these songs in *Israel's Mission to the World*, 1939, and *The Missionary Message of the Old Testament*, 1945.

⁴ The following are but a few of the more important monographs which have appeared during the present century, dealing with this subject: K. Budde, *Die sogenannten Ebed-Jahwe-Lieder und die Bedeutung des Knechtes Jahwes in Jes. 40-55*, 1900; J. Fischer, *Isaias 40-55 und die Perikopen vom Gottesknecht*, 1916, and *Wer ist der Ebed in den Perikopen Js 42, 1-7; 49, 1-9a; 50, 4-9; 52, 13-53, 12?*, 1922; S. Mowinckel, *Der Knecht Jahwäs*, 1921; O. Eissfeldt, *Der Gottesknecht bei Deuterojesaja*, 1933; J. van der Ploeg, *Les chants du Serviteur de Jahvé dans la seconde partie du livre d'Isaïe*, 1936; I. Engnell The *'Ebed Yahweh Songs and the Suffering Messiah in "Deutero-Isaiah"*, 1948 (reprinted from *Bulletin of the John Rylands Library*, xxxi, 1948, pp. 54-93); C. R. North, *The Suffering Servant in Deutero-Isaiah*, 1948.

THE ELECTION OF INDIVIDUALS

cussion here could only distract the reader from the main subject of this study.

Most writers have adopted the view that a common principle of interpretation must be applied to the four passages, though it is to be noted that some writers have adopted the principle that each is to be interpreted in relation to its immediate context, and that the Servant of one song is therefore not to be identified with the Servant of another.[1] We may content ourselves with recognizing a fundamental unity in the conception of the Servant in these passages, without attempting to determine whether the Servant was conceived of as the nation Israel, either ideal or actual,[2] or as a historical figure who preceded the prophet[3] or who was his contemporary[4] or whether he was thought of as an ideal figure

---

[1] Two recent writers have adopted this principle, but with widely differing results. E. J. Kissane (*The Book of Isaiah*, ii, 1944) finds the Servant in the first two songs to be Israel, in the third to be the prophet himself, and in the fourth to be the Messiah; while S. Smith (*Isaiah, Chapters* xl-lv, 1944) finds the Servant in the first song to be Cyrus, and in the remaining three to be the prophet himself. Cf. C. Bruston, in *Vom Alten Testament* (Marti Festschrift), 1925, pp. 37-44, and F. X. Peirce, *Ecclesiastical Review* xcii, 1935, pp. 83-95.

[2] Cf. K. Budde, *op. cit.*; J. Skinner, *Isaiah, Chapters* 40-66 (CambB), Revised ed., 1917, pp. lvi-lxvii (see also pp. 263-281); O. C. Whitehouse, *Isaiah xl-lxvi* (CentB), pp. 18-29; A. S. Peake, *The Servant of Yahweh*, 1931, pp. 1-74, A. Lods, *Les prophètes d'Israël*, 1935, pp. 276ff. (English Tr., *The Prophets and the Rise of Judaism*, 1937, pp. 246f.). For a modified form of collective theory, in which fluidity is recognized, cf. O. Eissfeldt, *Der Gottesknecht bei Deuterojesaja*, 1933, and "The Ebed-Jahwe in Isaiah 40-55", in *Expository Times*, xliv, 1932-33, pp. 261-268. Cf. too, N. Johansson, *Parakletoi*, 1940, pp. 49-62.

[3] Many candidates have been put forward, including Moses (E. Sellin, *Mose und seine Bedeutung für die israelitisch-jüdische Religionsgeschichte*, 1922), and Jeremiah (B. Duhm, *Die Theologie der Propheten*, 1875, p.298—later abandoned; in a modified form S. H. Blank, "Studies in Deutero-Isaiah", in *Hebrew Union College Annual*, xv, 1940, pp. 1-46; cf. too, F. A. Farley, "Jeremiah and 'The Suffering Servant of Jehovah' in Deutero-Isaiah", in *Expository Times*, xxxviii, 1926-27, pp. 521-524).

[4] Amongst the suggestions that have been made we may note Jehoiachin (E. Sellin, *Das Rätsel des deuterojesajanischen Buches*, 1908—later abandoned; cf. L. H. K. Bleeker, *Zeitschrift für die alttestamentliche Wissenschaft*, xl, 1922, p. 156; E. Burrows, *The Gospel of the Infancy*, 1940, pp. 59-80); Zerubbabel (E. Sellin, *Serubbabel*, 1898—later abandoned); Meshullam, the son of Zerubbabel (L. Palache, *The Ebed-Jahweh Enigma in Pseudo-Isaiah*, 1934); an anonymous leprous Rabbi (B. Duhm, *Das Buch Jesaia* [HK], 2nd ed., 1902); the prophet himself (S. Mowinckel, *Der Knecht Jahwäs*, 1921 [cf. "Die Komposition des deuterojesajanischen Buches" in *Zeitschrift für die alttestamentliche Wissenschaft*, N.F. viii, 1931, pp. 87-112, 242-260, esp. pp. 245ff., and *Det Gamle Testamente*, iii, *De senere profeter*, 1944, pp. 192ff.]); E. Sellin, "Tritojesaja, Deuterojesaja und das Gottesknechts-problem", in *Neue kirchliche Zeitschrift*, xli, 1930, pp. 73-93, 145-173; P. Volz, *Jesaia II* (KAT), 1932; K. Elliger, *Deuterojesaja in seinem Verhältnis zu Tritojesaja* (BWANT, 4 Folge, xi), 1933. For a full account of these and other views, with full references to the literature, cf. C. R. North, *The Suffering Servant in Deutero-Isaiah*, 1948, pp. 47ff., 72fl.

of the future, comparable with the Davidic Scion of other passages.¹ Even if—as I believe—the Servant began as a personification of Israel in the prophet's thought, it is hard to avoid the conclusion that he became a person by the fourth song.² This is not to deny the unity of the conception of the Servant in the four passages, but to recognize an element of fluidity within that unity,³ and an element of fluidity that is quite characteristic of Hebrew thinking.⁴ But whether the Servant was in all these songs an individual, or whether the conception came to a focus in the thought of an individual, it would seem right to consider the election of the Servant

¹ So J. Fischer, *Wer ist der Ebed?*, 1922; J. van der Ploeg, *Les chants du Serviteur de Jahvé*, 1936; C. R. North, "Who was the servant of the Lord in Isaiah 53?" in *Expository Times*, lii, 1940-41, pp. 181-184, 219-221, and *The Suffering Servant in Deutero-Isaiah*, 1948; P. Heinisch, *Theologie des Alten Testamentes*, 1940, pp. 316-319; A. H. Edelkoort, *De Christus-verwachting in het Oude Testament*, 1941, pp. 372-436; R. T. Murphy, "Second Isaias: The Servant of the Lord", *Catholic Biblical Quarterly*, ix, 1947, pp. 262-274. J. Lindblom (*Israels Religion i gammaltestamentlig tid*, 1936, p. 196) regards the Servant of Yahweh as "a parallel figure to the Messiah". Cf. too, H. Gressmann, *Der Messias*, 1929, pp. 308ff.; also I. Engnell, *The 'Ebed-Yahweh Songs and the Suffering Messiah* (and the Swedish article which formed the basis of this, "Till frågan om Ebed Jahvesångerna och den lidande Messias hos 'Deuterojesaja'", in *Svensk Exegetisk Årsbok*, x, 1945, pp. 31-65), where the figure is interpreted eschatologically, but brought into relation with cultic practice running back to ancient, and even pre-Israelite, days; also S. Mowinckel, "Til uttrykket 'Jahvæs tjener'" in *Norsk Teologisk Tidsskrift*, 1942, pp. 24-26, where some connexions with the Ras Shamra texts are noted; and H. S. Nyberg, "Smärtornas man: en studie till Jes. 52, 13-53, 12", in *Svensk Exegetisk Årsbok*, vii, 1942, pp. 5-82—an important article, in which many streams of influence, both Canaanite and Israelite, are found in the conception.

² Cf. J. Pedersen, *Israel III-IV*, 1940, pp. 604f.: "It is Israel embodied in a person who endures the fate of Israel, with the sufferings of the weak, and yet realizes the true law given by the only God. The prophet, in this account, surely had actual examples in view, men in whose life and fate he saw a typical realization of the nature of the true Israel, as it appeared among the peoples. And just as the description has been most personal, we see that it does not apply to a single chance individual. . . . The servant was Israel, who had yet a task among the Israelites and the peoples."

³ Cf. A. Causse, *Israël et la vision de l'humanité*, 1924, p. 54: "Altogether it appears that the idea of the Ebed Yahweh in the prophecies of Deutero-Isaiah is almost always imprecise and variable. This fluidity agrees with the lyrical and apocalyptic manner of the prophet. At the outset the Servant represents the exiled people, then the community of Yahweh, the minority of the *anavim*. At the end, it is a personal hero, the mysterious liberator, a hero comparable with the Messiah." Cf. W. Robinson, *The Biblical Doctrine of the Church*, 1948, p. 31; K. Hj. Fahlgren, *Ṣᵉdāḳā, nahestehende und entgegengesetzte Begriffe im Alten Testament*, 1932, p. 234; A. Bentzen, *Indledning til det Gamle Testamente*, I i, 1941, pp. 98-100; A. V. Ström, *Vetekornet*, 1944, p. 433 (English summary, the only part of this work which I have seen).

⁴ Cf. H. Wheeler Robinson, "The Hebrew Conception of Corporate Personality", in *Werden und Wesen des Alten Testaments* (ed. J. Hempel), 1936, pp. 49-62.

here, as the climax of Old Testament ideas on the election of individuals.

In the first of the songs the Servant is called the elect of God:

> Behold! My Servant whom I uphold!
> Mine elect, in whom my soul delighteth![1]

In the second we read that, like Jeremiah, he is chosen from birth for his service:

> Yahweh from the womb hath called me,
> Made mention of my name from my birth . . .
> And now Yahweh hath spoken,
> Who formed me from the womb as his servant.[2]

Here it is already clear that the election is for service. For the Chosen One is called the Servant. Nor is it to any easy path of service that he is called. Rather is it, as we find in the later songs, service that entails acutest suffering:

> My back have I given to the scourgers,
> And my cheeks to the pluckers;
> My face I have not hidden
> From shame and spitting.[3]

Or again:

> He was despised and forsaken of men,
> A man of pains and familiar with disease;
> And as one from whom men turn their faces
> He was despised and we esteemed him not . . .
> He was beaten,[4] yet meek was he,
> Nor opened his mouth in complaint;
> As a sheep that is led off to slaughter,
> Or a ewe that is dumb before her shearers.[5]

---

[1] Isa. 42 : 1.　　[2] Isa. 49 : 5.　　[3] Isa. 50 : 6.
[4] The Hebrew word used here is associated with labour under a taskmaster.
[5] The Hebrew repeats "and he opened not his mouth". Some editors think this was an accidental repetition, while others disconnect the preceding word from what goes before, and alter it to the masculine form, yielding "he was dumb". This would give very exceptional rhythmical weight to this word, which would be followed by a pause, since a single word would take the place of three rhythmically. Cf. C. R. North, *The Suffering Servant in Deutero-Isaiah*, 1948, p. 124.

By oppression and without justice was he taken,[1]
And who gave a thought to his fate?[2]
For he was snatched from the land of the living,
He was smitten for the sin of the people.[3]

His suffering has thus reached its extremest limits, and his mission has cost him his life. Let it not be forgotten that many a prophet was elect to suffering. Micaiah, as the result of his faithfulness to his mission, was cast into a prison;[4] and Jeremiah not only knew the misery of incarceration in a foul cistern, where he was almost starved,[5] but added to it the inner suffering that only such a sensitive soul could feel at all the loneliness of his lot. The prophet Uriah was put to death for his word,[6] and it is likely that the innocent blood with which Manasseh filled Jerusalem[7] included the blood of

---

[1] This line has been much discussed and many translations offered. The translation here offered takes the preposition *min* in two different senses. In the following line the same preposition has also two senses, both different from either of those found here. Since it admittedly has three senses in two lines, it is not difficult to find a fourth, and it may well be designed that this preposition stands four times in this verse and each with a different meaning.

[2] The Hebrew ordinarily would mean "to his generation", or "to his age", which does not yield a satisfactory sense. Amongst the many suggestions made we may note those of T. K. Cheyne, that for *dôrô* we should read *darkô=his way*, or *his fate* (*Introduction to the Book of Isaiah*, 1895, p. 428; cf. J. Fischer, *Das Buch Isaias*, ii, 1939, pp. 135f.), of R. Levy, that we should read '*adrô=the treachery shown to him* (*Deutero-Isaiah*, 1925, p. 264); and of G. R. Driver, that we should connect *dôrô* with Arabic *dawr=turn, time, change of fortune*, and render *his state*, or *condition* (*Journal of Theological Studies*, xxxvi, 1935, p. 403). This last seems the most satisfactory, and the above rendering rests on it. With it may be compared a suggestion recorded in *American Journal of Semitic Languages*, xxvii, 1910-11, p. 192, which equated the Hebrew with the Talmudic word *dûrâ=burden*. H. S. Nyberg (*Svensk Exegetisk Årsbok*, vii, 1942, p. 53) seems independently to have reached the same view as Driver.

[3] Isa. 53 : 3, 7f. The Massoretic text has "for the sin of my people" in the last line, and is supported by the Versions. C. C. Torrey (*The Second Isaiah*, 1928, p. 420) defends this reading, and thinks it is a vivid individualizing on the part of the separate speakers. Most editors, however, feel that it reads unnaturally, and many emendations have been proposed. K. Budde (*Die sogenannten Ebed-Jahwe-Lieder*, 1900, p. 12) read "for our sins"; F. Giesebrecht (*Der Knecht Jahwes des Deuterojesaia*, 1902, pp. 89ff.) "for their sins"; P. Volz (*Jesaia II*, 1932, p. 171) "for sins"; J. Fischer (*Das Buch Isaias*, (HSATes), ii, 1939, p. 136) "for the sin of his people"; E. J. Kissane (*The Book of Isaiah*, ii, 1943, p. 182) "with the rebellious". It seems to me simplest to omit a single letter—possibly detached from the following word which could then be read as a verbal form instead of a noun—and find an expression similar to "a covenant of the people" in Isa. 42 : 6, where we have seen that the word "people" may be used in the sense of "universal". This line would then mean "for the sins of all men". Instead of "he was smitten" most editors rely on the LXX and change to "he was stricken to death".

[4] 1 Kgs. 22: 27.   [5] Jer. 38 : 6,   [6] Jer. 26 : 23.   [7] 2 Kgs. 21 : 16.

THE ELECTION OF INDIVIDUALS

prophets. Moreover, tradition has it that Isaiah was martyred in that reign.[1] The Servant of Yahweh is not, therefore, the only one whose mission involves him in suffering and death. For the elect of God is not seldom elect to suffer.

The uniqueness of the Servant is that whereas others suffered in consequence of their mission, his suffering is the organ of his mission. The service for which he was chosen was a world-wide service:

> In faithfulness shall he bring forth judgement;
> He shall not burn low, or be bruised[2]
> Till he have set justice[3] on the earth,
> And for his law the isles shall wait.[4]

> Too light is it that thou shouldest be my Servant
> To set up the tribes of Jacob,
> And the preserved of Israel to restore;
> I will make thee the light of the nations,
> That my salvation may reach
> To the end of the earth.[5]

Moreover, his suffering is not incidental to this mission; it is its organ:

> He was pierced through our transgressions,
> Crushed through our evil deeds;
> The discipline of our well-being lay upon him,
> And by his stripes there was healing for us ...
> And he bore the sin of many,
> And for transgressors made intercession.[6]

The complaint against the Biblical doctrine of election that it is unjust is here more than anywhere shown to be beside the mark. For what is commonly meant by the complaint is

---

[1] Cf. Asc. Isa. 5 : 1 (in Charles's *Apocrypha and Pseudepigrapha of the Old Testament*, ii, 1913, p. 162).
[2] This translation rests on a generally accepted change of vowels, which reads the consonants as from the same root as is found in the previous line.
[3] The Hebrew word *mishpāṭ* normally means *judgement* or *justice* or *custom*. Here it probably means *true religion*, and for this development of meaning it is common to compare the Arabic *dīn*. Cf. H. W. Hertzberg, *Zeitschrift für die alttestamentliche Wissenschaft*, xli, 1923, p.41; R. Levy, *op. cit.*, p. 144; J. van der Ploeg, *Oudtestamentische Studiën*, ii, 1943, p. 155; C. R. North, *The Suffering Servant in Deutero-Isaiah*, 1948, pp. 140f.
[4] Isa. 42 : 3f.   [5] Isa. 49 : 6.   [6] Isa. 53 : 5, 12.

that it is unjust that the elect should be favoured. It has been insisted throughout these lectures that while there is favour and honour in being chosen by God, His election has always its reverse side in the service it involves. But here it would appear that if there is injustice, it is directed against the elect and not in his favour. His is a heritage of suffering, and to others—even to those who inflict the suffering on him—it brings a heritage of blessing. For justice is not the only Divine principle, or even the highest principle. That man should treat his fellow-men with injustice is sin, and an offence to God. This means that the maltreating of the Servant by men is sin, and therefore an offence against God. But that the Servant should willingly accept that suffering in obedience to his vocation is something far higher than justice. It is the fruit of his standing in the council of God, and the mark of his oneness with God. The same suffering viewed from the side of those who inflicted it is sin, and viewed from the side of the sufferer is the highest service of God and man. For God, who delights not in injustice, delights in the spirit of service that is here manifested.

In Israel's disloyalty to God, the heart of God was pained, and it has been said that His discipline of Israel was born of His love and of His unwillingness easily to relinquish her. In the Servant's suffering at the hands of those he served there is thus the reflection of the spirit of God. If the purpose of Israel's election is rightly said to have been to receive the revelation of God, to reflect His character and will in life, and to share with all men the treasure mediated unto her, then that purpose would seem to reach its climax in the Servant. The first revelation of God's grace in the time of Moses consisted in the deliverance of Israel from the Egyptian bondage. The great prophets had always perceived that He purposed a deeper deliverance from inner disloyalty of heart. The revelation of that deeper purpose was nowhere more manifest than in the work of the Servant. Again, none rose more nearly to reflect the character and the will of God, and for the understanding of the very heart of God there is nothing in the Old Testament which surpasses these songs. Finally the mission of the Servant is directed to the achievement of the world mission of Israel, whereby she should share with all men the glory of her heritage. If here is the crown of individual election in the Old Testament, here too is something that links most closely with the thought of Israel's election.

I have not here attempted to identify the Servant. Nor is it necessary to do so. For the grandeur of the conception is more germane to our present purpose than the identification of the figure. Nevertheless I may be pardoned for observing that I have already indicated that I find progress as well as fluidity in the concept, and the personification of Israel and at the same time the person of one who embodied in himself her mission, and who both represented her and surpassed her in his fulfilment of that mission. If the author supposed that any who had preceded him, or any of his contemporaries, or even that he himself, could truly be described in the terms of this account, he was merely an artist skilled in clothing with a beauty which he brought to his subject the realities on which he looked rather than a prophet of God, dealing in truth. If his thought were wholly of the people Israel, whether of the nation as he knew it or of the inner faithful core or of the Israel that should be, his thought bore little relation to the truth. Israel had never been such as he here depicted, and to this day there is no sign of his dream being fulfilled in her experience. It therefore seems to me that the only satisfying view is that he thought of an individual still future in his day in whom his conception should be realized, and we shall yet have to ask how far it was realized.

It may be answered that even though the figure of the Servant was but the beautiful dream of the poet, realized in concrete experience neither before his day nor since, we need not be surprised. Many of the expectations of the prophets proved to be mistaken, and it would be easy to collect prophetic words that have not been, and cannot now be, fulfilled. The enriching quality of the thought of these poems is what matters, rather than whether the ideal has become real. This far from satisfies me. It is true that many prophecies were not fulfilled. Sometimes this was because there was a contingent element in prophecy, either expressed or implied; sometimes because prophecy is given through the organ of human personality, and a message from God is expressed in terms that are supplied by a fallible speaker. The prophet's personality is never wholly suspended in his prophecy, which reflects in some measure his thought, his experience, his outlook, and his literary style.[1] But if the grandest conception to be found in all prophetic literature was but the empty dream of the singer, we should have a very different state of affairs. That imperfect men imperfectly express the word of the perfect God is intelligible; but that the perfection of this picture should be of man and should so surpass the reality known to God would be surprising. While, therefore, for my present purpose the identification of the Servant is immaterial, I am far from agreeing that it is finally unimportant, and the question whether or not the Servant has lived amongst men is of the highest importance for its religious consequences. To that question we shall have to return in our concluding lecture.

The Servant of Yahweh is a single figure without parallel in the Old Testament. He is chosen for his service, and his response to his election is complete. Others at whom we have looked sometimes responded and sometimes did not respond to their election. But always election and response in service and loyalty belong together, and the final repudiation of the service is equally the renunciation of the election. He who responds feels that he can do no other than respond, for he feels the constraint of the Divine call. Yet they who fail to respond are the evidence that election does not really turn man into a puppet and sweep away his will. Many are called, but few are finally chosen, because few there are who finally respond to the choice.

[1] Cf. G. A. Barton, *Studies in New Testament Christianity*, 1928, p. 3: "In predicting events of the distant future or in setting forth ideals that could only be realized in the lapse of centuries, no prophet has ever correctly predicted any considerable number of important details. The nature of the fulfilment can never be clearly discerned from the prophecy. It is only in looking back that we can discern that the prophecy has been fulfilled. It was the function of the prophet dimly to discern an ideal and to set it forth in such a way as to stir the faith and quicken the ethical life of his people. Psychologically it was only possible for him to clothe his vision of the ideal state in concepts current in his own time. Fulfilment has always been of a different, a more spiritual, a more glorious character than anything in the form of the prophecy would lead one to guess."

Chapter Five

ELECTION WITHOUT COVENANT

SO far our thought has been limited to the election of Israel and the extension of that election to such of the Gentiles as should come to share her faith and her covenanted response to God. That Israel was the Chosen People, and that she was chosen for service, is the clear teaching of the Old Testament as a whole. In its different parts there is a difference of emphasis as to the nature of the service, and some passages more emphasize the privileges of her election and others its obligations, yet no one could read the Old Testament as a whole and fail to realize that for its writers the failure to accept the obligations of the Covenant which was intimately associated with the election involved the forfeiture of all title to the privilege. By the grace of God the privilege might be continued for a time, or in modified ways, but it was a privilege to which the disloyal people could lay no claim. "There was", says R. B. Y. Scott, "nothing necessary or final about Israel's election, should she fail to serve the divine purpose."[1]

Similarly, when individuals within the elect people were chosen for service related to the purpose of Israel's election, the obligations of the Covenant lay upon them, and any repudiation of those obligations cancelled their election. In every case the obligations were related to the specific purpose of the election, and they demanded absolute obedience to the will of God in the fulfilment of the purpose.

Throughout the pattern of Old Testament thought, therefore, election is not blind favouritism. Neither is it an irrevocable reward which belongs either to the nation or to individuals. "Whatever the divine election of the Jewish people may mean", says Alan Richardson, "it certainly did

[1] Cf. *The Relevance of the Prophets*, 1944, p. 121.

not mean preferential treatment for them."[1] Nowhere in all this thought is there the slightest suggestion of any arbitrary singling out by God of one for honour and another for dishonour, for honour is but incidental to election whereas service is fundamental.

Nevertheless our study would be seriously incomplete if we failed to consider the Biblical teaching on election that lay wholly outside the Covenant that bound Israel to her God. For here we find that other nations could be chosen by God for a service that often carried no measure of privilege, and could even be called from the ends of the earth to do His will. The Assyrians and the Chaldaeans are frequently spoken of in this way. Instead of honour there is dishonour for them, and the issue of their service is that they are punished for rendering it. Nevertheless, it is not for dishonour that they are called, but for service. They are furthering the purposes of God, and for this alone can they be said to be chosen by Him.

It is easy to misunderstand the Old Testament prophets, and to suppose that they regarded the nations as mere puppets in God's hand, existing only for Israel's sake, though sometimes to serve her and sometimes to discipline her. This is because they were primarily concerned only with that aspect of the life of the nations that touched Israel. They were not abstract philosophers and theologians, but religious leaders, addressing their fellow-Israelites for their profit, and they dealt only in that which yielded profit for them. Hence, speaking generally, they only thought of the nations in relation to Israel.

In the book of Amos we read:

> For behold! I am raising against you,
> O house of Israel[2], a nation,

---

[1] Cf. *Christian Apologetics*, 1947, p. 144.
[2] The words "Oracle of Yahweh God of Hosts" stand in the Hebrew in the middle of this line. Some MSS. of the LXX omit them, and they are treated as secondary by some modern editors. Even if these words belong to the original form of the book of Amos, they are *extra metrum*, and so are left untranslated here. In some cases above, where similar formulæ are found *extra metrum*, but standing between lines, instead of within them, I have retained them in the text as parentheses.

And they shall oppress you from the entrance
of Hamath
Unto the wady of the Arabah.[1]

Here the unnamed nation is conceived of as performing God's purpose of discipline in relation to His people Israel. It is not to be supposed that Amos imagined that this was the sole purpose of the existence of the nation. He recognized that God is in control of all history, and that the migrations,[2] as well as the rise and fall, of nations have their place in His purpose. But in the complexity of the Divine purpose in raising up the oppressing nation, Amos declared that the discipline of Israel had a place. And since that alone was relevant to the prophet's message to Israel, that alone is mentioned.

Isaiah more specifically indicated Assyria as the instrument of God's will in relation to His people:

> And it shall be in that day,
> Yahweh will whistle for the fly
> That is at the source of the rivers of Egypt,
> And for the bee that is in the land of Assyria.
> And all of them will come and will settle
> In the ravines of the precipices
> And in the clefts of the rocks,
> And on all the thorn bushes,
> And on all the pasture lands.
> On that day the Lord will shave,
> With a razor that is hired from beyond the River,[3]
> The head and the hair of the body,
> And also the beard will he sweep away.[4]

---

[1] Amos 6 : 14.
[2] Cf. Amos 9 : 7.
[3] The Hebrew adds "Even with the king of Assyria", but almost all modern editors regard this as a gloss. So B. Duhm, *Das Buch Jesaia*, 2nd ed., 1902, p. 53; K. Marti, *Das Buch Jesaja* (KHC), 1900, p. 80; G. W. Wade, *The Book of the Prophet Isaiah* (WC), 1911, p. 50; G. B. Gray, *The Book of Isaiah, Chapters i–xxvii* (ICC), 1912, p. 139; G. H. Box, *The Book of Isaiah*, 1916, p. 49; O. Procksch, *Jesaia I* (KAT), 1930, p. 127; J. Fischer, *Das Buch Isaias* (HSATes), i, 1930, p. 75; E. J. Kissane, *The Book of Isaiah*, i, 1941, pp. 85f.
[4] Isa. 7 : 18–20.

Or again:

> Ah! Assyria, rod of my anger,
> And staff of my indignation!
> Against a nation profane do I send him,
> And commission him against a people of my wrath,
> To despoil them completely, and to plunder unsparingly,
> And to trample them down as the mire of the streets.[1]

Yet Isaiah made it abundantly clear that no honour for Assyria was involved in her performance of the Divine will. Her service rested on no covenant whereby she yielded herself freely and voluntarily to do His will. She was utterly indifferent to Him and His will, and was only concerned to live out the cruel purposes of her own heart:

> But he planneth not so,
> Not so doth he purpose in his heart;
> For in his heart is it but to destroy,
> And to cut off nations not a few.[2]

That Assyria can serve the purposes of God is but due to the greatness of His power and His wisdom, whereby He can integrate into His purpose that which by its own quality and nature is utterly alien to His will. No credit is due to Assyria for her service, but only punishment for the iniquity of her heart.

> And it shall be,
> When the Lord hath finished all his work
> On the mountain of Zion and on Jerusalem,
> I[3] will visit the fruit of the arrogance
> Of the heart of the king of Assyria,
> And the pride of his haughty eyes.[4]

---

[1] Isa. 10 : 5f.
[2] Isa. 10 : 7.
[3] The LXX here reads *He will turn*, whence many editors emend the Hebrew from '*ephqōdh* to *yiphqōdh*=*he will visit*. There is no need to emend the text, however. Similar transitions from the third person to the first person in prophetic oracles are by no means uncommon, as also are transitions from the first person to the third person. The prophet speaking as the mouthpiece of God can utter the word of God in the first person, identifying himself for the time being with the God whose message he bears, or he can use the third person of God, differentiating himself as the messenger from the God he represents. Cf. A. R. Johnson, *The One and the Many in the Israelite Conception of God*, 1942, pp. 36ff.
[4] Isa. 10 : 12.

Similarly Jeremiah and Habakkuk thought of the Chaldaeans as raised up by God to perform His purpose, yet to perform it unwittingly and to deserve only condemnation for their deeds. Speaking perhaps originally of the Scythians, rather than the Chaldaeans,[1] Jeremiah said:

> For behold I am summoning
> All the kingdoms[2] of the north,
> And they shall come and set up each his throne
> At the entrance to the gates of Jerusalem,
> And against all her walls round about,
> And against all the cities of Judah.
> And I will utter to them my judgements
> Upon all their wickedness in forsaking me,
> And in sacrificing to other gods,
> And worshipping the works of their hands.[3]

Or again:

> Behold I am bringing against you
> A nation from afar, house of Israel!
> A nation of long history it is,
> A nation from of old it is,[4]
> A nation whose language thou knowest not,
> Nor hearest what it says;
> Whose quiver is an open grave,
> Men of war are they all.[5]

---

[1] The common view that Jeremiah began his ministry at the time when the Scythian menace loomed large and that he later reissued the Scythian prophecies retouched to make them fit the new situation when Nebuchadrezzar was conquering Pharaoh Necho and possessing himself of the west (persuasively presented to English readers in J. Skinner, *Prophecy and Religion*, 1922) is strongly contested by some writers. Cf. F. Wilke, "Das Skythenproblem im Jeremiabuch", in *Alttestamentliche Studien R. Kittel zum 60 Geburtstag dargebracht*, 1913, pp. 222-254; also J. Lewy, *Forschungen zur alten Geschichte Vorderasiens*, 1925, pp. 51-55; P. Volz, *Der Prophet Jeremia* (KAT), 1922, pp. 57f.; A. C. Welch, *Jeremiah; His Time and His Work*, 1928, pp. 97-131; C. C. Torrey, "The Background of Jeremiah 1-10", in *Journal of Biblical Literature*, lvi, 1937, pp. 193-216; J. P. Hyatt, "The Peril from the North in Jeremiah", *ibid.*, lix, 1940, pp. 499-513; F.W. König, *Älteste Geschichte der Meder und Perser*, 1934, pp. 35ff.; W. Rudolph, *Jeremia* [HAT], 1947, pp. 41ff.; and W. A. L. Elmslie, *How Came our Faith*, 1948, p. 314 n.

[2] The Massoretic text reads "all the families of the kingdoms". This looks like a conflation of two readings "all the families" and "all the kingdoms". In Jer. 25 : 9 we have "all the families of the north", whereas here the LXX has only "all the kingdoms of the north". Hence many editors prefer to follow the LXX here and to suppose that the alternative reading arose by a scribal reminiscence of the other passage.

[3] Jer. 1 : 15f.

[4] This is more likely to have been said of the Chaldaeans than of the Scythians, and if this oracle was originally spoken about the Scythians this is probably one of the cases of retouching.

[5] Jer. 5 : 15f.

And with clearer and specific reference to the Chaldaeans:

> And Zedekiah the king of Judah
> And his princes will I give into the hand of their foes,
> And into the hand of them that seek their life,
> And into the hand of the army of the king of Babylon,
> That have gone up away from you.
> Behold! I am commanding and I will bring them back
> To this city and they shall fight against it,
> And shall take it and shall burn it with fire;
> And the cities of Judah will I give
> For a desolation, void of inhabitants.[1]

With equal clearness Habakkuk says:

> For behold! I am raising up the Chaldaeans,[2]
> The bitter and impetuous nation,
> That goes through the breadth of the earth,
> To possess dwellings not its own.[3]

Yet though Habakkuk could thus regard the Chaldaeans as raised up by God to perform His will upon Israel, he was deeply troubled at the thought that for all its sin Israel was more righteous than the instrument of the chastisement:

> O thou too pure of eyes to look upon evil,
> And who canst not gaze upon iniquity!
> Why dost thou gaze upon the faithless,
> Or keep silence when the wicked swallows
> Him that is more righteous than himself?[4]

The earlier prophets had not supposed that Assyria or Babylon were chosen for their worth to be the instrument of God's will, but had not been troubled by this moral problem.

---

[1] Jer. 24 : 21f.
[2] This is the reading of the text and there is no reason to question it. Duhm proposed to read "the Kittim" in order to bring the prophecy down to the Greek period (*Das Buch Habakuk*, 1906, pp. 19ff.), but an emendation which is based on the theory whose basis it itself provides can never be convincing. Sellin followed Duhm (*Das Zwölfprophetenbuch* (KAT), 1922, p. 340) but later abandoned this (2nd ed., 1929, p. 388).
[3] Hab. 1 : 6.
[4] Hab. 1 : 13.

To them it appeared to excite no wonder that God should choose these nations for His purpose and cast them aside when it was achieved. But to Habakkuk it was a serious problem. When he found his way through his problem he expressed himself in words that have aroused much discussion. Neither their translation nor their interpretation is at all certain, and it is with much diffidence that I would render:

> Behold! he whose soul is not upright within him shall fail;[1]
> But the righteous through his faithfulness shall live.
> And the faithless shall become nought,[2]
> The man that is haughty shall not abide;[3]
> Who enlargeth his desire as Sheol,
> And is himself as death and insatiable,
> And hath gathered unto him all the nations,
> And collected for himself all the peoples.[4]

[1] The R.V. renders the Hebrew of this line: "Behold, his soul is puffed up it is not upright in him." No antecedent for the pronouns is expressed, and no fate is pronounced. Among the many changes proposed by editors the simplest and most satisfactory seems to be that of Van Hoonacker (*Les douze petits prophètes* (EB), 1908, p. 477), which reads '*ullaph* for '*uppᵉlāh* and takes the following words as a relative clause with suppression of the relative particle, and yielding the translation given above. *La Bible du Centenaire*, ii, 1948, p. 792, follows the same view, save that it supplies the relative by reading '*ullaph zū*. Aquila appears to have read '*ullᵉphāh* (cf. *Jewish Quarterly Review*, N-S. vii, 1916–17, p. 297).
[2] The R.V. renders "Yea, moreover, wine is a treacherous dealer", but this seems inappropriate, and neither LXX nor Syriac has any reference to wine. Here again many suggestions have been made for the improvement of the text, of which the most satisfying appears to be that of H. C. O. Lanchester (*The Books of Nahum, Habakkuk and Zephaniah* [CambB], 1920, p. 78), which reads *w 'ephes yihyeh* for *weʾaph kî hayayin*. The suggestion of W. F. Albright (*Bulletin of the American Schools of Oriental Research*, No. 91, Oct. 1943, p. 40 n.) is very attractive. This reads *kᵉhîyôn* for *hayyayin* and yields "Though he be crafty as Hîyôn, a faithless man shall not succeed." Hîyôn does not appear elsewhere in the Old Testament, but stands as Hîyân in the Ras Shamra texts, where Albright finds him to be the archetype of all ingenuity, whether of hand or brain.
[3] The R.V. here has "a haughty man, and that keepeth not at home", with Marg. "He shall not abide" for the last words. I have here followed the R.V. marg., but have omitted *and* with LXX. The word rendered "he shall (not) abide" is a *hapax legomenon* from a noun meaning *a shepherd's shelter*, but it does not seem very probable that this could mean *abide* in the sense of *endure*. Van Hoonacker (*loc. cit.*, p. 478) suggests reading *yihyeh* for *yinweh*, so securing the meaning "he shall not live".
[4] Hab. 2 : 4f.

It is clear from this and from the verses that follow that the prophet recognized that evil is ultimately self-destructive, and he was as sure as Isaiah had been that the instruments of wrath would themselves become the object of a deeper wrath. They were chosen of God for no lasting service, and their election is in the completest contrast to that of Israel. Israel was chosen that God might lavish His love upon her, and that she might give Him her loyalty in response, and might serve Him by mediating the knowledge of His will to all the world; they were chosen to serve a temporary purpose, and without any expectation that they would make conscious response to God's will. They were what the New Testament calls "vessels of dishonour", serving God indeed, but with no exalted service. They were not puppets in His hand, compelled to do His will without moral responsibility for their deed, but chosen because He saw that the very iniquity of their heart would lead them to the course that He could use.

What Habakkuk meant by the words "But the righteous through his faithfulness shall live" will never be known with certainty. There are some who read a profoundly spiritual meaning into the passage, and find it to mean that the righteous shall find a deeper satisfaction in his righteousness than could be found in prosperity.[1] True as this is, it is doubtful if it is the meaning here, for Habakkuk is under no illusions as to the degree of Israel's righteousness. She is more righteous than her tormentor; but he certainly does not think of her in profoundly spiritual terms. By others the verse is held to mean that in contrast to the more wicked oppressor, who will perish, the righteous will survive.[2] This

---

[1] Cf. T. H. Robinson, *Prophecy and the Prophets*, p. 118. Cf. J. Hoschander (*The Priests and Prophets*, 1938, p. 122), who thus describes the content of *faithfulness* in the thought of Habakkuk: "It must denote a 'Faith' so firm and strong, so deeply rooted in heart and soul that no power is able to shake it, that no sufferings and no temptations can move it from its place. This is the faith by which the righteous is expected to live."

[2] Cf. J. M. Powis Smith, *The Prophets and their Times*, 1925, pp. 131ff. (2nd ed., 1941, pp. 159ff.) Cf. too, *La Bible du Centenaire*, ii, 1948, p. 792: "He who does not observe the right carries already in himself the seed of death, which will surely develop and bring about his destruction; the just, on the other hand, has life by reason of his fidelity." On the word '^{e}mûnāh cf. P. Humbert, *Problèmes du livre d'Habacuc*, 1944, pp. 149f.

is relevant to the whole range of the prophetic teaching on this subject. It means that Israel, because of the spark of righteousness and faithfulness still found in her despite her sins, yet may be of service to God, and for that will survive. Her survival can have no meaning, except in so far as it is related to the will of God; and it can only be so related when she yields herself in faithfulness to Him. Common to the prophets is the thought that only as Israel is loyal to her Covenant can her election continue; and here is the thought that her very life as a nation depends on her loyalty. The spark of loyalty that is in her, the relative righteousness as compared with the foe, offers her the chance of survival. But in that case, if she would know strength of vitality, she must find it in renewed and deeper loyalty, and in a fuller acceptance of the obligations of her Covenant.

All this conception of foreign nations being chosen by God to serve His purpose in relation to Israel is not confined to the prophetic teaching, but is found throughout the historical books that are dominated by the thought and outlook of Deuteronomy. Moreover, as we shall see below when we turn to the individual aspect of this sort of election, it belongs also to the story of the deliverance from Egypt. One of the most characteristic messages of the book of Deuteronomy is that Israel's well-being is bound up with her loyalty to her Covenant. So long as she is faithful to it, prosperity will attend her; but when she is unfaithful misfortunes of every kind will fall upon her. And in the long catalogue of those misfortunes which stands in chapter 28 we read: "Yahweh will raise against thee a nation from afar, from the end of the earth, as the vulture darteth, a nation whose language thou canst not understand; a ruthless nation that will have no regard for the aged, nor have pity on the child."[1]

When writers of the Deuteronomic school came to edit the historical records they desired to point this message, and underlined the connexion between faith and fortune. It was not because their foes were mightier than they that they were reduced to bondage, but because Yahweh raised them up to discipline His people. "The children of Israel did that which

[1] Deut. 28 : 49f.

was evil in the eyes of Yahweh, and forgot Yahweh their God, and served the Baals and the Asherahs. Therefore Yahweh's wrath was kindled against Israel, and he sold them into the hand of Cushan-rishathaim.[1] "And the children of Israel again did that which was evil in the eyes of Yahweh. And Yahweh made Eglon the king of Moab strong against Israel."[2] Just as Yahweh raises up saviours for Israel when His people return to Him in loyalty, so He raises up oppressors when they forsake Him. And on through all the story we find the same thing.[3] When Jehoiakim, who stands condemned in the record, rebelled against Nebuchadrezzar, it was Yahweh who sent against him the bands of Chaldaeans and Syrians and Moabites.[4] He chooses the peoples to do His will, and makes them serve His purpose.

It is not to be supposed, however, that the Biblical writers held a deterministic view of history that made God finally responsible for its whole course. They could hardly have complained that Israel did not do the will of God, if everything that happened accorded with that will. They recognized human responsibility for human acts, and passed moral judgement on those who wrought them. If God could integrate into His purpose acts which sprang from indifference to His will, that was the mark of His greatness. On the human plane such things are frequently experienced. A skilled chess player perceives the plan of his opponent and so determines his own plan that the very moves of the other serve his purpose. A skilled debater turns the very arguments of his rivals against them and uses them to the advantage of his own cause. A great general not merely beats off the attack of the enemy and launches his own attack, but skilfully turns every move of the foe to further his own plan. If these things can be done on the human plane, it should occasion no surprise that God can similarly integrate into His purpose acts which are directed against Him. When the Biblical writers use the language of election in relation to these things they mean no more than this. There is no con-

[1] Judges 3 : 7f.
[2] Judges 3 : 12.
[3] Cf. G. von Rad, *Deuteronomium-Studien*, 1947, pp. 52–64.
[4] 2 Kgs. 24 : 2.

scious call, no conscious response, no pledge and promise on either side. It is but that God chooses the free acts of men to execute His will.

It is a sad reflection that whereas the Chosen People often failed to do the will of God, we never read of these instruments of His discipline of Israel failing to do that will. That does not mean, however, that He found a larger obedience amongst others than in Israel. In all these acts there was no doing of God's will in a moral sense. They sprang from no understanding of God's character, and were in no sense the reflection of God's character in human life. They were but acts which were morally wrong, and which sprang from hearts that were selfish and evil, which God could yet use without the willing collaboration of their perpetrators. This election, therefore, while it was for service like all election, entailed no beneficent consequences for the elect, but only for Israel. To the nations whom God used there was given through His use of them no larger understanding of His nature, no call to embody His will in their life, and no summons to missionary activity on His behalf.

In the individual sphere, however, we find greater varieties of election outside the Covenant relation. Sometimes it is precisely like that at which we have just looked. Thus, Nebuchadrezzar is called the Servant of God when he is merely the leader of the Chaldaeans in that unwitting service which itself stands condemned. Jeremiah says: "Behold! I am about to send and take all the families of the north—this is Yahweh's oracle—and Nebuchadrezzar[1] the king of Babylon, my Servant, and I will bring them against this land and its inhabitants."[2] And again: "And now I have given all these lands into the hand of Nebuchadrezzar the king of Babylon, my servant."[3] And yet again: "And thou shalt say unto

---

[1] The Hebrew has "and unto Nebuchadrezzar", which fits the sentence badly syntactically. As the words "oracle of Yahweh, and unto Nebuchadrezzar the king of Babylon, my servant" are missing from LXX, many editors omit them here as an intrusion. This is a very inadequate reason for omitting, since the LXX has a much shorter text for the book of Jeremiah, and omits large numbers of such phrases. It seems simpler to change a single letter and restore syntactical regularity than to resort to needless surgery.
[2] Jer. 25 : 9.
[3] Jer. 27 : 6.

them, Thus saith Yahweh of hosts, the God of Israel, Behold! I am about to send and take Nebuchadrezzar the king of Babylon, my servant, and I will set[1] his throne over these stones which I[2] have hidden."[3]

It is a little surprising at first to find Nebuchadrezzar called the servant of Yahweh, that title which we have seen to belong to the noblest conception within the whole prophetic collection. But God has many servants, and their service is rendered on many levels, and it is in the quality of his service that the Suffering Servant of Deutero-Isaiah is differentiated far from Nebuchadrezzar, whose unwitting service brings him no honour and no reward, save a fleeting material power.

Of a somewhat different significance is the Divine use of Pharaoh. In the account of the mission of Moses we read frequently of God's "hardening the heart" of Pharaoh. Sometimes He announces to Moses in advance: "I will harden his heart"[4] and sometimes it is recorded that "the Lord hardened the heart of Pharaoh".[5] These passages would seem to suggest that Pharaoh's refusal to let the Israelites go was something for which not he but God was responsible, and he was but executing the will of God in all that he did. Such a view on the face of it would make nonsense of the whole story. Pharaoh was not the elect of God to chasten and discipline His wayward people, after the fashion of the Assyrians and the Chaldaeans, but the oppressor whose harshness aroused the pity of God and led to the rescue of His people. Here it is not the sufferings which are intended to instruct, but the deliverance, and it is the power of God over Pharaoh rather than through him which takes the centre of the interest. Moreover, that Pharaoh is

---

[1] Many editors needlessly read with the LXX and Syriac "he will set".

[2] Here we have a good example of the fluidity of prophetic pronouns. In the preceding "I will set" the prophet is the mouthpiece of God, to whom the pronoun refers; yet here, within the same sentence, he reverts to the use of the first personal pronoun with reference to himself. Some MSS. of LXX, followed by the Syriac, avoid this oscillation by reading "thou hast hidden". It is probable that it was this oscillation which caused these versions to alter both the preceding verb and this.

[3] Jer. 43 : 10.
[4] Ex. 4 : 21. Cf. 7 : 3.
[5] Ex. 9 : 12, 10 : 20, 27, 11 : 10.

not thought of as a mere puppet is made quite clear by the passages which state that Pharaoh hardened his own heart.[1] His act was none the less his own because God could use it. But for Pharaoh's oppression Israel would never have perceived that the God who elected her was a gracious and saving God. Without the oppression the whole mission of Moses would have no meaning, and the deliverance that issued in the Covenant of Sinai, with its rich and enduring significance for Israel and the world, cannot be conceived. As unwittingly as Nebuchadrezzar, Pharaoh served the purpose of God, and for the iniquity of his harshness, which aroused God's pity, he bears the full responsibility and cannot escape condemnation. He was but chosen by God so that through his acts Israel might learn the power and the character of God. "I have hardened his heart and the hearts of his servants that I might set these signs of mine in their midst, and that thou mayest recount in the ears of thy son and thy grandson how I acted masterfully in Egypt . . . that ye may know that I am Yahweh."[2] In one passage it is stated that God's purpose is that the Egyptians may know that He is Yahweh.[3] But here no more is meant than that they should be compelled to recognize and to respect the power of God, and not that they should be led to bow themselves before Him in conscious and willing service. But so far as Israel is concerned God's purpose is that they shall realize that He has chosen them and manifested His power on their behalf, and the very hardness of Pharaoh's heart but made more plain the greatness of God's power. And in the recognition of the love and the power of God lay the summons to Israel to make Him her God, and to yield Him covenanted and loyal service. Whereas, therefore, in the prophetic teaching God used alien empires to serve His purpose upon Israel, here he chose Pharaoh to serve His purpose on behalf of Israel. There He sought to instruct her in the folly of her way; here He sought to instruct her in the wonder of His grace. In neither case is there the slightest honour for

[1] Ex. 8 : 15, 32, 9 : 34.
[2] Ex. 10 : 1f.
[3] Ex. 14 : 4.

the instrument God uses, and the whole pattern and conception of election here is other than that we have considered in the previous lectures. It neither rests on, nor leads to, any covenant, and its very service is not obedience to the will of God but the sharpest opposition to His will.

Different again, however, is the election of Cyrus for service that carried a measure of honour. In the work of Deutero-Isaiah there are references to the Persian king as the elect of Yahweh, or as Yahweh's Anointed. Once more the purpose of the election has reference to Israel, but this time it is that Cyrus may be the instrument of God's gracious purpose, and of the deliverance and restoration of His people. Here, while it is stated that Cyrus did not know God, and hence could not be acting in conscious submission to His purpose, it is implied that the purpose of Cyrus's heart was in harmony with the purpose of God's heart. In the case of Assyria and Babylon, and of Pharaoh, the outer act could be integrated into God's purpose, though the motive and the spirit stood under His condemnation; here the spirit no less than the act is thought of as being in harmony with the Divine will. God does not whistle for him, as He is said to have whistled for Assyria; He takes him by the hand and leads him.

Without going so far as some who believe that Cyrus was the first model for the portrait of the Servant of Yahweh, from whom the prophet later turned in disappointment,[1] or going to the other extreme and eliminating Cyrus altogether from the prophecies of Deutero-Isaiah with Torrey,[2] we may find that the prophet conceived of him as the elect of God for a limited and specific purpose, which included the deliverance of Israel. He is spoken of in terms of honour, and is

---

[1] So M. Haller ("Die Kyroslieder Deuterojesajas", in *Eucharisterion* (Gunkel Festschrift), i, 1923, pp. 261-277; cf. *Das Judentum* (SAT) 2nd ed., 1925, pp. 21f). Cf. J. Hempel, "Vom irrenden Glauben", in *Zeitschrift für systematische Theologie*, vii, 1930, pp. 631-660; S. Mowinckel ("Die Komposition des deuterojesajanischen Buches", in *Zeitschrift für die alttestamentliche Wissenschaft*, N.F. viii, 1931, pp. 87-112, 242-260; W. E. Barnes, "Cyrus the 'Servant of Jehovah', Isa. 42 : 1-4 (7)", in *Journal of Theological Studies*, xxxii, 1931, pp. 32-39. Servetus went so far as to interpret Isa. 53 of Cyrus (Cf. L. I. Newman, *Jewish Influence on Christian Reform Movements*, 1925, pp. 582ff.).

[2] Cf. C. C. Torrey, *The Second Isaiah*, 1928, pp. 38-52.

promised a reward for the service he renders. His election involved his exaltation to imperial power over the nations, and he is promised Egypt and Ethiopia and Seba as a reward for his service to Israel.[1] Yet it was not for the possession of imperial power as an end in itself that the prophet thought of him as chosen by God. He was chosen for service, and his election had no meaning, save in so far as he became the instrument of God's will.

The first passage which most modern scholars interpret of Cyrus was traditionally interpreted of Abraham, and Torrey still in part defends this interpretation,[2] while Snaith holds that it should be interpreted of Israel;[3]

> Who hath roused up one from the east,
> Whom he calls in righteousness to his feet?[4]
> Nations he sets before him,
> And kings he subdues under him;[5]
> He makes them as the dust with his sword,[6]
> As the driven stubble with his bow.
> He pursues them and passes over in safety,
> By a path whereon he came not with his feet.[7]

Here I am not very confident of the interpretation of Cyrus, though I am still less confident of the interpretation

---

[1] Isa. 43 : 3.
[2] Cf. Torrey, *op. cit.*, pp. 310ff. So, too, Kissane, *The Book of Isaiah*, ii, 1943, pp. 20ff. My colleague Mr. P. R. Weis suggests that there may be some verbal reminiscences of Gen. 14 in the words *ṣedek*, *shālōm* and *melekh*, which stand in this passage.
[3] In an unpublished paper which will appear in the T. H. Robinson Festschrift, *Studies in Old Testament Prophecy*.
[4] This rendering which agrees with R.V. in taking the word *ṣedek* to be an adverbial accusative seems to me preferable to that favoured by several editors, who take the alternative sense of the verb and render "one whom victory meeteth at every step".
[5] The R.V. has "and maketh him rule over kings", but the form of the Hebrew verb is anomalous. Many editors read *yārōdh* for *yard* and so secure the sense given above. Other suggestions, which seem to me less likely, have also been made. The words *under him* are not represented in the Hebrew. While only metrical considerations suggest that any word has fallen out, I have added them with some diffidence, though they can only indicate a possible restoration.
[6] The R.V. has "he giveth them as the dust to his sword". The rendering given above is an alternative rendering, taking *ḥarbô* as adverbial accusative. Some editors take this word as the subject, and render "his sword maketh them as dust".
[7] Isa. 41 : 2f.

of Abraham.[1] I would therefore prefer not to build on this passage any idea of the election of Cyrus, but to turn to passages that may be used with more confidence.

> I am Yahweh, the maker of all things,
> Who stretched out the heaven by himself,
> Who beat out the earth—who was with me? . . .
> Who says of Jerusalem: It shall be inhabited;
> And of the cities of Judah: They shall be built,
> And their ruins will I raise up . . .
> Who says of Cyrus: He is my shepherd[2]
> And all my pleasure shall he perform . . .
> Thus saith Yahweh to his Anointed,
> To Cyrus, whose right hand I have taken,
> To subdue[3] nations before him,
> And the loins of kings will I ungird;
> To open doors before him,
> And gates shall not be closed . . .
> And I will give thee the stores of darkness,
> The hidden treasures of the secret places;
> That thou mayest know that I am Yahweh,
> Who called thee by name, the God of Israel,
> For the sake of Jacob, my servant,
> And Israel my chosen.
> And I called thee by thy name,
> And surnamed thee, though thou didst not know me.
> I am Yahweh, there is no other;
> And beside me there is no God.[4]

---

[1] The only element in the Abraham tradition which could have relevance to this description would be the story of the pursuit of Amraphel and his associates in Gen. 14. But this is so isolated an element in a tradition which is dominantly non-military that it would hardly justify this description. Moreover, Abraham could hardly be said to have been roused from the east for this incident.

[2] Many editors by the change of a vowel secure the reading "He is my friend". This would certainly yield an excellent sense, but since there is no reason to question the Massoretic reading, which also yields a perfectly satisfactory sense, it seems preferable to retain it.

[3] The grammatical form of the Hebrew verb is here abnormal. Hence some editors propose various emendations to secure forms from different verbs. This seems quite needless, since the verb employed in the Massoretic text is fully appropriate. A slight change of vowels could restore the normal form of the Infinitive, though since the present form is not wholly unparalleled there is no pressing necessity to make even that change. We should have expected *lāradh* instead of *lᵉradh*, however, and perhaps the preposition should be so pointed.

[4] Isa. 44 : 24, 26, 28, 45 : 1, 3-5.

ELECTION WITHOUT COVENANT

Here it is clear that the election of Cyrus is not something inconsistent with the election of Israel. It is, indeed subservient to that election, for it is for the sake of Israel, the elect, that Cyrus is called. He is chosen for his service before he has heard the very name of Yahweh, just as Moses was sent to an Israel that did not know Him as her God. It is of the Divine grace that he is chosen for his honourable task, since God saw that he would be serviceable unto Him. Yet there is nothing here comparable with the Old Testament teaching of the election of Israel. There is universal significance in his service:

> That men may know from the rising of the sun
> To its setting[1] that there is none beside me.[2]

Yet there is no suggestion that even Cyrus himself—let alone his people or his descendants—is thought of as called to a relation of covenanted loyalty to God, or of enduring obedience to His will. He is called to a single act of service, or to a series of acts that will culminate in that liberation of the Jews which shall so profoundly impress the whole world. He is first the recipient of the Divine grace in the wide conquests of his sword, and the service that is claimed of him is but that he shall be willing

> To say of Jerusalem: she shall be built!
> And to the Temple:[3] Thy foundations shall be laid.[4]

This digression from the thought of Israel's election confirms us in the view that all election is for service, though not all election is for honour. Sometimes it is the unwitting service which the pursuit of human purposes may render, and the praise or blame it earns depends on whether its character makes it harmonize with the will of God or whether He has

---

[1] The Hebrew reads "and from the setting" or "the west". The rendering above follows the suggestion of R. Levy (*Deutero-Isaiah*, 1925, p. 186) in omitting the preposition as a dittograph, leaving the *He locale* with its full locative force.

[2] Isa. 45 : 6.

[3] This rendering follows the R.V., which tacitly restores the preposition. The R.V. marg. tacitly emends the verb to a masculine form. It seems preferable to add the preposition and to retain the change of person, which is so characteristic of Hebrew poetry.

[4] Isa. 44 : 28.

to bend what is alien to His will yet to serve His purpose. In neither case does the election lead on to any covenant. In so far as there is merit in the service, it receives its reward from God, who is never in the debt of man. But it is no service that gives an enduring claim on God, or that leads to a permanent relationship between the elect and God.

Quite other than this is the election of Israel, which rests solely on the Divine grace, and which brings first of all the never-to-be-forgotten service which made Israel conscious that she was the elect of God, and which called for the consecration of herself to Him in a lasting covenant, whose blessings should be the inheritance of future generations and to which, therefore, their loyalty was due. Far higher, too, is the purpose of the election of Israel than any election that lay outside the Covenant. For no profoundly spiritual fruits of the latter election were gathered by the elect.

This is not to claim that there is no real election, save of Israel. It is but to say that the Old Testament is concerned with the election of Israel, and with the election of others only in so far as its purpose touches Israel. It neither affirms nor denies that God chose Greece to achieve cultural heights far beyond Israel's. For it is not interested in culture, but in religion. It claims that in the realm of the spirit Israel is the unique Chosen People, and that to her and through her in an unparalleled degree God designed to reveal Himself and His will. Nor can I see how this claim can be disputed. The spiritual quality of the Old Testament cannot be matched in any non-Christian sacred book, and no people can provide a succession of religious leaders comparable with the Hebrew prophets. To the question why Israel alone should have such a succession, the only satisfying answer is to be found in terms of her election. Yet that election involved a condition, and the prophets repeatedly declared that the condition was not fulfilled. And with the failure of the condition the election no longer held for the nation, though by Divine grace it could be continued for the Remnant to carry forward the heritage to the distant future, in which shone the light of a larger hope. To that Remnant we must return in our final lecture.

Chapter Six

THE HEIRS OF ELECTION

IN summing up the teaching of the prophets, R. B. Y. Scott says: "The religious group which only carries on the momentum in belief and practice of an age which has passed away, and has not made its own the covenant of the fathers, will find that the covenant is no longer valid, and the living God has passed on to seek a new people for himself."[1] It is the claim of the New Testament that this is what happened in the founding of the Christian Church, and that the Church is the heir of the election of Israel. It is therefore our task now to ask how far this claim can be justified, or how far it is merely the assertion of the self-esteem of the early Christians and their successors.[2] That Israel's claim to be the Chosen People rests on solid grounds, and that objective evidence in its favour can be produced, has already been said. It remains to be seen whether the Church can produce any equally objective evidence in support of its claim.

It is of importance to remember that the first evidence to which the Church appealed was supplied by Judaism itself, and was treasured in its own Scriptures. It was not simply that the Church and the Synagogue were two rival bodies, each claiming to be the People of God, but that the Church affirmed as confidently as the Synagogue that Israel was the Chosen People, but that the Church was the true Israel in accordance with the teachings of the Old Testament itself. For already there we find that significant loosing of election from mere physical descent in the constant teaching that only they who yield their loyalty to the Covenant and its obligations are the heirs of election, and that therefore not

---

[1] Cf. *The Relevance of the Prophets*, 1944, p. 210.
[2] For a valuable study of the relation of the Church's election to that of Israel, cf. W. Zimmerli, "Biblische Grundlinien zur Judenfrage", in *Judaica* i, 1945, pp. 93–117.

all Israel after the flesh belong to the Chosen People. T. W. Manson says: "In the doctrine of the Remnant a decisive step is taken towards the individualizing of religion; and this religious individualism modifies in one essential matter the idea of a people of God . . . The Remnant which was to survive the judgement would take the place formerly held by the nation as a whole. But there is this significant difference between the old dispensation and the new. Membership in the nation came by the accident of birth; in the Remnant it is a matter of deliberate choice by the individual. If our interpretation of Isa. 8 : 16ff. is correct, the vitally important thing is no longer to be a son of Abraham, but to be a disciple of Isaiah with all that that implies."[1]

Moreover, as we have seen, there was not merely the limitation of the election to some only of the nation, but there was also the extension of the election through proselytism to those who lay beyond the bounds of the nation. It is true that racial distinctions had been maintained, and that proselytes had still been regarded as not quite the same as those who were Jews by blood,[2] though they had been compelled to affirm their solidarity with the Jewish nation as well as with the Jewish faith. Nevertheless the whole idea of an exclusive national election has been undermined. They who belong to Israel after the flesh are born to a heritage which only becomes theirs when by the acceptance of the Covenant they claim it; and Gentiles who accept the Covenant may possess the heritage, since from the start it was destined for them, and it belonged to the purpose of Israel's election that she should mediate it to them. The New Testament is not, therefore, presenting a new point of view that

[1] Cf. *The Teaching of Jesus*, 2nd ed., 1935, p. 177.
[2] Cf. M. Simon (*Verus Israel*, 1948, p. 85): "The Israelites continue to constitute, by the fact of their birth, a sort of aristocracy, and the proselytes remain Jews of second rank." That there were differences of attitude has been said above, and the degree of differentiation applied to the proselyte varied greatly. Moreover, support could be found for those who emphasized the differentiation in the more nationalistic passages of the Old Testament. Cf. A. B. Davidson in Hastings' *Dictionary of the Bible*, i, 1898, p. 738 a: "While already in the Old Testament the Gentiles are fellow-heirs of salvation with Israel, the racial distinction is not obliterated. Jews and Gentiles do not amalgamate into one people or church—Israel 'inherits the Gentiles' (Isa. 54 : 3) . . . The nations occupy a subordinate place." Cf. Judah Ha-Levi (quoted by J. Jocz, *International Review of Missions*, xxxvii, 1948, p. 385): "With all this the one received into our faith is not made equal with the native."

is alien to the thought of Judaism when it declares the same thing.

We may first look at a few of the passages in which the claim is made. In the first Gospel we read: "Therefore I say unto you, the kingdom of God shall be taken away from you, and it shall be given to a nation that bringeth forth its fruits."[1] While this saying is put into the mouth of our Lord, following the parable of the Wicked Husbandmen, it is regarded by T. W. Manson as an editorial comment, since it has no parallel in Mark or Luke and it does not fit the parable itself, since there the wicked husbandmen are threatened with destruction and not merely with dispossession.[2] Whether it is actually a saying of our Lord's, perhaps originally separate from the parable to which it is now somewhat loosely attached,[3] or whether it is editorial, it expresses the belief of the Early Church that the inheritance of Judaism had become the inheritance of the Church. In a less disputed utterance of our Lord's we read: "I say unto you that many will come from the east and from the west, and will recline at table with Abraham and Isaac and Jacob in the kingdom of heaven; while the children of the kingdom"—i.e. those who by their blood should inherit the kingdom—"will be cast into the darkness outside".[4]

J. W. Bowman has recently argued that the reason for the choice of twelve disciples was to claim by symbolic action, akin to prophetic symbolism, that our Lord was the leader of the Remnant and therefore the founder of a new community that should replace the old.[5] Implicit or explicit in much of Christ's teaching is the claim that He supersedes the old Law. "Ye have heard that it was said ... but I say

---

[1] Matt. 21 : 43.
[2] Cf. Major-Manson-Wright, *The Mission and Message of Jesus*, 1940 ed., p. 516. Cf. G. D. Kilpatrick, *The Origins of the Gospel according to St. Matthew*, 1946, p. 30. C. J. Cadoux (*Historic Mission of Jesus*, 1941, p. 141) regards the verse as coming from M, which he defines as a collection of Sayings of Jesus of considerable authority, compiled at Jerusalem about A.D. 55–60 (p. 21).
[3] D. Buzy (in Pirot and Clamer's *La Sainte Bible*, ix, 1946, p. 287) notes that this verse bisects the little allegory of the stone, which is quite distinct from that of the vineyard.
[4] Matt. 8 : 11. This is assigned by Manson (*Mission and Message*, p. 416) to Q. So Kilpatrick, *op. cit.*, p. 118; Cadoux, *op. cit.*, p. 144.
[5] Cf. *The Intention of Jesus*, 1945, p. 185, Cf. R. N. Flew, *Jesus and His Church* 2nd ed., 1943, p. 38.

unto you."[1] Yet He does not simply dismiss the old Law and start *de novo* with another. He emphatically repudiates such an idea. "Think not that I came to destroy the law or the prophets; I came not to destroy, but to fulfil."[2] M. Goguel has observed: "It is often said—and rightly—that in his commentary on the Commandments in the Sermon on the Mount he substituted the ethic of intention and of the will for that of the act, or, in other words, he made morality an inward thing. Thus he has not merely transformed the moral side of life, but religion itself; the religion of the heart, of inner moral purity, replaces a religion of outward conformity to God's commands."[3] But this is precisely the inauguration of the New Covenant of which Jeremiah had prophesied, when the law should be inscribed on the living tables of human personality instead of on external tables of stone.

In the Pauline account of the Last Supper, we read that Jesus said: "This cup is the new covenant in my blood."[4] The same words stand in the Lukan account,[5] but in the accounts of Matthew and Mark the word "new" does not stand in the best manuscripts.[6] There must remain some doubt, therefore, as to whether our Lord used the word. But there is none that the Early Church accepted this connexion with the New Covenant of Jeremiah, and therefore believed that the Church entered into the inheritance of Israel.[7] The New Covenant was to supersede the Old Covenant, and therefore the Church believed that its election in Christ superseded the old election. That it was true to the essential thought of Christ, whether he used the word "new" on that occasion or not, seems to be clear. He always claims the heritage of the old Covenant, though He is not in bondage to it, and feels Himself free to advance beyond it in the laws He lays down for His followers. For the true Israel He claims to be the new Lawgiver, and they are Israel who hearken to His word.

[1] Matt. 5 : 21f., 27f., 33f., 38f., 43f.
[2] Matt. 5 : 17.
[3] Cf. *Life of Jesus*, English Tr., 1933, p. 556.
[4] 1 Cor. 11 : 25.
[5] Luke 22 : 20.
[6] Cf. A. Huck, *Synopsis of the First Three Gospels*, English ed., 1936, p. 186.
[7] Cf. Heb. 8 : 8-12; 2 Cor. 3 : 4-6.

THE HEIRS OF ELECTION

Our Lord addressed Himself exclusively to Jews[1] and only once, so far as we know, did He go beyond the borders of His own country during His ministry. He declared that He was sent to the lost sheep of the house of Israel,[2] and when He sent forth His disciples He commanded them to go only through the length and breadth of their land.[3] This has led to the view, widely disseminated through the influence of Harnack,[4] that while there is an implicit universalism in the Gospel, our Lord never gave expression to any explicit universalism, and that such words as the command of the Risen Christ in Matt. 28 : 19f. must therefore be quite unauthentic.[5] The thesis that the conscious thought of Jesus was in the world of Jewish particularism, while His implicit thought was universalistic, means that the Church has been truer to the essence of His teaching than He was Himself. It has been criticized by B. Sundkler[6] as resting on a false antithesis. Sundkler argues that our Lord thought of the Church as the Remnant that should inherit the mission

[1] Cf. J. Klausner, *Jesus of Nazareth*, English Tr., 1925, p. 368: "Jesus was a Jew, and a Jew he remained till his last breath."
[2] Matt. 15 : 24. Cf. C. H. Dodd, *History and the Gospel*, 1941 ed., p. 131: "Whether or not He used the express words, 'I am not sent but unto the lost sheep of the House of Israel', those words describe the limitations which He actually accepted."
[3] Matt. 10 : 5f.
[4] Cf. *Expansion of Christianity in the First Three Centuries*, English Tr., 1, 1904, pp. 40-48.
[5] The verses are regarded as editorial by Cadoux (*op. cit.*, p. 33), and Kilpatrick (*op. cit.*, p. 49), on internal grounds. D. Buzy (*La Sainte Bible*, ed. Pirot and Clamer, ix, 1946, p. 386) says: "We have here one of those exceptional cases where a text of capital importance is attested by all the manuscripts and witnesses, without a single known exception." H. de Lubac (*Le fondement théologique des missions*, 1946, p. 19) says: "Even supposing that Jesus had not formally given this command, the Church would have known equally well that this was its task." For a careful discussion of the authenticity of this passage cf. P. W. Evans, *Sacraments in the New Testament*, 1947, pp. 10ff., where the conclusion is reached (p. 21) that "the evidence is indecisive as to whether our Lord used the exact phrase reported in Matthew 28 : 19. But even were it finally proved that we have not Christ's *ipsissima verba*, we may still have his intention correctly reported.
[6] Cf. B. Sundkler and A. Fridrichsen, *Contributions à l'étude de la pensée missionaire dans le Nouveau Testament*, 1937. J. Klausner (*From Jesus to Paul*, 1943, p. 445) holds that the particularistic and universalistic tendencies ought not to be set against one another. He says: "In the Jewish Messianic conception throughout its history, the national and universal elements are so combined and fused together that they cannot be separated. ... These two aspects of the Jewish Messiah have always existed side by side, except that sometimes the politico-national aspect received more emphasis, and at other times the universalistic, spiritual aspects."

of Israel, and that while His own mission was to Israel, it had necessarily a universalistic significance, since it recognized that from Jerusalem as the centre of the world life-giving streams should pour forth for the renewal of the world.[1]

That Paul thought of the Church in terms of the Remnant is beyond dispute.[2] "They are not all Israel which are of Israel" he says,[3] and he goes on to note, as we have already noted above, that the limitation of the Abrahamic covenant to the seed of Isaac in itself implied that physical generation could not alone control the heritage of the election.[4] He cites Isa. 10 : 22,[5] and Isa. 1 : 9,[6] in which the doctrine of the Remnant was enunciated, to reinforce his argument, and finds in the seven thousand who had not bowed the knee to Baal in the time of Elijah the prelude to his assertion that "in the same way there is at the present time a remnant according to the election of grace".[7] But with the thought of the limitation of the election of Israel to but a part of the Israel according to the flesh he combined the thought of the extension of that election beyond the bounds of the nation to those amongst the Gentiles who should come to share the faith and the task of Israel. "Therefore is it of faith", he says, "so that it may be according to grace, to confirm the promise to all the seed, not alone that which is of the law, but also to that which is of the faith of Abraham, who is the father of us all."[8] In the same Epistle he speaks of some of the branches of the tree of Israel having been broken off through

[1] A. H. McNeile (*The Gospel according to St. Matthew*, 1915, p. 435), observes: "If the risen Lord commanded it in one of His latest utterances, the action of the apostles with reference to the Gentiles (see e.g. Gal 2 : 9, Acts 10, 11 : 1–18) is inexplicable." But surely it is precisely similar to their attitude on so many things, as they appear before us in the Gospels. They completely failed to understand our Lord's teaching about His own death, until the fact of the Cross made them think back over His teaching. It was as easy for them to preserve the memory of a missionary injunction and to think of it in an ideal rather than a practical way as it was for Judaism to preserve the Scriptures which set its missionary vocation before it without addressing itself seriously to its mission.

[2] Cf. W. D. Davies, *Paul and Rabbinic Judaism*, 1948, p. 75: "Paul saw in the emergence of the Church that the 'Israel of God' had entered upon a new phase in its history. The Church fulfils the functions of the faithful remnant, and is interpreted by Paul in terms of the remnant doctrine of the Old Testament."

[3] Rom. 9 : 6. [4] Rom. 9 : 7f. [5] Rom. 9 : 27.
[6] Rom. 9 : 29. [7] Rom. 11 : 4ff. [8] Rom. 4 : 16.

unbelief, and Gentiles being grafted in to take their place.[1] It is of the grace and goodness of God that they are grafted in, and it can only be as they respond to that grace by faith that they can remain in the tree. In all this there is nothing that is in the least degree alien to the teaching of the Old Testament.[2]

Nor does he stop with this general repetition of Old Testament principles. Instead he goes on to give it all specific application to the Christian Church. He contrasts the "Israel according to the flesh"[3] with the "Israel of God",[4] which is the Church. "For he is not a Jew who is one outwardly, neither is that circumcision which is outward in the flesh; but he is a Jew which is one inwardly, and circumcision is of the heart."[5] "Now we, brethren, are children of the promise, as Israel was. But as then he that was born after the flesh persecuted him that was born after the spirit, even so is it now."[6] "If ye are Christ's, then ye are the seed of Abraham, and heirs of the promises."[7] "Wherefore remember, that at one time ye who are Gentiles in the flesh, called Uncircumcision by that which is called the Circumcision in the flesh, made by hands, ye were at that time strangers to the covenant of promise, having no hope and being without God in the world . . . Ye are no longer strangers and sojourners, but are fellow-citizens with the saints and of the household of God."[8] "The Gentiles are fellow-heirs and of the same body and are sharers of the promise in Christ

---

[1] Rom. 11 : 17ff. Paul's spiritual principles are sounder than the metaphor by which he expresses them, which betrays an ignorance of the real effect of grafting in the botanical realm, unless, as J. Denney (*Expositor's Greek Testament*, ii, p. 680) argues, Paul deliberately used a figure which "turns on the fact that the process *was* an unnatural one".

[2] Cf. W. A. Irwin, *The Intellectual Adventure of Ancient Man*, 1946, p. 328: "Paul was expounding the best thought of his people when he distinguished between Israel after the flesh and after the spirit"; C. H. Dodd, *The Epistle of Paul to the Romans* (MC), 1942 ed., p. 160: "Here Paul is unquestionably at one with prophetic teaching in its main trend. His Christian experience has given him a key to the prophets which the rabbis had largely lost." Sanday and Headlam (*The Epistle to the Romans* (ICC), 5th ed., 1902, p. 317) say: "This doctrine of the 'Remnant' is as true to human nature as it is to Israel's history. No church or nation is saved *en masse*, it is those members of it who are righteous."

[3] 1 Cor. 10 : 18.   [4] Gal. 6 : 16.   [5] Rom. 2 : 28f.
[6] Gal. 4 : 28f.   [7] Gal. 3 : 29.   [8] Eph. 2 : 11f., 19.

Jesus."[1] Or again: "For we are the true circumcision, who worship God in spirit, and who glory in Christ Jesus, and have no confidence in the flesh."[2] Elsewhere he speaks of God's adoption of the Church of Christ. "If any man have not the spirit of Christ, he is not his. But if Christ be in you, the body is dead because of sin, while the spirit is life because of righteousness . . . For as many as are led by the Spirit of God, they are the sons of God. For ye did not receive the spirit of bondage again for fear, but ye received the spirit of adoption, whereby we cry, Abba, Father. The Spirit itself adds its testimony to our own spirit, that we are the children of God; and if children, then heirs, heirs of God and fellow-heirs with Christ."[3]

Beyond the Pauline Epistles we find the same thought. The Epistle of James begins: "James, a servant of God and of the Lord Jesus Christ, to the twelve tribes which are in the Dispersion, greeting."[4] Here the scattered Christian Church is claimed to be the true Israel. In the First Epistle of Peter that Church is declared to be the Chosen People of God. "Ye are an elect race, a royal priesthood, a holy nation, a special people, that ye may declare the excellences of him who called you out of darkness into his marvellous light."[5] It is by no accident that phrases from Ex. 19 : 5 are found here. E. G. Selwyn observes: "Since his purpose is to assert that the Christian Church has now inherited the peculiar character and privileges of Israel, Ex. 19, which records the divine establishment of Israel's status and call as a result of the deliverance from Egypt, is no doubt the ground-base of the passage."[6] Like the election of Israel, that of the Church

---

[1] Eph. 3 : 6.
[2] Phil. 3 : 3.
[3] Rom. 8 : 9f., 14-17.
[4] Jas. 1 : 1.
[5] 1 Pet. 2 : 9.
[6] Cf. *The First Epistle of St. Peter*, 1946, p. 278. Cf. F. W. Beare, *The First Epistle of Peter*, 1947, p. 101: "The entire description is taken from the Greek Old Testament, with slight adaptation; he claims for the Church that place in the divine economy which the teachers of Israel had set before their nation as the destiny to which it was called. . . . He has gone far beyond the thought of St. Paul. . . . His thought is not that the Church has now supplanted or superseded Israel, but rather that the Church has been the object of God's concern all the while."

is revealed in the mighty acts of grace, and its purpose is the proclamation of the revelation.

Throughout the New Testament the term "elect" is found many times for the Church, testifying to the belief that the Church was the elect of God, and in the Epistle to the Ephesians it is declared that that election belongs to the eternal purpose of God, and that it was made before the foundation of the world.[1] Yet never is this election thought of as a rival to that of Israel, but as the continuation of that election, to which the Church had become heir. It was in this belief that the Church continued to use the Jewish Scriptures. They were a part of its heritage, and it thankfully accepted them and all the enrichment they brought. Never does it become the Christian to speak slightingly of Judaism, for out of the womb of Judaism was Christianity born,[2] and into its heritage the Church entered. This is not to make Christianity just a natural development out of Judaism. Far from it, indeed! There was continuity; but there was also a new element. Neither must be emphasized to the exclusion of the other. The mission and message of Jesus can never be understood without relation to the background of Judaism out of which it came; but it can still less be understood only as the issue of that background. The work of Moses can never be understood without relation to the experience of his call in the wilderness, through which he embarked on something new and creative in religious history. Merely to regard him as the mediator to Israel of Kenite Yahwism is to miss his real significance. And as little can we ignore the new and creative element that was in Christ. The heritage that is ours in Christ, and the creative element in His message, and still more the dynamic element that was in His Cross and Resurrection, must be both cherished and preserved.

That the Church claimed that it was the spiritual Israel and the heir of the election, the Remnant that alone could claim the promises reinforced by those of the Gentiles who

[1] Eph. 1 : 14f.
[2] Cf. S. H. Hooke, *Judaism and Christianity, I. The Age of Transition*, (ed. W. O. E. Oesterley), 1937, p. 254: "It is necessary to remember that the Church emerged from the womb of Judaism, and that the metaphor has the profound truth in it that the bones of the Christian Church were shaped in that womb."

shared its faith, is hardly to be gainsaid.[1] And that faith has continued in the Church until the present day. The Church is not a society of like-minded people who meet for mutual edification, or even for worship. It is the Israel of God,[2] chosen and called by Him, and responding in a covenant that is both individual and corporate, chosen to receive of His grace, indeed, but also to feel the constraint of that grace and to render a service that is absolute and unconditional.

All this is a particular application of the Old Testament principles to which the New Testament appeals. So long as it is merely stated that not all Israel is Israel, and that they who are not of Israel may yet be of Israel,[3] appeal may be made to the Old Testament. But to go on from this and to state that the Church is the only true Israel is to make a claim which cannot be simply demonstrated by appeal to the Old Testament, and a claim which soon precipitated conflict between the Church and the Synagogue. Its formulation is not its establishment, and however firmly the Early Church believed it, we need to ask how far it can justify itself at the bar of reason, and how far it can claim the support of objective facts. We have seen that Israel's faith in her election did rest on something more than her subjective fancy. That did not wholly eliminate the subjective from it, for there must always be a subjective element in faith. But a faith that is wholly subjective, poised on nothing, and that belongs entirely to the world of fancy, is not the only sort of faith, or, indeed, any satisfying form of faith. Israel's faith was not of that kind, and unless the faith of the Church was at least as well grounded in concrete experience it must have a poor case to establish its claim to be the heir of Israel.

The Church soon became predominantly Gentile in its membership, yet is it not to be thought of as a Gentile society over against the Jewish society of the Synagogue.

---

[1] For a much fuller study of the New Testament thought of the Church as the New Israel, cf. R. N. Flew, *Jesus and His Church*, 2nd ed., 1943, *passim*. Cf. also C. H. Dodd, *The Bible To-day*, 1946, pp. 70f.; W. Robinson, *The Biblical Doctrine of the Church*, 1948, pp. 67f., 202ff.
[2] Gal. 6 : 16.
[3] Cf. Hosea 2 : 23, cited in Rom. 9 : 25.

The Founder of Christianity was a Jew. The first disciples were Jews. The great leaders of the first generation, who set the feet of the Church on its way, were all Jews.[1] That they were a Remnant of the Israel according to the flesh is clear, whether they were the Remnant that inherited the election or not. They stood within the Covenant of Israel, and they thought of themselves as the loyal Remnant, inheriting the election because they responded to its claim, and hailed the fulfilment of its promise, and because they conveyed the heritage to those Gentiles who shared with them their response. They thought of the Jews who refused to share their response as failing to fulfil the purpose of their election, and hence renouncing their election. This did not fill them with feelings of triumph, but with profound sorrow. To Paul especially it brought the deepest pain, and he longed inexpressibly for his fellow-Jews to share with him his response. He did not debate with the Jews in order to demonstrate his skill, but in order to win them to share the treasure he had found. He would cheerfully have accepted a curse upon himself if only that could have served.[2] Nor could he readily accept the view that Israel's rejection of Christ was final, but kept alive the thought of the possibility that she would yet accept Him and be grafted anew into the tree from which she had been torn.[3] Nevertheless it is clear that in Paul's thought it was not that the Church was co-elect with the Synagogue, but that the Church had inherited the Synagogue's election. The Jews who would not accept Christ had forfeited their election, and were branches torn out of the tree.

The earliest appeal of the Church in support of its claims was to the fulfilment of prophecy, and in the New Testament we find frequent citation of Old Testament passages that are held to have found their fulfilment in Christ. Many of these have little cogency for the modern reader and are without

---

[1] Cf. A. Deissmann, *Paul: A Study in Social and Religious History*, English Tr., 1926, p. 96: "Even when a Christian, Paul preserved the most genuine features of his Jewish nature. Therefore the theme 'Paul the Jew' is not to be interpreted as if Paul had been a Jew up to his conversion, but after that was a Jew no longer. Paul remained a Jew while also a Christian in spite of his passionate controversy against the law."
[2] Rom. 9 : 2f.
[3] Rom. 11 : 23f.

objective value for the establishment of the claim that the Church is the heir of Israel's election. Thus the first chapter of the New Testament states that our Lord's birth took place in fulfilment of Isaiah's prophecy to Ahaz.[1] In truth the question of the Virgin Birth of Christ can neither be established nor overthrown by appeal to Isa. 7 : 14 with which it can have nothing to do. It is improbable that Isaiah was referring to a supernatural birth, and quite certain that he was referring to one much nearer his own time than the birth of Jesus.[2] This kind of appeal to the Old Testament,

[1] Matt. 1 : 21ff.
[2] For ample references to the recent literature which has been devoted to the study of this prophecy cf. J. J. Stamm, *Revue de Théologie et de Philosophie*, xxiii, 1944, pp. 1–4. To this bibliography may be added K. Hj. Fahlgren, "Hā'almā", *Svensk Exegetisk Årsbok*, iv, 1939, pp. 13–24; A. Feuillet, "Le signe proposé à Achaz et l'Emmanuel," *Recherches de Science Religieuse*, xxx, 1940, pp. 129–151; S. Mowinckel, "Immanuelprofetien Jes. 7", *Norsk Teologisk Tidsskrift*, xlii, 1941, pp. 129–157; E. Hammershaimb, "Immanuelstegnet", *Dansk Teologisk Tidsskrift*, viii, 1945, pp. 223–244; C. Lattey, "The Emmanuel Prophecy: Isaias 7 : 14", *Catholic Biblical Quarterly*, viii, 1946, pp. 369–376; *id.*, "The Term 'Almah in Isa. 7 : 14", *ibid.*, ix, 1947, pp. 89–95; *id.*, "Various Interpretations of Isa. 7 : 14", *ibid.*, pp. 147–154; E. Power, "The Emmanuel Prophecy of Isaias", *Irish Ecclesiastical Record*, 5th series, lxx, 1948, pp. 289–304. It is of interest to observe the similarity between the interpretation of Lattey and that of Stamm in the article to which the above mentioned bibliography is prefixed, "La prophétie d'Emmanuel", *loc. cit.*, pp. 1–27. Lattey interprets by the principle of compenetration, holding that the child referred to was Isaiah's own son, Maher-shalal-hash-baz, but that that in the title Immanuel there is also a prophecy of Christ, and that the principle of compenetration can be applied to the mother no less than to the son (viii, pp. 375f.). By the principle of compenetration a double sense is found in prophecy, the one referring to the nearer and the other to the more distant fulfilment. Very similarly, but completely independently, the Protestant scholar Stamm holds that the primary reference of the prophecy was to the prophet's own son, but that it also contains an "obscure presentiment" of Christ, and that therefore Immanuel is a prophetic type of Christ. In Isa. 7 : 14 the name is everything and the bearer nothing; but in Christ such a distinction is impossible. He is not merely called Immanuel; he is Immanuel (p. 27). Both of these scholars agree that the primary reference is to a child to be born in Isaiah's own day. That the name is more fitting for our Lord than it was for any eighth-century child I fully agree, but this is scarcely to make the passage into a direct prophecy of Christ, and neither of these scholars affirms that it is. As so often our Lord "fulfils" the prophecy by clothing its thought with a reality greater than could have been guessed from the word itself. Feuillet (*loc. cit.*) distinguishes Immanuel from the child who eats curdled milk and honey, and identifies the latter with Isaiah's son Shear-jashub, while transferring the prophecy of the former to the end of the chapter. He says (p. 132): "If Immanuel is really the Messiah—and it is impossible to doubt it—it is no less inconceivable that Immanuel should be the child given as a sign to Ahaz and designated in verse 16." Fahlgren, in the article noted above, holds that the mother of the child in Isa. 7 : 14 is a woman attached to the cult, while S. H. Hooke (*Prophets and Priests*, 1938, pp. 29–31) holds that she was one who would take part in the sacred marriage ritual; and so Hammershaimb (*loc. cit.*) who cites Ras Shamra evidence in support.

which consists in taking a verse right out of its own proper context, and linking it to something quite unrelated to its thought by means of some verbal association, has no logical value whatever. It was psychological, and it can be paralleled from Jewish sources, where similarly fanciful links are often made.[1] That Jesus more truly deserved the name Immanuel than any child of whom Isaiah spoke, and deserved it in virtue of what He was in Himself rather than in view of the circumstances that attended His birth, is again quite irrelevant, and unwillingness to recognize any cogency in the appeal to Isa. 7 : 14 does not involve rejection of the fact of the Incarnation, or even of the Virgin Birth. So far as we know He was never called Immanuel during His life on earth, and in the New Testament He is nowhere else given this name. Moreover, not even the Evangelist claims that His mother ever gave Him this name,[2] or that there was more than an inexact fulfilment of the Old Testament passage.

If this were the only sort of appeal to prophecy, the case of the Church would be a weak one. The kind of psychological appeal which was once effective cannot be converted into a logical appeal with cogency for a different audience, and we but weaken our own cause when we confuse psychology with logic. Happily there is a more effective appeal to the Old Testament, and especially to its prophecies.

The predictions of the future found in the Old Testament prophets were of two kinds. They spoke mainly of the future that should issue out of the present, and this was predominantly described by the pre-exilic prophets as the harvest of sorrow that should be produced by the sowing of folly in their time. In this prophecy there was a contingent element,

---

[1] Cf. J. Massie, in Hastings' *Dictionary of the Bible*, i, 1898, p. 65a: "The Palestinian Jews allegorized the Old Testament, finding a hidden sense in sentences, words, letters, and (in the centuries after Christ) even vowel-points, in order to satisfy their consciences for the non-observance of laws that had become impracticable, or to justify traditional and often trivial increment, or to defend God against apparent inconsistency, or the writers or historical characters against impiety or immorality; or, generally, for homiletical purposes." J. Bonsirven (*Exégèse rabbinique et exégèse paulinienne*, 1939, p. 209) complains that this is too sweeping a statement, and that Jewish writers were restrained in the resort to allegory.

[2] Cf. Isa. 7 : 14; "she shall call his name Immanuel."

and moreover the mediation of the message through the organ of the prophet's personality sufficiently explains why no exact fulfilment of many of their words has taken place, or is now to be expected. But there were other prophecies of the Golden Age that lay beyond the sorrows on the far horizons of time. There was no attempt to link that Golden Age with their own day by any causal links, and they never supposed it would come by merely human efforts. It is widely recognized to-day that this eschatological element belonged to early prophecy as well as late, though it became more marked as prophecy developed into apocalyptic. The difference between prophecy and apocalyptic is not, as is sometimes supposed, that the latter is eschatological while the former is not, and we should always beware of confusing the terms eschatology and apocalyptic. The difference is rather that whereas the prophets thought the Golden Age was on the far horizon, the apocalyptists believed they had reached the horizon, and the Golden Age was about to dawn. But in both prophecy and apocalyptic there was this forward look to a future which should transcend the present, and in which the hopes of the Old Testament should have their fulfilment.

These hopes were expressed in a variety of terms, and it is difficult to imagine any literal fulfilment of them all. Some of them centred in a Davidic leader, who should inaugurate an enduring reign of peace and righteousness, when the very face of Nature would be transformed. In the book of Daniel, the Davidic leader does not figure, and the coming kingdom is spoken of as a stone cut without hands,[1] or as one like unto a son of man coming with[2] the clouds of heaven.[3] These are figures for the kingdom, rather than for any individual leader of the kingdom. Moreover, there are prophecies such as Jeremiah's prediction of the New Covenant, which are unrelated either to a Davidic leader or to catastrophic events

[1] Dan. 2 : 45.
[2] This is a rendering of the Aramaic text, which is represented in the Greek of Theodotion and the Vulgate, and which stands in the New Testament in Mark 14 : 62, Rev. 1 : 7, and in 4 Ezra (=2 Esdras) 13 : 3. On the other hand the LXX has "on the clouds", and so the Syriac, and this is followed in the New Testament in Matt. 22 : 30, 26 : 64, Rev. 14 : 14, 16.
[3] Dan. 7 : 13.

in the political life of the nation. The prophecy of the New Covenant is introduced by a formula[1] which places it vaguely in the future, unrelated to the events of the prophet's own day, very similar to all these promises. In addition there are the passages that speak of the Suffering Servant, in whom Israel's mission will reach its supreme fulfilment.

The Church claimed that Christ gathered all these prophecies into Himself, and that in Him and in His Church they all found their fulfilment. That they found no literal fulfilment in all their details is manifest, but it would be hard to imagine any situation which could at once have fulfilled all of these. All that could be claimed was that the essential hope of these prophecies found in Him its realization. It could not be claimed that the only conceivable fulfilment was the fulfilment in Christ. But it may be claimed that the only fulfilment which has yet been seen in history was the fulfilment in Him. There have been others who have claimed to be the Davidic Messiah, but the event has proved their claims to be ludicrous. The claim of the Church that all these hopes met in Christ is certainly not ludicrous. Either they were fulfilled in Him, therefore, or they are yet unfulfilled. And since it is unlikely that any living Jew could produce convincing evidence of his descent from David, any demonstrably literal fulfilment is not now to be expected. In other words, either these prophecies were fulfilled in Christ, or they can never be fulfilled in history.[2]

It is significant that J. H. Greenstone, who records the modifications of the messianic idea found in some circles in modern Jewry, and its replacement by Zionism in others,

[1] P. A. Munch (*The Expression Bajjōm hāhū*, 1936) has argued that this expression is not an eschatological *terminus technicus*, as had been maintained by H. Gressmann (*Der Messias*, 1929, pp. 82ff.), but can always be understood as a temporal adverb. A. S. Kapelrud (*Joel Studies*, 1948, p. 165) observes: "Characteristic of both is that they are right in some of the instances treated, and that both press their point far too much." Kapelrud soundly concludes (p. 166) that "we cannot content ourselves with explaining the expression on the basis of one principle only", and that in historical narrative it is a temporal adjective while in prophetic contexts it has an eschatological meaning. Cf. G. Pidoux, *Le Dieu qui vient*, 1947, pp. 14f.

[2] Cf. L. Magnus, *The Jews in the Christian Era*, 1929, p. 397: "There can be no more false Messiahs."

says: "However, the belief in a personal Messiah, whose advent is to be accompanied by many miracles and wonders, is still potent, and keeps many of the orthodox Jews out of the Zionist camp."[1] He himself thinks that Zionism may contribute towards the full realization of that hope, which he declares to be "the establishment by the Jews of a world-power in Palestine to which all the nations of the earth will pay homage".[2] Such a messianism is merely the aspiration for world dominion, which has proved a snare to so many nations. That it is not the messianism of the Old Testament is clear from the fact that some of the most enthusiastic of the Zionists, as Greenstone himself acknowledges,[3] have been Jews who are themselves estranged from Judaism, giving rise to the fear that the movement would lead to a breaking away from the religion of Israel. In the teaching of the Old Testament, as we have seen, it is made clear that they who are disloyal to the Covenant cannot claim the heritage of the promises, and still less can they who are not concerned to go up to the house of the Lord themselves, or to learn His law, be seriously mentioned in connexion with Old Testament messianism, one of whose features was to be the universalizing of the faith of Israel. The messianism of the Old Testament was fundamentally and profoundly religious, and no movement which is not essentially and fully religious in its inspiration and character can offer any pretence to be the heir of its tasks or its promises.

Either the messianic prophecies of the Old Testament were fulfilled in Christ, or they can never be fulfilled in history. Yet this leaves unanswered the question how far they were fulfilled in Him. It is true that He did not rule an earthly kingdom from the throne of David, as some of the prophecies had foretold. It is true that all earthly empires did not totter before Him and collapse in swift disaster. But here we must remember that there is a variety of pictures of the messianic age in the Old Testament, and that in the thought of our Lord these were brought together for their mutual

[1] Cf. *The Messiah Idea in Jewish History*, 1943, p. 276.
[2] *Ibid.*, p. 278.
[3] *Ibid.*, p. 273.

modification, and it was in that mutually modified form, based on the amalgam of Old Testament hopes, that the Church claimed that in Him they found their fulfilment. Wheeler Robinson observes that "He seems to have had little use for the 'Davidic' form",[1] and while this is true to a point, it is of importance to note that the characteristic title by which He was known from the foundation of the Church is that which became especially attached to the hope of the Davidic Leader—Messiah, or Christ.[2] In the Gospels He is stated to have claimed the title at His trial,[3] and while He discouraged its use amongst His followers the reply to Peter's confession at Caesarea Philippi involves its acceptance.[4] The Early Church can only have thought of Him as the Davidic Messiah in a modified sense, and the Gospels indicate how reluctantly the disciples came to accept any modification. It is therefore almost certain that the modification existed first in His thought, and that it was on this account that He discouraged the use of the term which was most closely associated with hopes He did not purpose to fulfil. The Servant Songs governed His conception of His kingdom, and so far as we know He was the first to bring the Servant concept and the Messiah concept into association for the modification of the whole thought of the Messiah's mission.[5] Some years ago it was argued with great improbability that the Suffering Servant passages had not seriously

---

[1] Cf. *Revelation and Redemption*, 1942, p. 198.
[2] For a valuable study of the Messiahship of Jesus, cf. W. Manson, *Jesus the Messiah*, 1943; and for a review of the theories on the Messianic consciousness of Jesus that have exercised scholars for the past hundred years, cf. E. Sjöberg, "Ville Jesus vara Messias?" in *Svensk Exegetisk Årsbok*, x, 1945, pp. 82-151.
[3] Cf. Mark 14 : 62, Matt. 26 : 64.
[4] Matt. 16 : 15ff., Mark 8 : 29f., Luke 9 : 20f.
[5] Cf. J. W. Bowman, *The Intention of Jesus*, 1945, p. 10: "Jesus and he alone was responsible for the fusion of the two prophetic concepts noted (i.e. Suffering Servant and Messiah)." Several writers have argued that before the ministry of Jesus these two concepts were already fused. Cf. C. C. Torrey, *Journal of Biblical Literature*, xlviii, 1929, p. 25: "These three conceptions (i.e. Davidic Messiah, Suffering Servant and Son of Man) had been combined, speculated upon, and fashioned into a many-sided doctrine, held and cherished by the Jewish people long before the beginning of the Common Era." Cf. W. Manson, *Jesus the Messiah*, 1943, pp. 98ff., 113ff., 171ff. Some have gone to the other extreme (see following note) and have denied that the bringing together of these conceptions took place until after the ministry of Christ.

influenced our Lord,[1] but if we are to argue on the basis of our records—and we have no other basis on which to offer valid argument—we must recognize that they profoundly influenced Him, and especially in the latter part of His ministry, after Caesarea Philippi. "Accepting the form" (of the messianic expectation), says Wheeler Robinson, "He transformed the content of Messianic belief, by interpreting His Messiahship in the light of the Suffering Servant of Isaiah 53."[2] The title which He preferred to assume was "Son of Man"[3] and the fact that He openly used this while He discouraged the use of "Messiah" sufficiently indicates that the two titles could not have been regarded as equivalent in His day.[4] Yet the Son of Man stands in Dan. 7 : 13 as

[1] Cf. C. T. Craig, "The Identification of Jesus with the Suffering Servant", *Journal of Religion*, xxiv, 1944, pp. 240-245. Cf. too, the reply of J. W. Bowman, *ibid.*, xxv, 1945, pp. 56-58. B. W. Bacon (*Journal of Biblical Literature*, xlviii, 1929, pp. 60ff.) holds that the Servant Christology is a post-resurrection creation, and therefore younger than the Son of Man Christology. Cf. F. J. Foakes Jackson and K. Lake, *The Beginnings of Christianity*, i, 1942 ed., pp. 383ff. Against this cf. J. Moffatt, *The Theology of the Gospels*, 1912, p. 149: "The suffering Servant conception was organic to the consciousness of Jesus"; A. M. Ramsey, *The Gospel and the Catholic Chnrch*, 1936, p. 17; V. Taylor, *Jesus and His Sacrifice*, 1943 ed., pp. 39-48. C. R. North, *The Suffering Servant in Deutero-Isaiah*, 1948, pp. 24f.

[2] Cf. *Revelation and Redemption*, 1942, p. 198.

[3] S. J. Case ("The Alleged Messianic Consciousness of Jesus", in *Journal of Biblical Literature*, xliv, 1927, pp. 1-19) doubts whether Jesus ever used the title "Son of Man" either of Himself or in the third person, and thinks "it was far easier for Christians in the latter half of the first century to designate Jesus 'Son of Man' than it would have been for him in his own lifetime so to style himself" (p. 17). But this takes no account of the fact that we have no evidence whatever of Christians using this term to designate Him in the latter half of that century. Outside the Gospels it is used only once on the lips of Stephen (Acts 7 : 56), and within the Gospels it is not put into the mouth of the disciples, as it ought to have been if the alleged later usage were being read back into an earlier age.

[4] W. D. Davies (*Paul and Rabbinic Judaism*, 1948, p. 279) holds that "already before the Christian era the ideas of the Messiah and of the Son of Man had been merged, although it would be incorrect to think of this merging as a precise identification". As he holds that I go too far in denying that before the time of Christ there was any equation of the term Son of Man with the Messiah in the technical sense of the term (*ibid*), I am at a loss to understand his position. Apparently the equation of the terms is affirmed, though not the precise identification of the figures they denote. But if the terms were in any sense equated before the time of Christ it would seem to make nonsense of our Lord's use of the one, and injunctions to His disciples to see that they did not mention the other. It would also reduce Peter's confession at Caesarea Philippi to a mere glimpse of the obvious, if our Lord had already frequently used of Himself a term which was recognized to be equated with the one which Peter used. Nor are we in better case if we deny the authenticity of our Lord's use of the term Son of Man of himself prior to Caesarea Philippi, or of his injunction not to tell anyone that He was the Messiah. For that would merely mean that

the symbol for the coming kingdom, and was associated in some way in the minds of His hearers with that kingdom. It seems to me probable that there was a measure of fluidity in the significance of the term,[1] just as we have seen that there was in the term Servant of Yahweh in Deutero-Isaiah, so that it could stand as a symbol for the Kingdom or as a term for the representative of the kingdom.[2] T. W. Manson has stressed the collective use of the term in the Gospels,[3] and it seems to me undeniable that there is such use.[4] In its personal use we find that here again the concept of the Suffering Servant modifies our Lord's thought, and He expresses the mission of the Son of Man in terms of the suffering of the Servant.[5] Further, it is probable that the prophecy of

the Evangelists or the Early Church were unaware of the equation, despite its long establishment. I still prefer to adhere to the view that while the concepts of the Messiah and the Son of Man were related in that both had to do with the coming kingdom, they were different concepts, and that the Son of Man began as a term for the corporate body of the saints as invested with power but was later individualized, and in the Gospels has still a fluidity of use that enables it to stand now for one and now for the other. P. Parker ("The Meaning of 'Son of Man'", in *Journal of Biblical Literature*, lx, 1941, pp. 151–157) goes to the other extreme and holds that on the lips of Jesus the term Son of Man was never related to an apocalyptic or messianic meaning, and in the Gospels has such a meaning only in three unauthentic passages.

[1] Cf. S. A. Cook, *Introduction to the Bible*, 1945, p. 118.
[2] Cf. S. Hanson, *The Unity of the Church in the New Testament*, 1946, p. 11: "The same pertains to Ebed JHWH and the Son of Man, viz. that they are corporate personalities having individual traits." Hanson also finds this same feature in the figure of the Messiah. Cf. what I have written in *The Relevance of Apocalyptic*, 2nd ed.,1947, pp. 32f., and A. Bentzen, *Messias, Moses redivivus, Menschensohn*, 1948. Cf. too, Á.V. Ström,*Vetekornet*, 1944, p. 433: "Here we are above all interested in the corporate identity of individual and group, being represented by the Servant, Isa. 53 . . . and the Son of Man in Daniel, 1 Enoch and 4 Esra" (I have not had access to the Swedish text of this work, but only—by the author's kindness—to the English summary). See also M. Black, "The 'Son of Man' in the Old Biblical Literature", in *Expository Times*, lx, 1948-49, pp. 11-15.
[3] Cf. *The Teaching of Jesus*, 2nd ed., 1935, pp. 227f. Also "Mark 2 : 27f." in *Coniectanea Neotestamentica XI in honorem Antonii Fridrichsen sexagenarii*, 1948, pp. 138–146. Cf. too, J. R. Coates, *The Coming of the Church*, 1929, pp. 30–37; C. J. Cadoux, *The Historic Mission of Jesus*, 1941, p. 100; W. E. Wilson, "The Coming of the Son of Man", in *The Modern Churchman*, xxxvi, 1946, pp. 56-66.
[4] Cf. what I have written in *The Relevance of Apocalyptic*, 2nd ed., 1947, pp. 120ff.
[5] Mark 10 : 45, Matt. 20 : 28. On the bringing together of the figures of the Suffering Servant, and the Son of Man cf. R. Otto, *The Kingdom of God and the Son of Man*, English Tr., Revised ed., 1943, pp. 249ff. A. Loisy (*L'Évangile selon Marc*, 1912, pp. 309ff.) supposes that Mark 10 : 45 reflects the influence of Paul, and observes that "the idea of the life given as a ransom belongs to a different stream of thought from that of service". One would have supposed that the idea of service could be found without difficulty in the Servant of Yahweh, who also gave his life for others (cf. Isa. 53 : 5f., 10f.), and there is no reason to suppose that the Fourth Servant Song could not influence our Lord.

the New Covenant exercised an important influence on His thought.

The bringing of all these elements together meant that he conceived of the kingdom as established by suffering rather than by physical power, and its citizens as won to individual adhesion rather than as gathered by the annexation of states. Nor was this wholly alien to the thought of many of the other Old Testament passages. The passage duplicated in Isaiah and Micah promised universal peace only when all nations voluntarily go up to the house of the Lord and learn His law. The essence of the Golden Age is thus found to lie in a spiritual change in men rather than in a new political régime. It is therefore not surprising that our Lord only inaugurated the foundation of the kingdom, rather than its full consummation. A spiritual change in men is something that by its nature cannot be effected in a moment. Hence the Church placed the full consummation in the future. Yet its thought is not on that account to be likened to that of Judaism, which, in so far as it still cherishes the hope of these Old Testament prophecies, places their whole fulfilment in the future. For the Church the fulfilment has begun, is now continuing, and will one day be complete.

Nor should we forget that our Lord's thought of His mission in terms of the Suffering Servant can claim a very real objective and historical vindication. That the great fourth Servant Song profoundly influenced His thought seems to me undeniable, and it can provide the materials of His expectation that suffering was to be the organ of His service. In that Song the Servant is depicted as suffering death for no wrong that he had wrought, a death that is described as a sin-offering for others, whose sins he bore. By that death he brings acquittal to men of other nations, and not alone of Israel, but to men who acknowledge before his stricken figure that he suffered for them, and at the hand of their sin. This thought became not an ideal but a reality in the case of Jesus, and it has been a reality in the case of no other person of history. Jeremiah and Jehoiachin and Zerubbabel and all the others who have been put forward as the originals of the portrait completely failed to justify its hope.

None of these so impressed men of all nations that by their sufferings they fulfilled the mission of Israel. But Jesus did suffer death for no crime that justified death, and His death did become the organ of redemption to countless millions of men of all generations from His day to ours. This is not merely a matter of Christian faith; this is a matter of objective experience. It does not matter by what theory the Cross is interpreted. The fact is indisputable that before His Cross millions have experienced an inner revolution in their hearts, and their consciousness of an inner change has been confirmed by the witness of others, who have seen a manifest change in all the quality of their life. That they have become new men and new women is undeniable, and the newness is visible to those who have not shared its experience. It is as objective a change as anything we can meet in our experience of others. And that it is a change connected somehow with the Cross of Christ is as little to be denied.

Here, it is to be observed, we have something of the same pattern as the deliverance of Israel in the time of Moses. Moses came in the name of God promising deliverance, and the event responded both to his word and to Israel's need. To describe the natural conditions that effected that deliverance as fortuitous leaves out of account the prior assurance of Moses that deliverance was sure, though no material power to deliver was in his hand. His confidence could not of itself control Nature and thus effect deliverance; nor could a fortuitous wind explain his prior confidence.[1] It is the same here. To suppose that it is but a hallucination which connects the change in men with the Cross of Christ simply will not do. In the first place a hallucination that has been shared by countless millions of people in many lands and in many ages would have as good a claim to be treated as objective as most of the phenomena which scientists investigate. It has been experienced by ordinary men and women, under ordinary circumstances, under no conditions of secrecy and in the fullest light of day. Moreover, it would be a hallucination that has proved so profoundly beneficial to men that all

[1] Cf. what I have written in *The Rediscovery of the Old Testament*, pp. 61ff. (American ed., pp. 85ff.).

who care for the well-being of men ought to welcome it unashamedly. But in the second place, we should still have to reckon with the fact that Jesus believed His death would be mightily effective, and that it has in fact proved to be infinitely more effective than any other death of history. His faith has been vindicated in objective historical fact. The subsequently experienced power of the Cross could not explain our Lord's confidence that it would have the power which the death of the Servant in the fourth Servant Song was depicted as having; on the other hand, if His confidence was empty and insubstantial, then it could not give such power to his death. Here, then, is a very important objective justification of the faith of the Church.

Nor is this all. The Old Testament pattern is followed in many other respects.[1] In the days of Moses God first delivered Israel and then Israel responded in gratitude by committing herself in the Covenant in willing faith and obedience unto God. And here the grace of God is first manifested in Christ, and supremely in His death, which calls forth the response in faith and obedience from those who are saved. The New Covenant is no more conditional than the Old. It is the unconditional pledge of loyalty, in response to the grace

[1] I need scarcely say that I am not here reverting to the allegorical method once so popular. By that method meanings were brought to Scripture which could by no conceivable device be found there. The connexion between text and interpretation was wholly external, and reflected only the ingenuity and the piety of the interpreter. By this method, e.g. the Shulammite's navel in Cant. 7 : 2 (Heb. 3) could be interpreted of the Great Sanhedrin by Ibn Ezra (cf. H. J. Matthews, *Abraham ibn Ezra's Commentary on the Canticles after the First Recension*, 1874, Hebrew part, p. 21), of the baptismal font by Symon Patrick (cf. *The Books of Job . . . and the Song of Songs paraphras'd*, 1727, ed., p. 532 a), and of the cup from which the Church revives men by Hengstenberg (cf. *Das Hohelied Salomonis ausgelegt*, 1853, p. 186). What I am here referring to is the pattern of salvation reflected in the Old Testament revelation of God. If He is to be seen in His works on the plane of history, and if His character is One, it is to be expected that that unity will appear through all the diversity of the events whereby He reveals Himself. I am not claiming that the Old Testament events were a prefiguring of New Testament events or teaching but that they were a revelation of God, and that the same God revealed Himself in the New Testament events, and that the revelation in the latter case was not unrelated to the revelation in the former. It is perhaps necessary for me to make this clear since one of my reviewers suggested that in an earlier work I was opening the door to allegory, when my argument was poles asunder from allegory. What I have called the pattern in the Old Testament is not something I have brought to it from the New, but something which is plainly there in the texture of the story.

manifest in the already achieved salvation. On the other hand, it is just as conditional as the old, in that the continuance of its blessings can no longer be claimed when its pledge is broken. The Church is therefore the heir of Israel in the very nature of its establishment.

Moreover, the Church not alone claimed to be the heir of Israel's election; she accepted the obligation of Israel's mission. It was not that she claimed to replace Israel in the seat of privilege, but that she acknowledged her call to take up the service to which Israel had been called. And again it is an undeniable, objective fact that in notable ways the Church has performed that service to a degree vastly greater than Judaism has ever even attempted to carry it through. To say this is not to undervalue all that the world owes to Judaism, and I would not for one moment forget it. If the Church claims to have received a great heritage from Judaism, there is every call to her to honour that Judaism which preserved its heritage and passed it on to her. Yet it seems to me still a simple and undeniable fact that the Church did accept the mission of Israel, and did address itself to it in a way and to a degree that Judaism has never done—though I would add that I am far from suggesting that the Church has done anything like all that she might have done. Her fulfilment of her mission is still partial, and her only ground for glory is in what Christ has done for her and not in what she has done for Him.

Israel's election was to service. And the first element of that service was to receive and cherish the revelation of God given in history and in experience, and especially the revelation mediated to her in the persons of the great prophetic figures of her story from Moses on. That revelation was embodied, in so far as the revelation of a personal God can be embodied in anything that is not itself fully personal, in the Scriptures of the Old Testament. And the Church received her first Bible from Judaism. She did not, of course, rob Judaism of it, but it continued to be the Bible of Judaism while it became the Bible—and later part of the Bible—of the Church. To the revelation of God there embodied there was added the revelation of God in Christ, which was also given in the life of Israel, and was passed from Israel to the Church. This part of her heritage Judaism did not herself cherish. Nevertheless we must remember that it was received by the Church from Judaism, though not shared with Judaism. "Thus we have the phenomenon of a Jewish ideal", says J. H. Greenstone, "developed on Jewish soil, which has influenced Jewish life and habit, and has been influenced by them, giving birth to a creed which, becoming later antagonistic to its parent, assumes an entirely separate existence."[1] That Judaism has cared so little for One who, on the lowest count, is the greatest of her sons, and the One who has most powerfully influenced the world, is a singular fact. For the revelation of God given in the New Testament was given to Israel. If, then, the first element of the service of the elect was to receive and cherish the revelation of God given to Israel, then the Church performed it more fully than did Judaism.

The second main element noted in the preceding chapters was to reflect the will and character of God in life. In receiving the Jewish Scriptures the Church accepted the high standards of ethical conduct laid down in the Old Testament. "It cannot be emphasized too strongly", says W. F. Albright, "that the true greatness of Jesus's ministry does not lie in His ethical teachings. The ethics of Jesus agree strikingly, if compared in detail, with contemporary Jewish ethical teaching."[2] In the new revelation of the character of God in Christ there were new demands which not all Christians have ever accepted, any more than all Christians or all Jews have ever conformed to the full heights of the ethical demands of the Old Testament. Both Judaism and Christianity have accepted the highest ethical demands of the Old Testament as binding on all their adherents, and in so far as they have not been accepted in practice, men have been false to the religion they have professed.

But the reflection of God's character is not merely a matter of ethics; it is still more a matter of religion. To walk humbly with God is essential to the doing of justice and the loving of

[1] Cf. *The Messiah Idea in Jewish History*, 1943, p. 79.
[2] Cf. *From the Stone Age to Christianity*, 2nd ed., 1946, p. 302.

mercy,[1] and walking humbly with God involves fellowship with Him and worship of Him. Here it may be said that the Church did not accept the inheritance of Judaism. The Church entered into the heritage of the Synagogue, and modelled its form of worship largely on that of the Synagogue, though we should not forget the element of Temple inspiration which has found a place in the ritual of some branches of the Church. But all the animal sacrifices of the Temple were abolished for the Church. Yet the worship of the Synagogue is nowhere prescribed in the Old Testament, whereas the offering of sacrifices is prescribed. Here, then, it would seem that the Church repudiated a part of the inheritance of election.

Judaism too has ceased to offer animal sacrifices. Yet there is little in common between her ceasing to do so and that of the Church. Judaism ceased to offer sacrifices when the Temple was destroyed, and when it was no longer possible for her to offer them on the one legitimate altar which she recognized. It was by sheer force of circumstances, and not because for her sacrifices were abrogated, that she ceased to offer them. For her the law of sacrifice remained the law of God; yet she was unable to continue the service which God still demanded of her in an unabrogated law.

For the Church, on the other hand, animal sacrifices had ceased to have meaning because for her the law of sacrifice was abrogated in the sacrifice of Christ. For her God was not so self-stultifying as to continue to demand what men could not perform. For her the New Testament was a part of her Bible, and not force of circumstances but the revealed will of God had abrogated sacrifice. It was abrogated because its meaning was taken up into the sacrifice of Christ, which thus in a real way "fulfilled" the law of sacrifice for the Christian Church. Here, therefore, while Judaism was compelled involuntarily to abandon this element of her service, the Church had already transmuted it, and voluntarily abandoned it in its old form to perpetuate its significance in the new form. And the new form was not something thought up for the purpose. It was, as has been said above, rooted in

[1] Mic. 6 : 8.

the concrete historical fact of the Cross, and in the experienced power of that Cross. It was of the very essence of the new element of her heritage which Judaism refused to share.

The third main element of the service to which Israel was called was to mediate to all men the law of her God, and to spread the heritage of her faith through all the world. While Judaism had welcomed proselytes, and some Jews must have sought them, Judaism was never a strongly missionary faith in the sense of undertaking a campaign to win the world. Even Pharisaism, which was the noblest flower of Judaism, despite the condemnation in the New Testament of some of its Palestinian representatives in the time of our Lord, is said by W. F. Albright to have been unsuited to become the vehicle of a great and world-wide evangelistic movement.[1] For in Pharisaism the element of particularism, which had done great service in preserving Judaism from the perils that might easily have otherwise engulfed it, was too firmly established to be sacrificed when it had served its usefulness and was no longer necessary to cramp the mission to the world that had been entrusted to Judaism.[2] "The error of Israel", says Y. Raguin, "is to have wished to retain Yahweh as a definitive possession, when He was only given to her to be revealed to all."[3] Here again, however, the Church accepted the mission of Israel in a way that the Synagogue never did. A Jewish writer has observed that "whereas the Pharisaic champions of Judaism were content with a single proselyte as a representative of the convertible pagans, the conversion of the heathen to the true faith became the central point of the New Testament".[4] From the start the faith of the Church

[1] Cf. *op. cit.*, p. 301.
[2] Cf. what I have written in *Israel's Mission to the World*, 1939, pp. 50ff., 73ff.
[3] Cf. *Théologie missionnaire de l'Ancien Testament*, 1947, p. 48. Cf. B. J. Bamberger, *Proselytism in the Talmudic Period*, 1939, p. 3: "Whereas Christianity and Islam were from the start universal and world-conquering faiths, in which missionary work was a central and essential element, Judaism began as a national faith, which even after it had been universalized by prophetic teaching never lost its particularistic color." Cf. H. G. May, *Journal of Bible and Religion*, xvi, 1948, p. 105b: "Old Testament religion even at its best found it difficult to escape completely from nationalism."
[4] Cf. A. Jellinek, *Beth Ha-Midrasch*, 2nd ed., v. 1936, p. xlvii. Cf. H. F. Hamilton, *The People of God*, ii, 1912, p. 13: "The universalism of Christianity consisted in raising these uncircumcised Gentile believers to that highest level of privilege"—I would add, and responsibility—"which the Jewish propaganda

was an essentially missionary faith,[1] and while the strength of its missionary zeal has varied greatly from age to age, when it has been truest to its genius it has been most missionary. "As Israel of old was chosen to keep alive in the hearts of men the hope of a coming saviour of the world, so the Church is chosen to bear abroad into all the world the gospel of a universal redemption, forbidden to leave out one single soul from the vast circle of her intercessions", says J. O. F. Murray.[2] It is undeniable that the Church has been the means of winning vast numbers of men from almost every race of men to worship the God of Israel and to enter into the inheritance of her religion. Through the Church Gentiles from every corner under heaven have been brought in spirit to Zion, and have learned the law of God. The Jewish Bible has been translated into innumerable languages and has become the cherished Scripture of multitudes who would never even have heard of it through Jews alone. These are objective facts. It is not merely that the Church believed she was commissioned to take over the task of Israel. She did in fact take it over from an Israel that was less willing to undertake it; and she has indisputably fulfilled that task in a great, though still insufficient, measure.

If, therefore, Israel's faith in her election was not just the reflection of her self-esteem, neither is the Church's faith in hers to be traced to such a cause. In both cases there lay behind it a combination of subjective and objective factors, and in both cases the election was election to service. All complacency in her election in Israel was sternly rebuked by the prophets; and in the Church complacency is no more tolerable. Indeed, any such complacency betokens the forfeiture of her election. The Church that is truly conscious

---

denied to them. . . . The dispute" (i.e. between the Synagogue and the Church) "arose because the universalism of Christianity went far beyond that of the Jewish propaganda." Cf. also C. H. Dodd, *The Bible Today*, 1946, p. 119: "Its effect is to universalize the meaning of the revelation which was given to particular people at particular times."

[1] Cf. R. Liechtenhan, *Die urchristliche Mission*, 1946, where it is maintained that the mission to the world undertaken by the Early Church was rooted in the nature of the Gospel as it was conceived by our Lord, and that it was carried out by a Church which responded to the constraint of its Lord.

[2] Cf. Hastings' *Dictionary of the Bible*, i, 1898, p. 681 b.

of her election is in earnest with her mission to reveal the will of God and to claim for Him men of every race. The sense of her high privilege is matched by the sense of her responsibility. And when she fails to live up to her responsibility she repudiates her election, just as Israel did. In a passage to which reference has already been made, Paul warned the Romans not to glory over the branches which had been plucked from the tree of election, but to realize that if God had not spared those branches, neither would He spare the newly grafted ones, if they ceased to manifest true faithfulness unto Him.[1] And loyalty to God always involves the discharge of the task which is the corollary of election.

It cannot be too strongly emphasized that if the Church is the heir of the election of Israel it is also the heir of the warnings that her heritage is cast away if she is not loyal to the purpose of that election. Her election is conditional on her desiring to retain it, and that can only be tested by her desire to fulfil its obligations. In the closing book of the New Testament we read of the Church at Loadicea, which is threatened with being spewed out of its Lord's mouth because of its unfaithfulness to its responsibilities.[2] A holy zeal in cherishing the revelation of God given to Israel and in Christ, an eagerness to reflect the character and will of God in every aspect of its life, both corporate and individual, and a passionate devotion to the task of winning the world, are the essential marks of the loyal Church, and the Church that has not these marks is the Church that thereby declares that she does not value her election. Indeed, we should rather say that it is in the measure of her possession of these marks that she is true to her election. Any lukewarmness is intolerable, since a lukewarm response to the amazing grace of God betokens either blindness to that grace or contempt for it. And since there is no limit to the fullness of the possession of these marks, no Church can rest content. And in particular no Church that perceives that Israel's supreme error was in failing to recognize the goal of her hopes and in failing to fulfil the world mission for which she believed she

[1] Rom. 11 : 18–22.
[2] Rev. 3 : 16.

was destined can be other than in earnest with her missionary work without standing self-condemned.

Along two lines, indeed, we are brought to this challenge. It is characteristic of the thought of the New Testament to speak of the Jewish Remnant and those Gentiles who came to share their faith, who together comprised the Church, as being "in Christ". The Church was to be an extension of the personality of Christ, infused with His spirit and the organ of His activity in the world.[1] For when the Church is in Christ, and Christ in the Church, then it is lifted into His purpose and becomes the instrument of His service. "The Son of Man is come to seek and to save that which was lost."[2] "The Son of Man came not to be ministered unto but to minister, and to give his life a ransom for many."[3] If a redemptive purpose, and a universally redemptive purpose, possessed His heart, then it must possess the heart of the Church that is "in Christ". And if that purpose so possessed His heart that He did not withhold from it His very life, it must possess the heart of the Church that is "in Christ" to the utmost degree. A Church that spends more on its pleasures than on the evangelization of the world cannot be "in Christ" who gave Himself for the redemption of that world. Election lays a terrifying responsibility on the elect.

Along a second line we are brought to the same point. In the concept of the Suffering Servant we found a fluidity that began with the thought of the mission of the whole of Israel,

---

[1] Cf. W. D. Davies, *Paul and Rabbinic Judaism*, 1948, p. 201: "The solidarity of all Christians with one another and with their Lord, through the one Spirit, is such that Christians as a Body no less than as individuals constitute a temple of the Holy Spirit." E. Percy, in a valuable study (*Das Leib Christi in den Paulinischen Homologumena und Antilegomena*, 1942) stresses the New Testament conception of the Church as the Body of Christ, rightly maintaining that it is not merely an aggregation of individuals who are "in Christ", but that the community is the Body of Christ. It is also true, as I have said in reviewing this book, that "we have an individual and direct, as well as a corporate and Church-mediated, relation with Christ" (*Expository Times*, lviii, 1946–47, p. 221). It is important, however, to recognize, in contrast to the extreme individualism of an earlier day, this other side of the teaching of the New Testament. Cf. too, for a good statement of this side of its teaching, E. Schweizer, *Das Leben des Herrn in der Gemeinde und ihren Diensten*, 1946. See also Å. V. Ström, *Vetekornet*, 1944, p. 434 (I have not had access to the Swedish text referred to on this page of the English summary).
[2] Luke 19 : 10.
[3] Mark 10 : 45.

but which rose to the thought of one who should supremely represent the nation and who should carry out its mission to a degree no other should attain, who should be himself the true Israel. Yet having found in Christ the fulfilment of this hope, the supreme Servant of the Lord, we should not forget that element of fluidity. If He is the Servant, so too is it of the essence of the mission of the whole of Israel to be the Servant.[1] And if the Church is the Israel of God, then is the Church called to enter into the task of the Suffering Servant.[2] That it cannot enter into that task in the measure of Christ is no reason why it should not enter into it to the utmost degree possible. And the task of the Servant was to suffer. The Church is therefore called to enter into the sufferings of the Cross in some measure, and to agonize for the world's redemption. This is something more than giving a measure of its interest, or even a measure of its wealth. It is to take the burden of the world's need on its own heart in a profound and passionate eagerness to serve and to save.

The Biblical doctrine of election is therefore penetrated through and through with warning. To be the elect of God is not to be His pampered favourite. It is to be challenged to a loyalty and a service and a sacrifice that knows no limits, and to feel the constraint of the Divine love to such a degree that no response can seem adequate and no service worthy. The constraint is not of our choosing. It is laid upon us. We can resist it, but if we do so resist it we act disgracefully. For we have received of the grace of God, and its obligation already lies upon us.

Nor is this obligation one which lies merely upon the Church. It might seem at first sight that this is patently wrong. In the teaching of the New Testament the Church is the elect, and the Church consists of those who have yielded

---

[1] In writing of the Servant of Yahweh in Deutero-Isaiah, H. de Lubac says: "Sometimes it is clear that an individual is intended, and sometimes it is the people itself that seems quite certainly designated. Perhaps it is well that a certain ambiguity remains, perhaps this very ambiguity has a profound significance: how should the prophetic spirit have separated Christ from his Church?" (*Le fondement théologique des missions*, 1946, pp. 23f.).

[2] Cf. W. Robinson, *Whither Theology?* 1947, pp. 58f.: "What we have to understand is that Jesus, at the moment of His death, was not only the Messiah, the Son of God, but the true Israel of God gathered into one Man . . . And after His death and resurrection we see the 'New Israel' re-formed in Him."

themselves to the power of Christ, and to His obedience. Those who are not of the Church owe Christ no service, and He has no claim on them. Yet if we look back to the Old Testament teaching we find that which leads us farther than this. The election of Israel passed only to the generations and the individuals that were loyal to the Covenant, though through the Remnant it might be transmitted to generations yet to be. But it was not that each generation and each individual was free to decide whether they wished to stand within the Covenant and within the election or not. Each generation and each individual had received a rich inheritance from the past mercies of God to the fathers of which they could not wholly divest themselves or be robbed even by God, and they heaped shame and curse upon themselves when they did not recognize the constraint of their heritage. In the same way every generation of children born within the Church and nurtured in its fellowship has received a heritage that demands a response in obedience. Indeed, every generation of children born in such a country as ours, whether born within the fellowship of the Church or not, is in debt to Christ. All have received of the inheritance of the election. For we are not merely individuals who begin each one a new and independent course of life, and who at some time are confronted with the free choice of the commitment of our loyalties, but members of a corporate society into whose life the stream of the past and the present has come, and who enter into a vast heritage for which we have not laboured, upon whom great obligations lie by the very fact of our being, and not through our own choice; and amongst these obligations is the sacred duty to respond to the grace of God which has so richly blessed us, and in such countless ways. The Biblical doctrine of election is therefore of great practical moment to the Christian preacher, charging him not merely to appeal to men to yield to the grace of Christ and so to experience His redemption, but also to establish God's claim on men by what He has wrought for them, whether they respond or not, and summoning them from the dishonour of withholding their response to His grace; charging him, too, to warn those who have responded in the Covenant of loyalty that the demands of the Covenant are exacting and continuous, and that the continuance of the high privilege of their election depends on the yielding of that continued loyalty.

Finally, something must be said of the election of individuals in the New Testament. The Church is elect because it is the company of the elect. Some are elect for special service. Thus our Lord chose twelve disciples to be with Him and called them to be His intimate associates.[1] But again they were chosen for service rather than for privilege. They were sent forth in pairs to be the heralds of the kingdom,[2] and they were the repositories of teaching that could not be appreciated by more miscellaneous audiences.[3] Later seventy were chosen to be sent forth in the Master's name and service.[4] Barnabas and Saul were chosen for the special work to which they were appointed.[5] But beyond this, every one who belonged to the fellowship of the Christian Church was thought of as elect. They were not men and women who chose to be Christians, or who of their own initiative decided to attach themselves to the Church, but men and women on whom the constraint of God had been laid, who were chosen in Christ and redeemed by Him, and who in individual loyalty had responded to that grace and pledged themselves without reserve to the obedience of their Lord. They were not picked out for privilege from the mass of men in whom God had no interest. They were chosen and called for service. It was realized that the grace of God became effective for them when they yielded to that grace, and that it can only become effective for those who do so yield.

In this there is nothing arbitrary, but rather something inevitable. For what is the nature of salvation? It is not something concrete and external that can be conferred on men. It is the recreation of personality, and the union of personality with God in Christ. The Christian is not simply one who yields allegiance to Christ. He is a new creature in Christ. The death of Christ became the organ of his death

---

[1] Mark 3 : 13f.; Luke 6 : 12f.
[2] Mark 6 : 7; Matt. 10 : 1, 5; Luke 9 : 1f.
[3] Matt. 13 : 11; Mark 8 : 31; Matt. 16 : 21; Luke 9 : 21f.
[4] Luke 10 : 1.
[5] Acts 13 : 2.

to the old self,[1] and of his rebirth to a new self that was infused with the presence and power of Christ.[2] In a profound way he entered into the experience of the death and resurrection of Christ,[3] so that His death became the organ of the soul's approach to God and of God's approach in grace to him, so that he rose with Christ to a newness of life whose fundamental quality was just that it was a sharing of His life.[4] Henceforth Christ lived in the Christian, who now lived out the purposes of his Lord, and reflected in himself something of the glory of Christ.[5] His life is said to be hid with Christ in God,[6] and he is said to be indwelt by the spirit of Christ, or by the Spirit of God.[7]

All of this might seem to savour of mere mysticism, and to be identical with what can be found in so many religions. Yet while there is a mystical element in it, it is to be differentiated from ordinary mysticism. Paul says: "I have been crucified with Christ; nevertheless I live: yet not I, but Christ liveth in me. And the life which I now live in the flesh I live by the faith of the Son of God, who loved me and gave himself for me."[8] Here we observe that the experience is rooted and grounded in a historical fact—in the fact of the Cross of Christ and in the power of God mediated through that historical event.[9] It begins with the Cross of

---

[1] Rom. 6 : 4-6.   [2] Rom. 6 : 8-11.   [3] Gal. 2 : 20; Phil. 3 : 10; Rom. 8 : 17.
[4] 2 Cor. 5 : 17; Rom. 6 : 4; Col. 3 : 10.   [5] 2 Cor. 3 : 18.   [6] Col. 3 : 3.
[7] Rom. 8 : 9-11; Eph. 2 : 22; 1 Cor. 3 : 16.   [8] Gal. 2 : 20.
[9] G. Widengren (*The Great Vohu Manah and the Apostle of God*, 1945, p. 72) says: "We have been able to ascertain in the Avesta the existence of an ancient doctrine, according to which man has a part of a cosmic Mind, *Vohu Manah*, within him, his own individual *manah* being fundamentally identical with the universal principle, which is a collective body, constituted by all the existent *manah*-s of all human beings, dead and living.... Vohu Manah as a person besides his collective body acts as a saviour towards the members of this body, namely the single *manah*-s." Å. V. Ström rightly notes the difference between this and the New Testament teaching in the historical foundation of the latter. He says: "In Semitic thought (e.g. in the Old Testament) we find a collectivistic view of all human relationship, above all verified in the corporate conception of the relation between prince and people. In Iranian and Gnostic religion, as well as in post-exilic Judaism, there is developed a corporate cosmology and soteriology of mythic structure. In the New Testament and in early Christianity we meet with an identification of the risen Lord and his Church, this identification being on the one hand a connection of concrete-human Jewish and mythic-cosmic Iranian collectivism, but on another hand something entirely new and unique, because the Saviour is a historic person" (*Vetekornet*, 1944, p. 435—I have only had access to a reprint of the English abstract of this work).

Christ, and to it it returns, and the experience of union with Him springs out of response to the amazing love there revealed. In the fourth Gospel we find the same thought. There Christ says: "I am the Vine, ye are the branches; he that abideth in me and I in him, the same beareth much fruit . . Ye did not choose me, but I chose you, and appointed you, that ye should go and bear fruit."[1] The union with Christ here again arises out of the electing love of God in Christ, and its purpose is not mere rapture, but fruitfulness.

None of this can have any meaning so long as a man closes the citadel of his heart against God. His opening of his heart is the necessary condition of his salvation, though not the organ of his salvation. When he does so open it he feels the constraint of the Divine grace so overwhelmingly that nothing else seems possible for him. Yet that is by the paradox of experience, to which attention has been already drawn. God does not really compel any to accept His grace, because a compelled loyalty is no real loyalty, and only when grace finds its response in loyalty is the Covenant complete. The initiative in redemption is ever with God, and that is why every redeemed man is conscious that if he chooses God, it is because God has first chosen him; if he loves God, it is because He has first loved, and all human love of Him is but the response to that love.

Too often men think of salvation as a gift of satisfaction which God hands out to men, and it is therefore supposed to be a mark of favouritism that He should give it so some and not to others. Every selfish instinct leads men to suppose that those who are not among the elect are missing something which they fain would have. It would be hard to diverge farther from the truth. Selfishness can have no place in election, for its very essence implies the antithesis of selfishness. Its end is not an eternity of easeful bliss, but a life of service, and it lifts all who respond to it in loyalty into the purpose that governs the election of the whole Church. They are individually called, therefore, to receive and to cherish the revelation of God's grace and character, to reflect His will and nature in their individual lives, and to take some

[1] John 15 : 5, 16.

share in the task of making Him known to all men and claiming all men's loyalty for Him. In so far as they repudiate any or all of these elements of the purpose of their election they repudiate the election itself, and men who in their hearts repudiate their election can scarcely lay upon God any charge of injustice in that they are not elect.

What God gives to the elect is Himself, and men who want His gift but not His presence want a contradiction in terms. The supreme blessing of God is the gift of His Spirit, and He cannot dwell in the hearts of men who at the same time wish to be far from Him. But when the Spirit of God does possess a man, then the purpose of God becomes operative in him, and he is lifted to share the love of God. He begins to agonize for the world's redemption with something of the agony of God's heart as revealed in the Cross of Christ. He is not content to cherish the thought of the universal kingdom of God as a distant dream. He recognizes that this is the age of the kingdom, established by Christ and spreading through all the world, and destined to spread yet more widely as the Church gives itself individually and collectively more completely to its service.[1]

Once more, therefore, no room can be found for complacency in the elect.[2] Throughout the Bible in both Testaments the doctrine of election, whether corporate or individual, does not beget any self-satisfaction. We find throughout the same emphasis on the fulfilment of the purpose of the election, if the election is not to be forfeited. For we have already noted that the message to one of the seven Churches of Asia was "I will spew thee out of my mouth"[3] owing to the very complacency that filled its heart. Just as the prophets in the moment of their consciousness of their election to their office felt a trembling humility and a burning sense of the

---

[1] Cf. E. Schweizer, *Das Leben des Herrn in der Gemeinde und ihren Diensten*, 1946, p. 90: "There are in the Church no idle members, as there are in the body no members without function."

[2] Cf. S. A. Cook, *Introduction to the Bible*, 1945, p. 132: "The story of the Election and Rejection of a Chosen People, as we read it in the Bible to-day, is one never to be read in a spirit of self-satisfaction and self-glorying, least of all in an age of trial and testing when one epoch of world-history is passing over into another."

[3] Rev. 3 : 15.

task to which they were called, so should all the elect who comprise the Church of Christ feel an ever renewed humility of spirit and wonder at the greatness of their privilege, together with a burning of heart at the greatness and urgency of the task to which they are elect. When the will of God no longer dominates the life, and the purpose of God no longer glows in the heart, when the abounding joy in God's fellowship in Christ is no longer experienced, then the New Covenant is rejected, and election is cast away because it no longer has any meaning. And when a Church turns in on itself and becomes a mutual improvement society, and regards itself as a little Ark of safety in a troubled world, instead of charged with a mission to the world, it turns its back on its election. The corollary of election is ever purposeful service, and its demand is for consecrated zeal. It carries in its heart a note of warning and of challenge, and it is fundamentally practical in its significance. This Biblical doctrine of election may be proclaimed without apology, and its proclamation is greatly to be desired to yield the foundation of a revived doctrine of the Church.

INDEXES

(a) SUBJECT

Aaron, 46n., 101
Abiathar, 101f.
Abraham, 19f., 23ff., 33ff., 43f., 65ff., 70, 93, 98, 135f., 140f., 144f.
Adonijah, 99, 101
Ahab, 71
Ahaz, 150
Ahijah, 97, 99f.
Allegorical interpretation, 151, 160n.
Amalekites, 97
Amos, 53, 56, 69n., 72, 74n., 75, 104f. 110, 122f.
Amraphel, 136
Animism, 28f.
Anthropomorphism, 52f.
Assyrians, 122ff.

Baal, 61, 71f., 130, 144
Baalism, 29
Baasha, 98
Babylonians, 126
baḥar, 48n., 63n.
Barak, 96
Barnabas, 126
berîth, 47n., 49n.

Caligula, 93n.
Canon, 85n.
Chaldaeans, 122, 125f.
Church, heir of election, 15, 139ff., 161; and missionary vocation, 92f.; and Remnant, 139ff.
Covenant, and election, 15n., 23, 33n., 34, 37f., 43, 45f., 68, 121; not a bargain, 46f.; breakable by Israel, 47; but not of right, 49; repudiation morally reprehensible, 51; obligation persists, 48f., 168f.; not immediately repudiated by God, 52, 99, 118; unconditional, 33n., 43, 46, 49f., 160; yet conditional, 49, 99, 129, 160f.; bilateral? 49; response of gratitude, 43, 48, 108, 160; to be renewed by each generation, 47f.; basis of, 67; renewal of, 76f.; New Covenant, 59, 76f., 142, 152f., 158, 160; and Remnant, 83f. (*see also* Remnant); implicit, 98
Cushan-rishathaim, 130
Cyrus, 81n.; and election 17, 135ff.
David, 98ff.; covenant with, 98f.; House of, 98ff.; Scion of, 99f., 114

Decalogue, 35, 37, 54ff.
Deutero-Isaiah, 21, 61ff., 78f., 81, 84, 86, 93, 111ff.
Deuteronomy, 129; Deuteronomist, 100
Diaspora, 89
Discipline the fruit of love, 53, 74

Election, neglect of doctrine, 15f.; election and grace, 18, 32, 33n., 35, 39, 48n., 49n., 52f., 57; and pride of race, 15f., 18f., 37f., 66, 71, 93f., 165; in Abraham, 19f., 21ff., 34f., 43; through Moses, 19, 30ff., 35, 37f., 43; of Israel in weakness, 18, 35, 42; not arbitrary, 32f., 34, 38f., 41n., 59n., 107, 117f., 121f.; not automatic, 33f., 47, 71, 99; not for worth, 34, 38; for purpose, 35, 38, 41, 44, 62, 68, 70, 75, 78, 88, 100, 111; to treasure revelation, 53, 118, 161; to obey God's will, 45, 48n., 53; to reflect God's character, 58f., 118, 162f.; to serve world, 60, 62ff., 66n., 67, 78f., 118, 164f.; grounds of faith in, 37ff.; for service, 41, 43, 45, 51f., 53f., 59, 95, 102, 108f., 115ff., 137, 161f.; election and revelation, 42, 48, 53; election of other nations, 39, 40n., 122ff., 138; carries privilege, 45, 121, 166, 172f.; yet not always, 137f.; carries obligation, 45f., 69, 121, 166; terminable by Israel, 47, 49; terminated by repudiation of obligation, 51, 68, 97, 102f., 120, 121; election and discipline, 53, 74; and covenant, 15n., 33n., 34, 37f., 43, 45f., 68; narrowed to Remnant, 70ff., 86, 93, 140 (*see also* Remnant); extension beyond Israel, 67, 86, 93, 140; election and proselytes, 87, 89, 140; of individuals in O.T., 95ff.; in N.T., 170ff.; of judges, 95; of kings, 95ff.; of priests, 100ff.; of prophets, 103ff.; of Suffering Servant, 111f.; without covenant, 121ff.; national, 122ff.; individual, 131ff.; of Nebuchadrezzar, 131ff.; of Pharaoh, 132ff.; of Cyrus, 135ff.; of Church, 139ff.; election and warning, 168, 173

175

INDEX

Eglon, 130
Eli, 101f.
Elijah, 71f., 103, 144
Elisha, 72n.
'*emûnah*, 128n.
Esau, 33, 71, 99
Exodus, 19, 35f., 37f., 42, 44, 60
Ezekiel, 20f., 77, 79, 81, 84, 90, 100f., 105n., 106
Ezra, 84f., 86n., 87

Gideon, 61, 95
Golden Age, 65, 69f., 81, 151f., 158

Habakkuk, 125ff.
Haggai, 85
Harran, 28f., 30, 32
ḥesedh, 22n., 49n., 57n., 58
Hezekiah, 55n., 60
History and revelation, 36, 42f., 47n.
Hîyôn, 127n.
Hosea, 20f., 50, 52, 57, 69n., 74n., 106

Immanuel, 150f.
Isaac, 24, 30n., 33f., 70, 141
Isaiah, 50, 58f., 64, 69, 73ff., 80n., 103, 106, 108f., 123f., 150, 158 (*see also* Deutero-Isaiah and Trito-Isaiah)
Israel, the true, 33, 114n., 145f., 148

Jacob, 24, 28, 30n., 33ff., 46f., 71, 99, 141
James, Epistle of, 146
Jehoiachin, 100, 113, 158
Jehoaikim, 100, 130
Jeremiah, 18, 20, 40f., 44, 51f., 59, 76f., 84, 100, 104f., 106f., 109f., 113, 115f., 125f., 142, 152f., 158
Jeroboam, 97f.
Jesus and Remnant, 141f.; and Suffering Servant, 158ff.
Jethro, 26f.
Jezebel, 72
Jochebed, 36n.
John the Baptist, 102
Jonah, 67f., 86
Joseph, 30n.
Josiah, 100
Judah, 27, 99
Judaism and particularism, 85f.; and proselytes, 87, 89ff.

Kenites and Yahwism, 26ff., 35ff., 42f., 55, 147

Levites, 100

Malachi, 85

Manasseh, 117
Marduk, 17
Meshullam, 113
Messiah, Davidic, 65, 80, 89, 114, 152f., 156ff.
Micaiah, 71, 116
Micah, 21, 57, 63f., 74n., 79f., 158
mishpaṭ, 117n.
Monotheism, 60ff.
Moses, 19f., 21, 23, 25, 27, 30ff., 35ff., 45, 46n., 48, 55f., 57n., 60, 87, 105, 108, 113, 118, 133, 137, 147, 159f., 161

Nahum, 69
Nathan, 98f.
Nebuchadrezzar, 80n.; and election, 130, 131ff.
Nehemiah, 84f., 87
Noah, 25

Obadiah, 72

Patriarchs, historical, 23f.; religion of, 28f.; traditions of, 24; and election, 19f., 21ff.
Paul, 40f., 89, 107, 142, 144f., 149, 170f.
Peter, 155, 156n.; Epistle of, 146
Pharaoh, 23, 37; and election, 132ff.
Potter, Parable of, 40f., 51, 128
Predestination, 16, 41n.
Pride of Race, 15f., 18f., 37f., 66, 71, 93f., 165
Prophecy, argument from, 149ff.
Prophets and revelation, 56ff.; election of, 103ff.; cultic, 103f.; false, 103ff., 109
Proselytes, 87, 89ff.

Ras Shamra, 26, 28, 36n.
Remnant, 70ff., 143ff.; saved, 70, 81; saving, 81; for purpose, 70, 75, 99; heirs of promises, 70, 81; sometimes loyal, 72, 81, 94; sometimes unrepentant, 73; sometimes justifying survival, 74ff.; few, 74f.; future Remnant, 78, 81, 94; conquering Remnant, 80; Isaiah and Remnant, 73, 81, 140; missionary, 82, 86, 90, 92f.; in Babylonian thought, 83; exiled Remnant, 84, 86; Remnant and Church, 141f., 143ff.
Ruth, 88

Sacrifice in Judaism and Christianity, cessation of, 163f.
Samson, 96
Samuel, 96f., 105

INDEX

Saul, 96f.
Scythians, 125
Sennacherib, 69
Seraphim, 58, 108
Servant, Suffering, 111ff., 155ff.; and Church, 167ff.
Shaddai, 21, 29, 60f.
Shammai, 92
Shear-Jashub, 74
Shulammite, 160n.
Sociality of man, 31, 33, 44, 169
Solomon, 99
Son of Man, 156ff.
Supper, Last, 142
Synagogue, 85f., 163
Syncretism, 29, 60f.

Terah, 28f.
Tiglath-pileser I, 16f.

Trito-Isaiah, 81, 112

Universalism, 62f., 65ff., 70n., 82, 87, 89f., 92, 143
Ur, 28f.
Uriah, 116

Yahwism, Origins of, 25ff.; and Kenites, 26ff., 35ff., 42f., 55; and ethics, 56f.; at Ras Shamra? 26
Yw, 36n.

Zadok, 101
Zadokites, 100ff.
Zechariah, 85, 87f., 90
Zechariah, father of John the Baptist, 102
Zerubbabel, 113, 158
Zionism, 153f.

(b) AUTHORS

Albright, W. F., 15n., 26n., 29n., 60n., 86n., 127n., 162, 164
Alt, A., 29n.
Aquila, 127n.
Auvray, P., 101n.

Bacher, W., 86n.
Bacon, B. W., 156n.
Baentsch, B., 46n.
Bamberger, B. J., 91, 92, 164n.
Barnes, W. E., 22n., 134n.
Barton, G. A., 27n., 120n.
Batten, L. W., 55n.
Bauer, H., 26n., 36n.
Baumgartner, W., 26n., 29n.
Bea, A., 26n.
Beare, F. W., 146n.
Beer, G., 45n., 46n., 54n.
Bennett, W. H., 45n., 46n., 54n., 66n.
Bentzen, A., 23n., 85n., 112n., 114n., 157n.
Berry, G. R., 22n., 55n.
Bertholet, A., 101n.
Billerbeck, P., see Strack, H. L.
Black, M., 157n.
Blank, S. H., 82n., 113n.
Bleeker, L. H. K., 113n.
Bonsirven, J., 19n., 49n., 90n., 93n., 151n.
van den Born, A., 101n.
Bousset, W., and Gressmann, H., 90n.
Bowman, J. W., 141, 155n., 156n.
Box, G. H., 73n., 112n., 123n.
Briggs, C. A., 22n.
Browne, L. E., 86n.
Brunner, E., 36n.

Bruston, C., 113n.
Buber, M., 26n.
Budde, K., 26n., 112n., 113n., 116n.
Burney, C. F., 27n.
Burrows, E., 113n.
Burrows, M., 22n.
Buttenweiser, M., 23n., 84n.
Buzy, D., 141n., 143n.

Cadoux, C. J., 92n., 141n., 143n., 157n.
Calès, J., 22n.
Calvin, J., 41n.
Case, S. J., 156n.
Causse, A., 87n., 90n., 114n.
Cave, S., 45n.
Cheyne, T. K., 116n.
Coates, J. R., 157n.
Cobb, W. H., 84n.
Cook, S. A., 15n., 157n., 173n.
Cooke, G. A., 101n.
Craig, C. T., 156n.

Dahl, N. A., 19n., 69n., 87n.
Daiches, S., 57n.
Danell, G. A., 19n., 73n.
Davidson, A. B., 140n.
Davies, W. D., 144n., 156n., 167n.
Deissmann, A., 149n.
Denney, J., 41n., 145n.
Derenbourg, J., 91n., 92n.
Dhorme, P. (E.), 24n., 28n., 29n.
Dittmann, H., 71n.
Dodd, C. H., 41n., 47n., 59n., 143n., 145n., 148n., 165n.
Driver, G. R., 116n.

M   177

INDEX

Driver, S. R., 45n., 46n., 54n., 66n.
Ducros, P., 49n.
Duhm, B., 22n., 73n., 113n., 123n., 126n.
Dussaud, R., 26n., 28n.

Edelkoort, A. H., 114n.
Eerdmans, B. D., 23n., 26n., 29n.
Eichrodt, W., 15n.
Eisendrath, M. N., 70n.
Eissfeldt, O., 27n., 45n., 46n., 54n., 66n., 72n., 80n, 87n., 112n., 113n.
Elliger, K., 81n., 113n.
Elmslie, W. A. L., 81n., 112n., 125n.
Engnell, I., 23n., 73n., 112n., 114n.
Evans, P. W., 143n.

Fahlgren, K. Hj., 114n., 150n.
Farley, F. A., 113n.
Feuillet, A., 150n.
Finkelstein, L., 86n., 91n., 92n.
Fischer, J., 73n., 112n., 114n., 116n., 123n.
Flew, R. N., 141n., 148n.
Friedländer, M., 91n., 92n.

Galling, K., 19
Giesebrecht, F., 116n.
Ginsberg, H. L., 28n.
Glahn, L., and Köhler, L., 82n.
Goguel, M., 142
Gordon, C. H., 26n.
Graetz, H., 91n.
Gray, G. B., 73n., 123n.
Greenstone, J. H., 153, 154, 162
Gressmann, H., 17n., 71n., 80n., 112n., 114n., 153n. *See also* Bousset, W.
Gruffydd, W. J., 35n.
Gunkel, H., 22n.
Guthe, H., 22n., 73n., 80n.

Haldar, A., 83n., 103n.
Ha-Levi, Judah, 140n.
Haller, M., 134n.
Hamilton, H. F., 49n., 164n.
Hammershaimb, E., 150n.
Hanson, S., 20n., 157n.
Harford, J. Battersby, 101n.
Harnack, A., 143
Harper, W. R., 50n.
Headlam, A. C. *See* Sanday, W.
Hebert, A. G., 19n.
Heinisch, P., 114n.
Hempel, J., 134n.
Hengstenberg, E. W., 160n.
Herntrich, V., 101n.
Hertzberg, H. W., 117n.
Hirsch, E. G., 74n., 91n.

Hölscher, G., 101n.
Hooke, S. H., 22n., 24n., 25n., 74n., 147n., 150n.
Van Hoonacker, A., 22n., 50n., 57n., 84n., 127n.
Hoschander, J., 128n.
Huck, A., 142n.
Humbert, P., 128n.
Hyatt, J. P., 125n.

Ibn Ezra, 160n.
Irwin, W. A., 19n., 20n., 46n., 101n., 145n.

Jack, J. W., 28n.
Jackson, F. J. Foakes, and Lake, K., 156n.
Jacob, E., 20n.
Jellinek, A., 91, 164n.
Jocz, J., 94n., 140n.
Johansson, N., 113n.
Johnson, A. R., 22n., 103n., 110n., 111n., 124n.

Kapelrud, A. S., 73n., 153n.
Kautzsch, E., 28n.
Kilpatrick, G. D., 141n., 143n.
Kissane, E. J., 73n., 113n., 116n., 123n., 135n.
Kittel, R., 22n., 73n.
Klausner, J., 143n.
Knight, H., 103n.
Köhler, L., 49n. *See also* Glahn, L.
König, E., 45
König, F. W., 125n.

Lagrange, M. J., 63n.
Lake, K. *See* Jackson, F. J. Foakes
Lanchester, H. C. O., 127n.
de Langhe, R., 26n., 29n.
Lattey, C., 150n.
Leslie, E. A., 30n.
Lévi, I., 92n.
Levy, R., 62n., 63n., 116n., 117n., 137n.
Lewy, J., 125n.
Liechtenhan, R., 165n.
Lindblom, J., 50n., 74n., 80n., 114n.
Lods, A., 22n., 29n., 113n.
Loewe, H. *See* Montefiore, C. G.
Lofthouse, W. F., 112n.
Lohmeyer, E., 47n.
Loisy, A., 157n.
de Lubac, H., 91n., 143n., 168n.
Luckenbill, J. J., 17n.

McCullough, W. S., 81n.
Macmillan, Lord, 49n.

178

INDEX

McNeile, A. H., 45n., 46n., 54n., 144n.
Magnus, L., 153n.
Manson, T. W., 79, 81, 140, 141, 157
Manson, W., 155n.
Margolis, M. L., 64n.
Marti, K., 22n., 31, 37n., 50n., 73n., 80n., 123n.
Massie, J., 151n.
Matthews, H. J., 160n.
May, H. G., 62n., 90n., 164n.
Maynard, J. A., 84n.
Meek, T. J., 27n.
Meinhold, J., 55n.
Menes, A., 86n.
Messel, N., 101n.
Meyer, E., 35n.
Moffatt, J., 20n., 156n.
Möhlenbrink, K., 46n.
Montefiore, C. G., 20n., 66n., 90n., 91n.
Montefiore, C. G., and Loewe, H., 19n.
Moore, G. F., 86n., 90n., 91
Morgenstern, J., 51n., 55n., 82n., 90, 112n.
Mowinckel, S., 55n., 71n., 80n., 103n., 104n., 112n., 113n., 114n., 134n., 150n.
Munch, P. A., 153n.
Murphy, R. T., 114n.
Murray, J. O. F., 34n., 165

Newman, L. I., 93, 134n.
North, C. R., 20n., 31, 46n., 63n., 67, 112n., 113n., 114n., 115n., 117n., 156n.
Noth, M., 36n., 46n.
Nowack, W., 22n., 50n.
Nyberg, H. S., 50n., 114n., 116n.

Odeberg, H., 81n.
Oesterley, W. O. E., 22n., 33n.
Oesterley, W. O. E., and Robinson, T. H., 28n., 45n., 46n., 54n., 66n., 80n., 101n.
Otto, R., 157n.

Palache, L., 113n.
Parker, P., 157n.
Paton, L. B., 27n.
Patrick, S., 160n.
Peake, A. S., 72n., 77n., 113n.
Pedersen, J., 19n., 29n., 87n., 114n.
Peirce, F. X., 113n.
Percy, E., 167n.
Pfeiffer, R. H., 27n., 55n., 80n., 93n.
Pidoux, G., 153n.
van der Ploeg, J., 112n., 114n., 117n.

Porteous, N. W., 36n., 39n., 48n.
Power, E., 150n.
Procksch, O., 73n., 123n.

Quell, G., 47n., 63n.

von Rad, G., 48n., 130n.
Raguin, Y., 164
Ramsey, A. M., 156n.
Richardson, A., 121
Robertson, E., 73n., 96n.
Robinson, H. Wheeler, 31n., 49n., 105n., 110n., 114n., 155, 156
Robinson, T. H., 22n., 50n., 79n., 106n. See also Oesterley, W. O. E.
Robinson, W., 114n., 148n., 168n.
Rogers, R. W., 17n.
Rudolph, W., 106n., 125n.
Ryle, H. E., 66n.

Sanday, W., and Headlam, A. C., 41n., 145n.
Schmidt, H., 106n.
Schofield, J. N., 26n., 35n.
Schweizer, E., 167n., 173n.
Scott, R. B. Y., 46n., 104n., 121, 139
Seeligmann, I. L., 73n.
Seierstad, I. P., 109n.
Seinecke, L., 84n.
Sellers, O. R., 106n.
Sellin, E., 22n., 53n., 80n., 113n., 126n.
Selwyn, E. G., 146
Servetus, 134n.
Simon, M., 140n.
Simpson, C. A., 35n., 46n., 54n.
Sjöberg, E., 155n.
Skinner, J., 24n., 32n., 66n., 77n., 80n., 113n., 125n.
Smith, G. A., 22n., 77n.
Smith, H. P., 28n., 35n., 48n.
Smith, J. M. Powis, 16, 22n., 50n., 66, 80n., 94, 128n.
Smith, S., 113n.
Snaith, N. H., 22n., 112n., 135
Spicq, C., 107n.
Stade, B., 26n.
Staerk, W., 63n.
Stamm, J. J., 150n.
Strack, H. L., and Billerbeck, P., 91n.
Ström, Å. V., 114n., 157n., 167n., 171n.
Sundkler, B., 143

Taylor, V., 156n.
Torrey, C. C., 63n., 81n., 84n., 86n., 116n., 125n., 134, 135, 155n.

de Vaux, R., 24n., 26n., 29n., 70, 71n., 81n.

INDEX

Vincent, A., 26n.
Virolleaud, Ch., 26n., 28n.
Volz, P., 31n., 113n., 116n., 125n.

Wade, G. W., 22n., 73n., 80n., 123n.
Walvoord, J. F., 33n.
Weill, R., 24n.
Weis, P. R., 135n.
Welch, A. C., 125n.
Wellhausen, J., 23
Wensinck, A. J., 26n.

Whitehouse, O. C., 113n.
Widengren, G., 65n., 171n.
Wilson, W. E., 157n.
Wilke, F., 125n.
Wright, G. E., 15, 22n., 43n., 46n., 60n.

Young, E. J., 111n.

Zeitlin, S., 86n.
Zimmerli, W., 139n.

(c) SCRIPTURE

Genesis
4 : 1	27n.
11 : 10ff.	34n.
11 : 31	28n.
12 : 1	29
12 : 2f.	32
12 : 3	65
13 : 18	28n.
14	135n., 136n.
14 : 13	28n.
14 : 17	28n.
15 : 2	25n.
15 : 7	21, 25n.
15 : 14	28n.
18 : 1	28n.
18 : 18	32, 66n.
20 : 1ff.	34n.
20 : 7	31n.
20 : 12	34n.
20 : 17	31n.
21 : 29ff.	28n.
21 : 33	28n.
22 : 17f.	32
22 : 18	66n.
25 : 22	86n.
26 : 4	33, 66n.
27 : 14	33
28 : 11–22	28n.
28 : 13	21
28 : 14	66n.
28 : 20f.	46
35 : 4	28n.
35 : 8	28n.

Exodus
3	105n.
4 : 21	132
6 : 2f.	21, 29
6 : 3	25n.
7 : 3	132n.
8 : 15, 32	133n.
9 : 12	132
9 : 34	133n.
10 : 1f.	133
10 : 20, 27	132
11 : 10	132
14 : 4	133n.
19	146
19 : 4f.	45
19 : 5	54, 146
20	55
20 : 3	54n.
20 : 6	56
23 : 10–19	55n.
24 : 9–11	46n.
30 : 23–26	55n.
32	61n.
32 : 13	33n.
34	55
34 : 6f.	54
34 : 14	54n.

Leviticus
18 : 9	34n.
19 : 2b–18	55n.
19 : 18	56n.
26 : 42	33n.

Numbers
3 : 2	101n.
12 : 6ff.	31n.
12 : 6f.	110
18 : 1ff.	101n.
18 : 23	101n.

Deuteronomy
1 : 8	33n.
4 : 31	33n.
4 : 37	23n.
5	55n.
5 : 2f.	48
6 : 5	56n.
6 : 10	33n.
6 : 17f.	54
7 : 6	18
7 : 7f.	18
7 : 8	23
9 : 5f.	18n.

INDEX

9 : 27	33n.		19 : 10	72n.
10 : 15	23n.		19 : 18	72n.
13 : 1–3	105n.		20 : 38	104n.
18 : 5	31n.		21 : 17ff.	104n.
18 : 6f.	100n.		22 : 6	72n.
18 : 20–22	105n.		22 : 27	116n.
28 : 49f.	129			
32 : 9	33n.		*2 Kings*	
33 : 10	102		5 : 9ff.	104n.
34 : 10	31n.		8 : 13	72n.
			9 : 6	72n.
Judges			13 : 23	33n.
1 : 16	27n.		21 : 16	117n.
3 : 7f.	130n.		23 : 29	100n.
3 : 12	130		24 : 2	130n.
4 : 6–9	96n.			
4 : 11	27n.		*1 Chronicles*	
6 : 15	96n.		6 : 4ff.	101n.
6 : 25	61n.		16 : 16–18	33n.
13 : 3–5	96n.		24	102n.
			24 : 6	102n.
Ruth			24 : 10	102n.
1 : 16f.	88f.			
			2 Chronicles	
1 Samuel			13 : 22	86n.
2	101			
2 : 27–36	101n.		*Ezra*	
3	105n.		2 : 36–39	102n.
8 : 4–9	96n.		8 : 17	86n.
9 : 16	96			
10 : 5, 10	104n.		*Psalms*	
12 : 22	33n.		2 : 7f.	17
12 : 23	31n.		33 : 12	33n.
13 : 8–14	97n.		105 : 5–10	22f.
15	97n.		105 : 43	23
16 : 1–13	96n.			
19 : 18ff.	104n.		*Song of Songs*	
21 : 1–9	102n.		7 : 2 (Heb. 3)	160n.
22 : 9–19	102n.			
			Isaiah	
2 Samuel			1 : 2	50
7 : 8f.	98		1 : 4	50
7 : 12f.	98		1 : 9	73, 144
12 : 1	104n.		2 : 2–4	64n.
24 : 11	104n.		2 : 2f.	64
			4 : 3	75
1 Kings			5 : 24	51
1 : 10–39	99n.		6	106n.
11 : 29–31	97n.		6 : 3	56
11 : 36	99		6 : 5	58, 108
11 : 38	98n.		6 : 7	108
13 : 18	105n.		6 : 9	109
13 : 20f.	104n.		6 : 13	73
13 : 21	105n.		7 : 3	74n.
14 : 1ff.	104n.		7 : 14	150, 151
14 : 7–11	97n.		7 : 18–20	123
16 : 1–4	98n.		8 : 16ff.	140
18 : 4	72n.		8 : 18	74n.
18 : 19	72n.		9 : 6	65n.

INDEX

10 : 5f.	124	53 : 7f.	115f.
10 : 7	124	53 : 10f.	157n.
10 : 12	124	53 : 12	117
10 : 20-22	74	54 : 3	140n.
10 : 22	144	56-66	81n.
11 : 6-8	65n.	56 : 7	65n.
11 : 9	94n.	60 : 11f.	19n.
13f.	81n.	61 : 1-4	112n.
14 : 1	88	61 : 1-3	112n.
17 : 7	75	61 : 5f., 9	19n.
19 : 16-25	65n.	66 : 18-20	82
27 : 5	75		
36 : 19f.	60n.	*Jeremiah*	
37 : 31f.	75	1 : 4-10	106n.
40-66	84n.	1 : 5f.	18
40-55	90n., 112n.	1 : 5	107
40 : 2	78n.	1 : 9	109
41 : 2f.	135	1 : 15f.	125
41 : 8f.	21	2 : 2	20
41 : 8	62	3 : 20	51
41 : 9	62	3 : 21	51
42 : 1-7	112n.	4 : 23-25	76
42 : 1-4	111n., 112n.	5 : 1	76n.
42 : 1	78f., 115	5 : 15f.	125
42 : 3f.	117	6 : 27-30	76n.
42 : 4f.	78f.	7 : 13	53n.
42 : 5-9	112n.	7 : 23	52n.
42 : 6-8	63	7 : 25	53n.
42 : 6	116n.	11 : 7	53n.
43 : 3	135n.	14 : 14	109n.
43 : 10	63	15 : 1	31n.
44 : 1	62	16 : 3f.	44n.
44 : 8	61	18 : 1f.	51n.
44 : 24, 26	136	19 : 4	40
44 : 28	136, 137	20 : 9	106
45 : 1, 3-5	136	22 : 18f.	100n.
45 : 5	61	22 : 28-30	100n.
45 : 6	137	23 : 3f.	77
45 : 22f.	62	23 : 9-40	105n.
46 : 1f.	81n.	23 : 16	109
47	81n.	23 : 18	110
49 : 1-9	112n.	23 : 22	110
49 : 1-6	111n., 112n.	24	84n.
49 : 5-7	112n.	24 : 21f.	126
49 : 5	115	25 : 4	53n.
49 : 6	117	25 : 9	125n., 131
49 : 7	112n.	26 : 2	104n.
49 : 8-13	112n.	26 : 5	53n.
50 : 4-11	112n.	26 : 23	116n.
50 : 4-10	112n.	27 : 6	131
50 : 4-9	111n.	29 : 19	53n.
50 : 6	115	29 : 27	104
51 : 2	21	31 : 29f.	44n.
51 : 9-16	112n.	31 : 31-34	77n.
52 : 13-53 : 12	111n., 112n.	31 : 33f.	59
53 : 1-12	112n., 156	32 : 33	53n.
53 : 3	115f.	35 : 14f.	52f.
53 : 5f.	157n.	36 : 26	77n.
53 : 5	117	38 : 6	116n.

182

INDEX

43 : 10	132
44 : 4	53n.

Ezekiel

1	106n.
8	101
11 : 14–20	84n.
11 : 19f.	77
20 : 5	20f.
36 : 22–25	78
37 : 11–14	77n.
40–48	101n.
40 : 2	64n.
44 : 6–9	90
44 : 10–14	101n.

Daniel

2 : 45	152n.
7 : 13	152n., 156

Hosea

1 : 2	106n.
2 : 23	148n.
6 : 7	50
8 : 1	50
11 : 1	20
11 : 8f.	52
12 : 9 (Heb. 10)	21
12 : 13 (Heb. 14)	31n.
13 : 4	21n.

Amos

3 : 2	18n., 53
3 : 7	111
3 : 8	106
3 : 12	72
4 : 11	72
5 : 15	76
6 : 14	122f.
7 : 13	104n.
7 : 14f.	106n.
9 : 7	123n.

Micah

4: 1–4	64n.
4 : 3f.	64
4 : 13	88n.
5 : 7–9 (Heb. 6–8)	79f.
6 : 8	57, 64n., 163n.
7 : 20	22

Habakkuk

1 : 6	126
1 : 13	126
2 : 4f.	127
2 : 14	94n.

Zephaniah

2 : 3	76

Zechariah

2 : 11 (Heb. 15)	87
8 : 20–23	88
14 : 10	64n.

St. Matthew

1 : 21ff.	150n.
5 : 17	142
5: 21f., 27f., 33f., 38f., 43f.	142n.
8 : 11	141
10 : 1, 5	170n.
10 : 5f.	143n.
13 : 11	170n.
15 : 24	143n.
16 : 15ff.	155n.
16 : 21	170n.
20 : 28	157n.
21 : 43	141
22 : 30	152n.
23 : 15	90n., 91n.
26 : 64	152n., 155n.
28 : 19f.	143

St. Mark

3 : 13f.	170n.
6 : 7	170n.
8 : 29f.	155n.
8 : 31	170n.
10 : 45	157n., 167
12 : 29ff.	56n.
14 : 62	152n., 155n.

St. Luke

1 : 5	102n.
6 : 12f.	170n.
9 : 1f.	170n.
9 : 20f.	155n.
9 : 21f.	170n.
10 : 1	170n.
11 : 51	85n.
19 : 10	167
22 : 20	142n.

St. John

8 : 39	93
15 : 5, 16	172

Acts

3 : 10	89n.
7 : 56	156n.
10	144n.
11 : 1–18	144n.
13 : 2	170n.

Romans

2 : 28f.	145
4 : 16	144

INDEX

6 : 4–6	171n.
6 : 4	171n.
6 : 8–11	171n.
8 : 9–11	171n.
8 : 9f., 14–17	146
8 : 17	171n.
9 : 2f.	149n.
9 : 6	144
9 : 7f.	144n.
9 : 21	40
9 : 22	41n.
9 : 25	148n.
9 : 27	144n.
9 : 29	144n.
11 : 4ff.	144
11 : 17ff.	145n.
11 : 18–22	166n.
11 : 23f.	149n.

1 Corinthians
3 : 16	171n.
10 : 18	145
11 : 25	142

2 Corinthians
3 : 4–6	142n.
3 : 18	171n.
5 : 17	171n.

Galatians
2 : 9	144n.
2 : 20	171
3 : 29	145
4 : 28f.	145
6 : 16	145, 148n.

Ephesians
1 : 14f.	147n.
2 : 11f., 19	145
2 : 22	171n.
3 : 6	145f.

Philippians
3 : 3	146
3 : 10	171n.

Colossians
3 : 3	171n.
3 : 10	171n.

1 Timothy
1 : 15	107

Hebrews
8 : 8–12	142n.

James
1 : 1	146

1 Peter
2 : 9	146

Revelation
1 : 7	152n.
3 : 15	173
3 : 16	166n.
14 : 14, 16	152n.

4 Ezra (2 Esdras)
6 : 55, 59	33n., 93n.
13 : 3	152n.

Ascension of Isaiah
5 : 1	117n.

Assumption of Moses
1 : 12	93n.
4 : 2	33n.

Psalms of Solomon
9 : 16–19	33n.
11 : 8f.	33n.
12 : 7	76n.
13 : 9–11	76n.
14 : 2, 7	76n.

www.ingramcontent.com/pod-product-compliance
Lightning Source LLC
Chambersburg PA
CBHW050807160426
43192CB00010B/1667